For Diane,

ECONOMIC DIPLOMAT

With warmest good wishes
from the author,

Nicholas Bayne

March 2018

# ECONOMIC DIPLOMAT

The Memoirs of
Sir Nicholas Bayne KCMG

The Memoir Club

© Sir Nicholas Bayne 2010

First published in 2010 by
The Memoir Club
Arya House
Langley Park
Durham
DH7 9XE
Tel: 0191 373 5660
Email: memoirclub@msn.com

British Library Cataloguing in
Publication Data.
A catalogue record for this book
is available from the
British Library

ISBN: 978-1-84104-208-4

Typeset by TW Typesetting, Plymouth, Devon
Printed by J F Print, Sparkford, Somerset

*To Dee and our descendants*

# Contents

# List of Maps and Plates

**Maps**

**Plates**

*Between pages 78–79*

1. In the ruins of Delphi
2. As Falstaff in the Eton school play
3. After the Eton wall game
4. Courting Dee by the Cherwell
5. At the site of Troy
6. At our wedding in Abbotsham
7. Manila: presenting diplomas to Colombo Plan scholars
8. Father Holland and the plane in which he flew us round the Sulu archipelago
9. After climbing Mayon volcano
10. First session of Berlin negotiations
11. Paris: as Father Christmas
12. Meeting President Mobutu of Zaire
13. Family on the residence veranda, Kinshasa
14. Cutting the ribbon at the new British embassy in Brazzaville

*Between pages 174–175*

15. Spinal unit at Gahini hospital, Rwanda
16. Young male gorilla on Mount Visoke
17. At Chetwynd House before Tom's wedding

# Foreword

When Nicholas Bayne entered the world in 1937 most of the globe, whose diplomacy he would spend much of his life helping to manage, was still colored pink. Many of his immediate ancestors had helped administer the far-flung British Empire, and although the Empire was gone by the time Nicholas entered the Foreign Office in 1961, its legacy still loomed large. As Ambassador Bayne's multi-faceted career now moves past its half century mark, Britain still punches above its weight in world affairs. This weight has however been diminished by the rise first of the United States and then of a united Europe and what once we called 'the Third World'. The Empire has long since vanished, but certainly not British influence. How British leaders and diplomats so successfully managed that remarkable transition during the second half of the twentieth century is an important issue for diplomatic historians. For Americans (who may face a similar challenge in the twenty-first century) the answer may hold important, though subtle lessons. For anyone wishing to explore those lessons Ambassador Bayne's engaging memoirs offer a ring-side seat.

Memoirs are the backstairs of history, according to the Victorian novelist and poet George Meredith. So in these memoirs we see, refracted in the miniature of a single life, intimations of broader social and political trends. In his early years we see that winsome combination of intellect, accomplishment and interest in public affairs that has long been more common in Britain than elsewhere and seems peculiarly Victorian, with the young Nicholas tacking back and forth between the opposing attractions of reflection and action, of Oxbridge and Whitehall. In the newlyweds' tales of the Philippines and in tiffs with the Beatles' entourage we glimpse unexpected perspectives on Britain's swinging sixties. We become close witnesses of the high-tension politics of the East-West Cold War as the rapidly rising young diplomat is dispatched to Bonn. The international megatrends of interdependence and globalization appear recurrently as both backdrop and foreground in Bayne's stints in Whitehall (both in the Treasury and in the Foreign Office) and in Paris at the OECD. The increasing interpenetration of domestic and international politics, another master trend of the last half century, is embodied in Bayne's entertaining accounts of globe-trotting British politicians and of the vexing discordances of global and parochial pressures. Economic diplomacy, once a quasi-commercial backwater in the world's foreign ministries, has become the unsettled core of contemporary international relations. A recounting of Ambassador Baynes' career provides a veritable textbook account of this domain, as his masterful concluding chapter here demonstrates.

Given Ambassador Bayne's personal engagement with all the major themes that have increasingly preoccupied theorists of international relations, it is hardly surprising that after a thoroughly successful career in the foreign service, he returned to the intellectual and academic pursuits that had attracted him as a young man, helping others to benefit from his experiences and reflections. One of the highlights of my own life and career has been the opportunity to learn from Nicholas, a terrific teacher and a loyal friend. I am honored to help bring his instruction to a wider audience, in the form of this uncommonly thoughtful memoir.

Robert D. Putnam
Harvard University 2010

# Preface

My father had an eventful life in the Royal Navy. He fought at the Battle of Jutland in World War I. He visited Yokohama just after the great earthquake of 1923. In World War II he ran a programme to arm merchant ships, so that they were not tied to convoys. But after he retired in 1947 he seldom spoke of his naval career and I did not think to ask him about it until it was too late. So my original reason for writing these memoirs is to provide some record for my children and grandchildren of what I did during my own life in the Diplomatic Service.

I did not have such an exciting career as he did. Yet my life offers an instructive comparison. He served in the armed forces in a half-century dominated by conflict. He contributed to Britain's victory in two world wars and helped to maintain international order in the years between. My career unrolled during a half-century of world peace, when war was confined to local outbreaks in Korea, Vietnam, the Gulf and Yugoslavia. As a British diplomat from 1961 onwards, I helped to maintain that peace during the uneasy confrontation between democratic West and communist East. This was misleadingly called the Cold War. In fact it was a peaceful contest between political and economic systems: democracy against ideologically-based despotism; open market economies, with some government intervention, against central planning and control of all economic activity. I became increasingly involved with the economic strand in this rivalry. This ended with the total collapse of communism in Europe. By the time I retired in 1996, the open economic system prevailed across the globe, more widely in fact than democracy.

In mid-career I had the chance of a year off for some research, in which I wrote a book with Professor Robert Putnam, who has contributed the Foreword to these memoirs. I continued to publish occasional articles on international economic policy till I retired and then began writing with greater frequency. I became a guest lecturer at the London School of Economics, teaching a course for graduates called 'Economic Diplomacy'. In this I drew on my earlier experience and used it to interpret contemporary events.

In these memoirs I want to think back over what I have seen and done and what I have taught and written. I shall offer some reflections on the conduct of international economic policy from the oil crises of the 1970s to the financial collapse of the early 2000s. That is why I have called the book 'Economic Diplomat'. It will not be easy to make this interesting and keep my readers' attention. As Lord Salisbury said in his essay on Castlereagh:

> A diplomatist's glory is the most ephemeral of all forms of that transient reward. There is nothing in the achievement that appeals to the imagination: nothing which art can illustrate, or tradition retain, or history portray.

In the face of these obstacles I have tried to lighten the weighty analysis with more personal material and anecdotes of family life.

I was worried at first about the sources for these memoirs, as I have never kept a diary. But I found plenty of written records from my early life, largely preserved by my parents. For my diplomatic postings abroad I have good sources too, in letters written home from Manila, Bonn, Paris and Kinshasa. The documentation becomes more haphazard during my spells in London, and at times I have had to rely on my memory, which I know to be capricious. If errors have crept in, I apologise in advance to anyone I have misjudged or misreported and especially to anyone I have inadvertently omitted. Diplomacy is a collective activity, and it would be wrong for me to claim sole credit for a shared achievement.

I am greatly indebted to my wife Diana (Dee) for her encouragement and moral support and to my brothers Christopher and David for providing family papers. All of them, together with my sons Tom and Dick, have read the whole book and given me valuable suggestions. I am most grateful to my cousin Dominic Grieve MP, for giving me access to the Hodgkinson papers collected by his father Percy Grieve. I owe my thanks also to Christopher Audland, Jim Bartleman, Simon Broadbent, John and Julia Boyd, Patrick Holdich and Stephen Woolcock for their comments on specific chapters; to Jim Daly for providing FCO clearance; and to the Memoir Club for their skill in converting my scrappy material into this elegant volume.

*Hampton Court*
*June 2010*

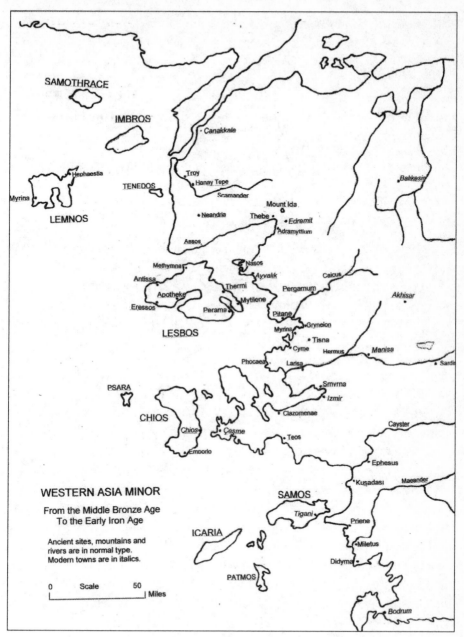

1. *Western Asia Minor from the Middle Bronze Age to the Early Iron Age*

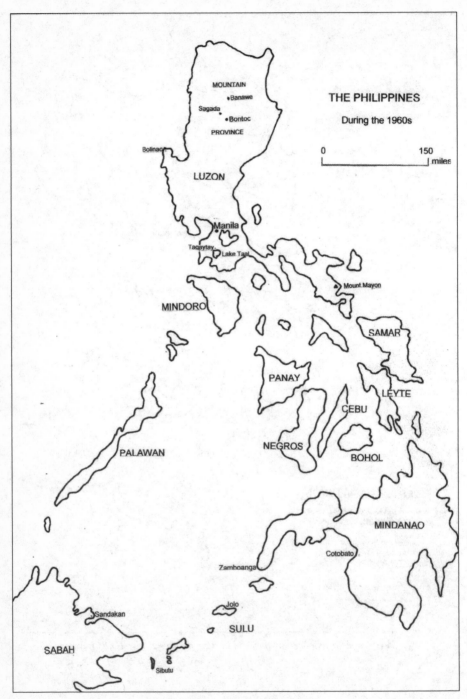

2. *The Philippines during the 1960s*

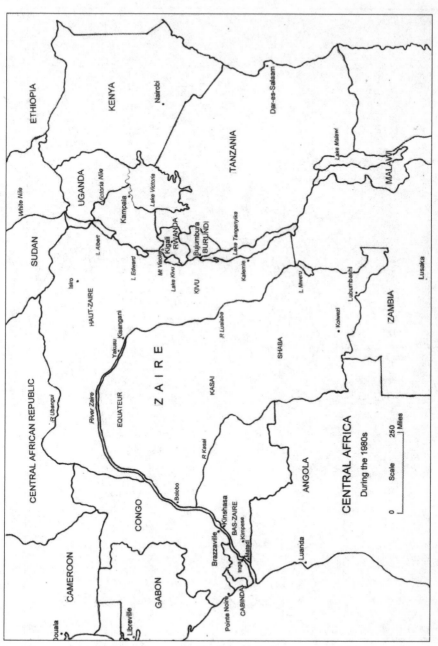

3. *Central Africa during the 1980s*

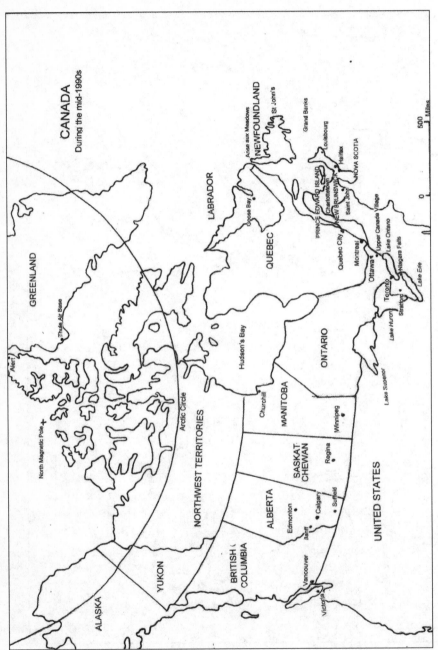

4. *Canada during the mid-1990s*

CHAPTER 1

# Diplomatic heredity

I BECAME A DIPLOMAT IN A spirit of experiment, but I have never regretted my decision. Diplomacy has given me a more rewarding life, I believe, than archaeology, which was my initial preference. Though I did not know it until late in life, my heredity had prepared me perfectly for a life of public service overseas, with academic pursuits on the side. The review of my ancestors that follows makes this plain.

The Bayne family originates in the highlands of Scotland, as a sept of the Clan Mackay. The Mackays trace their ancestry back to Lulach, the son of Lady Macbeth by her first husband. Lulach succeeded Macbeth as King of Scotland in 1057, but only lasted a few months. Over the next two centuries the clan constantly rose in rebellion, to reclaim the throne, until it was driven into the northernmost limits of Scotland. In 1431 Morgan and Neil Mackay led an uprising against their uncle, the clan chief Angus Dhu Mackay. But they were utterly defeated at the battle of Drum-na-Coup, called the 'Bannockburn of the North'. Morgan, Neil and Angus Dhu were all killed. Neil's eldest son John Bane Mackay sought asylum in Caithness. His descendants, calling themselves Bane and later Bayne, settled at Dingwall, a royal burgh in Easter Ross north of Inverness.

In 1542 King James V granted Tulloch Castle at Dingwall to Duncan Bane, who became the first Laird of Tulloch. But eventually the family ran out of heirs and cash, so that in 1760 Kenneth Bayne, the ninth Laird, surrendered both title and castle to the Davidsons. Meanwhile John Bayne, a descendant of an earlier laird, became the first Presbyterian minister in Dingwall in 1716. His grandson Ronald Bayne (1752–1821) followed the same vocation and married a great-niece of the great classical scholar Dr Richard Bentley. Ronald's son Charles John Bayne (1797–1832) likewise became a minister. Charles John's second son Peter Bayne (1830–96), born in Dingwall, was my great-grandfather.

Peter Bayne broke away from this stay-at-home tradition. He trained for the ministry, but became a writer and journalist instead. He moved to Edinburgh to edit a religious newspaper and then to London. His editorial ventures there were not successful, but he became leader-writer

1

for the *Christian World* and published books on religion, history and
literary criticism. He went to Berlin to study German and there met his
first wife, Clotilde Gerwien. My grandfather Charles Gerwien Bayne
(1860–1947) was their second son. Peter Bayne wanted his sons to have
more settled professions than he had and encouraged Charles to join the
Indian Civil Service (ICS). In many ways my grandfather's career
matches my own.

Charles Bayne was posted to Burma and arrived there late in 1880.
Five years later, after the third Burmese war, the province trebled in size
and its colonial government expanded to match. Charles had already
revealed the bureaucratic gifts that were valued in the central Secretariat:
an analytical mind, fluency on paper and a strong sense of duty. He was
called to Rangoon and stayed there for twenty years. His first chief, Sir
Charles Crosthwaite, had to pacify a rebellious province and ruthlessly
imposed methods he had used elsewhere in India. Charles served him
faithfully as Secretary, but he had more sympathy with those who
favoured a lighter touch and more respect for local traditions. As
Revenue Secretary in the 1890s, with economic responsibilities, he
sought to improve conditions for Burmese rice growers and to protect
the teak forests from predatory exploitation.

By the end of the decade, improved communications by railway and
telegraph had reduced the independence of district officers and increased
the pressure on the thinly staffed Secretariat. The gifted Chief Secretary,
Edward Symes, broke down under the strain and had to go home.
Charles became acting Chief Secretary for two years, until Symes came
back, only to shoot himself within a week. Charles was confirmed as
Chief Secretary in these tragic circumstances, but suffered a breakdown
too. After a spell of leave, he served two more years as Chief Secretary,
but was then sent home again, to prevent another collapse. He finally
returned in 1904 as acting Financial Commissioner, i.e. the province's
finance minister. He tried again to promote legislation to protect the rice
farmers, but expatriate interests in Burma opposed it and the Indian
government in Calcutta were lukewarm. Charles could have been
confirmed as Financial Commissioner, had he wished. But he became
eligible for his pension in 1906. Rather than put his health at risk again,
after two breakdowns, he chose to retire.

The Burmese historian Htin Aung wrote: 'The period 1890 to 1920
could be called the Golden Period of British rule.' But in fact the

decisions taken then lie at the root of Burma's problems today. The reforms imposed by Crosthwaite destroyed the traditional foundations of the Burmese state without putting anything durable in their place. The boom in rice and timber enriched expatriate exporters and financiers but ruined the indigenous farming population. Charles Bayne realised that Crosthwaite's policy was ill-judged and later did all he could to protect the forests and the native rice growers. But his strong sense of duty meant that he felt obliged to carry out colonial government policy, even when he disagreed with it. He may have left Burma when he could because he feared for the future.

Another powerful motive for retiring was to get back to his absorbing pursuit of research into English Tudor history. This had served as an effective therapy when he was home from Burma on health grounds. Within eighteen months of his return he had an erudite article published in the *English Historical Review*. A long double article followed and then a full-length book called *Anglo-Roman Relations, 1558–1565*. All these works dealt with the early reign of Elizabeth I. After World War I he changed his period and completed another book on the judicial role of Henry VII's Council. After long struggles, he got it published as the introduction to a collection of legal documents called *Select Cases in the Council of Henry VII*. The process was delayed by World War II and kept him occupied till he died in 1947, just short of his eighty-seventh birthday.

Charles Bayne put his bureaucratic skills to good use in writing history. He assembled a wide range of original texts, extracted the maximum evidence from them and developed rigorous arguments that challenged the conventional wisdom. Throughout the twentieth century the greatest English historians of the Tudor period, from Albert Pollard to David Starkey, drew on his work and recognised their debt to him. I can just remember him, as a frail old gentleman with a large moustache who lived off soup and rice pudding. I only learnt of his achievements much later, when I was better able to appreciate them.

Charles Bayne married Alice Augusta Hodgkinson (always called Augusta or Gussie), the sister of an ICS colleague, in Rangoon in January 1890. The Hodgkinson family originated in Lincolnshire and were recorded as landowners there from the seventeenth century. George Hodgkinson (1787–1856) became a solicitor in Newark and married Julia Beevor. Through her I can trace my descent back to Joan Beaufort, daughter of

John of Gaunt and Katharine Swinford, and thus to the royal house of England. Their eldest son George Christopher Hodgkinson (1815–80), my great-grandfather, took Anglican orders and entered the teaching profession. As Principal of the Diocesan Training Institution at York he was accused of introducing dangerous high church doctrines. The Archbishop of York and the Bishop of Ripon exonerated him completely, but he left to become headmaster of King Edward VI Grammar School at Louth, retiring only just before he died.

George Christopher Hodgkinson married Isabella Lydia Spence, who was descended from a famous family of Scottish naval explorers. John Ross, her great-uncle, had led an expedition into the Arctic which was trapped in the ice for four years. James Clark Ross, her uncle, discovered the North Magnetic Pole while on John Ross's expedition and later explored the coasts of Antarctica. (I crossed the track of my explorer uncles when I went to the Canadian North in 1994.) The Hodgkinsons had a large family of three sons and seven daughters; Augusta, my grandmother (1864–1941) was the youngest girl. The eldest son, George James Spence Hodgkinson (1845–91) entered the Indian Civil Service. He became a divisional commissioner in Burma and Charles Bayne worked under him. He never married, but invited four of his sisters out to join him and found husbands for them all. Augusta joined her brother in Rangoon in 1888 and Charles began courting her while holding down a demanding job in Crosthwaite's Secretariat. In due course Augusta accepted him, George gave his approval and Sir Charles released him for marriage and leave.

Augusta stayed with Charles throughout his ICS career, though Burma was thought very unhealthy for women. They had three children: Alice, Margaret (called Madge) and my father Ronald, born in 1897. I know what my grandmother looked like but very little about her personality. She was clearly a great support to my grandfather, with social gifts that made up for his rather retiring character. Later she was incapacitated by heart disease, which made her a semi-invalid. I am sure she saw me, as she was proud of all her grandchildren, but I have no memory of her and she died when I was five.

My mother's family was more exotic. She was born Elizabeth (Betty) Fleischmann in May 1905 and her ancestors were German merchants. A pedigree of 1897 traces the Fleischmann family back to the 1600s at

Kulmbach, a town on the river Main now in north-eastern Bavaria. Initially the family were goldsmiths, but Johan Salomon Fleischmann (1707–60) set up as a merchant instead. The business passed via Christoph Valentin (1745–1810) to Leonhard (1783–1847), who proved a black sheep, if the pedigree can be trusted. He produced two daughters and a son, Friedrich (1805–72, my great-great-grandfather) before he married their mother.

In the atmosphere of family scandal Friedrich preferred to leave home. He moved three hundred miles down the Main to settle at Marktbreit, upstream of Würzburg and still in Bavaria. It was a trading town, situated at the start of the shortest land route connecting the Main with the Danube. Friedrich prospered as a wholesaler, served as mayor, married and had five children, including Friedrich Karl, my great-grandfather (1843–1907). But in 1864 the railway reached Marktbreit, and destroyed at a stroke the town's commercial advantage. The trading houses migrated north and young Friedrich Karl followed them. He next appears in the 1871 English census, living in Liverpool.

Friedrich Karl Fleischmann (called just Friedrich from now on) joined the firm of Heilbut Symons and Co, the world's largest rubber importers. At that time all good quality rubber came from the jungles of the Amazon and was exported from the ports of Belem and Manaus. Ernesto Schramm, the largest Belem export house, regularly bought a quarter of the crop for Heilbut Symons, who shipped it to Liverpool, London and New York and sold it there. Friedrich never went to Brazil, but was involved with shipping, insurance and sales on both sides of the Atlantic. He became a naturalised British subject and married Annie Ashcroft (1847–1924), who was born in Bootle. They had two sons, Noel (1878–1949, my grandfather) and Oscar (1880–1944), who were sent to Rugby School and Magdalen College Oxford. Friedrich began collecting oil paintings, mainly English landscapes by the Norwich School.

Around 1895 the Fleischmann family moved to London. Friedrich was now a partner in Heilbut Symons and a very wealthy man. He leased a large house in Kensington, No 6 Collingham Gardens, with room to house his family and display his pictures. His collecting became more ambitious, as he moved into eighteenth century English (Gainsborough and Reynolds) and seventeenth century Dutch paintings (Rembrandt and Jakob Ruisdael). He died in August 1907, aged sixty-four, and his estate amounted to over £400,000 before tax, a huge sum for the time.

His fortune supported his descendants for another century and my brothers and I still own a dozen of his pictures. But we know very little about him as a person and even his name does not survive. In August 1914, as Britain went to war with Germany, Annie Fleischmann resumed her maiden name of Ashcroft by deed poll and all her descendants took the surname Ashcroft also.

Friedrich Fleischmann settled substantial sums on his sons, so that neither had to earn his living. Noel, my grandfather, took a first-class degree in chemistry at Oxford, followed by research at University College London. But his real passion was mineralogy, which occupied him for the whole of his life. He began by collecting zeolites, crystalline rocks that bubble when heated. Over fifteen years he built up a collection of some 2,000 zeolites, which he presented to the Natural History Museum as World War I interrupted this activity. He spent the war in civilian work for the government and, when peace returned, began to specialise in the minerals of Swizerland. He spent every summer there between the wars, combining mineralogy with mountaineering and photography. By 1938 his Swiss collections totalled 6,000 items, while he provided photographs for the scholarly work *Die Mineralien der Schweizeralpen*. At intervals he would present his finds to the Natural History Museum, and when he died in 1949 he left them all his remaining specimens, notes and papers. He was by far the largest benefactor to the Mineralogy Department up to that time, and his gifts are still preserved as the Ashcroft Collection.

In July 1904 Noel Ashcroft married Muriel im Thurn (1880–1975), who lived next door in No 5 Collingham Gardens. The im Thurn family originally came from Schaffhausen, a town on the upper Rhine between Basel and Konstanz, now in Switzerland. The im Thurns emerged in the 1200s among the noble families in the town, which later received a charter from Rudolf of Hapsburg. When the Swiss cantons rose in revolt, troops from Schaffhausen had to join the Hapsburg army and the nobles, including the im Thurns, suffered heavy losses. In peace-time too they lost ground. The Hapsburg dukes encouraged the political rise of the bourgeoisie and the nobles found their privileges curtailed. Many of them left to become mercenaries in the armies of foreign powers.

Johan Caspar im Thurn (1766–1850) made his career as a lieutenant in the Dutch army. He retired to Schaffhausen to become a money broker, but went bankrupt and died in exile. His third son Johan Conrad im Thurn (1809–82) had to make his own way in the world. He began as a salesman for a Stuttgart firm that sent him to London. There he set up his own trading house, J C im Thurn & Co, based in Fenchurch Street. He married his cousin Mary Catherine im Thurn (1823–95): her father Friedrich Ludwig im Thurn (1779–1831) had served with the British army in the West Indies, while her mother was Scottish. Johan Conrad and his bride settled in a large house in Dulwich and they had eight surviving children. The eldest son, John Conrad (1846–1920, my great-grandfather) joined his father in the firm. Johan Conrad's trading and financial interests spread ever wider, from Swedish forests and Swiss railways to projects in China, Japan and South America.

Suddenly the family fortunes crumbled. J C im Thurn & Co suffered heavy losses in coffee trading and Chilean railway investments. Early in 1875 the firm could no longer meet its payments on the Frankfurt stock exchange and had to be rescued by the Bank of England. Old Johan Conrad retired, while John Conrad the younger gradually rebuilt the firm and paid off its debts. He married Sarah Knowles, whose father was a merchant banker, and they had eight children: Herbert, Margaret, Muriel (my grandmother), Dorothy, John (who joined the navy), Donald, Gladys and Richard. They were a long-lived family and I knew most of my im Thurn great-aunts and uncles as I was growing up.

Some time in the 1890s the im Thurns moved to 5 Collingham Gardens, where they were next door to the Fleischmann family. Both Noel and Oscar Fleischmann fell in love with Muriel im Thurn. Muriel preferred Noel, accepted his proposal and they were married in July 1904. Some letters between them survive from this period and show them both very much in love: Noel is overwhelmed by his good fortune, while Muriel sounds calm and confident. They set up house in Bayswater, where their first three children were born. My mother Betty came first, followed by Diana and Anthony, with Michael as an afterthought in 1920. During World War I Muriel took her children to the Sussex coast for holidays and their letters too survive, urging their father to join them. Between the wars the family travelled several times to Kejimkuyik in the wilds of Nova Scotia. Muriel and the children went canoeing and camping, while Noel preferred fishing and photography. I went myself to Kejimkujik sixty years later and found it hardly changed from his photos.

★ ★ ★

One common heritage I have from all four grandparents is a readiness to travel and to work abroad. Over many generations my forbears had made their lives in the same place, in Scotland or Lincolnshire, Bavaria or Switzerland. But in the nineteenth century it became possible to move around freely and London acted like a magnet. The Bayne, Fleischmann and im Thurn families each migrated some five hundred miles, as Dingwall, Marktbreit and Schaffhausen are all roughly equidistant from London. (Augusta Hodgkinson only came from Nottingham, but made a detour via Burma.) One migration was enough and later generations did not settle abroad again. But many of them spent their working lives overseas and others showed a persistent yearning to visit foreign parts.

Otherwise their genetic legacies diverge. The Baynes and Hodgkinsons reveal a strong professional and public service strain. They became civil servants, teachers, lawyers and ministers of religion. They rarely went into business and then with poor success, like Peter Bayne's editorial ventures. An academic gene surfaces at times among the Baynes, no doubt originating from the same strand as the learned Dr Richard Bentley of Trinity, my six-times-great-uncle. It was strong in Peter and Charles Bayne and has reappeared with me. With my Fleischmann ancestors, however, a business gene is dominant, though they also served as mayors and were close to the Lutheran church. The im Thurns, originally nobles, became mercenary soldiers (which is also a sort of business) and then moved into finance. Sometimes they were undone by rash speculation, but the family always recovered. The business and financial gene from the Fleischmann and im Thurn lines has reappeared in my brother Christopher and my son Tom, but not in me. I have kept to the travelling, academic and public service traditions of my ancestors.

CHAPTER 2

# Wartime childhood

I WAS BORN ON 15 FEBRUARY 1937, in time for lunch, my mother said. She was staying in the London house of her parents, 1 Egerton Gardens in Kensington. This was her normal base when my father was at sea, and my brother Christopher had lived there since his birth in 1933. I remember nothing of Egerton Gardens, however, as next year we moved to Devon. My father, then Commander RN, was posted to the battle cruiser HMS *Resolution*, based in Plymouth. (One of its 15-inch guns is mounted outside the Imperial War Museum.) We lived in Crapston on the edge of Dartmoor. My earliest memory is recoiling from the sea, crying 'Too deep! Too deep!' This would have been at Woolacombe in North Devon, in August 1939.

When World War II broke out, my mother joined the WRNS and became a cipher clerk. She and my father worked long hours in Plymouth, so that Christopher and I were looked after by Nanny Davis. A few more memories survive from Crapston. At Christmas I remember pushing through a forest of adult legs to get a sight of the decorated tree. In February 1940 I had a birthday cake with three candles, while our dog Peter got a cake with one candle. (This was the only time we owned a dog.) In the summer my grandmother decided that Christopher and I should go to friends of hers in Boston, as Britain was too dangerous. We got as far as Liverpool, but my parents changed their minds, because they knew too much about the risk of U-boat attack. We went instead to the island of Eigg in the Inner Hebrides. I remember a stark house of granite, with stone balls on the gateposts, and a walk to the sea where we played trains. Nanny Thair joined us, who had been my mother's nanny and was then about sixty. On Eigg she received a telegram and showed me the crown at the top of it. 'This is from the King,' she said, 'because I am a hundred years old.' I believed her completely.

In 1941 my father was promoted to Captain and moved to the Admiralty to run a programme called Defensively Equipped Merchant Ships (DEMS). My mother went with him and I moved to Yorkshire. My great-uncle Admiral John im Thurn lived at Stainforth in the Ribble

9

valley, with his wife Margery and sister Margaret (Auntie Mar). Nanny Thair and I stayed with Mr and Mrs Foster in the village; he was a dairy farmer and she ran the post office. I have happy, if blurry, memories of Stainforth. Nanny taught me to read and books have been a pleasure and a comfort ever since. Mr Foster milked his cows by machine and I liked seeing the milk poured into great silver churns. I took part in haymaking and was fascinated by the noisy, throbbing threshing machine. Mrs Foster had a big warm kitchen where she made bread. I worshipped her fourteen-year-old daughter Kathleen, who would sit combing her long red hair. (In 1990 I went back to Stainforth and found Kathleen Foster, now married, occupying her mother's place in the post office.)

Christopher started boarding at Stone House School, evacuated to Ingleborough Hall at Clapham, five miles away. He joined me in Stainforth for the school holidays. We played by the beck in the village, crossed by stepping-stones, or watched immense goods trains go by on the railway from Carlisle. The beck joined the river Ribble, on whose banks my father, in a rare appearance, built us a house of rocks thatched with reeds. At intervals Nanny would dress us up and take us to visit Uncle John and the aunts in the big house. At last the threat of war receded and early in 1943 I came south again to Oxford, where my grandparents were already living. Nanny and I lodged with Mrs Massey and her two boys on Boar's Hill. I went to school for the first time, but only remember the long, cold walk to get there. In the summer we all migrated to Croyde in North Devon. There I was bored by the village school and one day was sent home in disgrace. I skulked in the bushes until I could go back with the others, but my sins were soon found out.

My nomadic life was coming to an end. In September 1943 I joined my mother in Oxford. I started at the 'baby school' for the Dragon, Oxford's most famous preparatory school, and thrived on proper schooling at last, sharpening my wits against the brainy children of dons. The school production of *Macbeth* gave me an enduring taste for Shakespeare, though I liked the witches and the fighting at the end better than the long speeches. My parents hoped I could continue in the Dragon School, but there was no room for me as a boarder. So after my younger brother David was born in September 1944 I went to join Christopher at Stone House.

I adapted readily to boarding school life and Christopher kept a fraternal eye on me. The work was easier than at the Dragon and I moved briskly up the school. At games I did less well. Though I hero-worshipped Stanley Matthews and Denis Compton, I was not much good at either football or cricket. However, a good turn of speed and fierce tackling later earned me my rugby colours. The school occupied a small stately home situated just below Ingleborough, one of Yorkshire's 'three peaks'. The winters were intensely cold for a small boy in shorts and I envied the snug plus-fours that Christopher wore. In the summer we swam in a lake fed by the snow-melt from Ingleborough, which was even worse. The water seldom rose to 15 degrees Celsius and we usually swam at around 10°C. I have been a reluctant swimmer ever since. (In 2008 Christopher and I went back with a group of our contemporaries and found everything still very recognisable.)

In summer 1946 Stone House moved back to its original site at Broadstairs in Kent. We could look out to sea from the school's windows and observe wrecks on the Goodwin Sands. There were more hard winters and we all got chilblains. I remember the masters well and three deserve my special gratitude. John Richardson the headmaster, always called 'JLR', combined good discipline with a cheerful atmosphere in the school. Theo Buckworth, a strict and austere man, communicated to me his love for the classics. Andrew Winser, the flamboyant English master, staged *Julius Caesar* and *King John* and gave me a taste for writing and drama. I was, I confess, a feckless boy, easily led by others into schemes of mischief. JLR, as schoolmasters did then, used the cane as a deterrent. After he beat me once, I took care never to risk being beaten again.

A debate developed over whether I should take the scholarship to Eton, where my Uncle Michael had been. JLR and Theo Buckworth thought I should wait till I was thirteen, so that Stone House would get the glory if I won. But my parents insisted that I should have a first shot when I was twelve. Thus in June 1949 I went up to take the Eton scholarship. I did not get onto the published list, but performed well enough to secure a place in the school from which I could sit the exam again a year later. So I left Stone House, with a good foundation for what would follow.

During the holidays my mother, my brothers and I first lived in furnished flats and then moved to a house in Frenchay Road, between Woodstock Road and the Oxford canal. My father joined us for most weekends. Granny and Grandpa were in nearby Upland Park Road, where my mother's sister Aunt Diana and brother Uncle Michael were frequent visitors. (Her other brother, Uncle Anthony, was with the navy in the Pacific.)

For the first time I got to know my parents properly. My father had been educated at Osborne and Dartmouth and spent his adult life in the Royal Navy as a gunnery officer. As a midshipman at the Battle of Jutland he had been in a 6-inch gun turret on HMS *Canada*. Later he had seen the German warships scuttled at Scapa Flow. Between the wars he had served at Gibraltar and Malta and in the South China Fleet. At home his habits of naval discipline left me rather in awe of him. He was good at maths, physics and engineering and produced meticulous drawings. Socially he was rather diffident and retiring and his greatest pleasure was his garden.

My mother had read French and Italian at Girton College Cambridge, before women were allowed to take degrees. She was more outgoing than my father and missed the lively London social round she had known before the war. She had accompanied my father on his naval postings when she could and enjoyed her spell in the WRNS when the war started. Being a housewife in wartime Oxford did not come naturally to her, but she made the best of it and took advantage of whatever cultural life the city had to offer. My parents were never very demonstrative to each other or to their children. Only when I became a parent myself did I realise the sacrifices they had made in bringing us up during wartime.

My grandmother was the dominant figure in the family and remained so till her death many years later, aged ninety-four. Grandpa was always very kind to us, but his mind was on his scholarly pursuits. Granny was active and energetic and put herself out to entertain and educate her grandchildren. Back in London after the war ended, she often invited us for visits. My earliest memories of these are of delicious food in restaurants; later came trips to museums, the theatre and the opera.

Aunt Diana was also a strong influence on me, as she first aroused my interest in archaeology. She had been on excavations in Britain and Cyprus in the 1930s. She worked at the RAF photographic interpretation centre at Medmenham and saw the photos taken after the dam-busters' raid. When the war ended she spent a year as an English teacher in Finland and wrote a book about her experiences. Eventually she got back to archaeology, working for Kathleen Kenyon at her excavations at Jericho.

Life remained austere in Oxford after the war, but I remember my earliest girl-friends, In Frenchay Road I showed off my bicycle to Joyce, when I was nine. I had taken ages to learn how to ride it, until my father took me in hand, but I could now go out on excursions as far as Eynsham and Witney. My grandmother resurrected her pre-war Wolseley saloon for us, though it only went fifteen miles to the gallon and petrol was still rationed. My father always drove at 37 m.p.h., which he claimed gave the best fuel consumption; my mother sometimes got up to 50.

In 1947 I had the most memorable experience of my life so far. My grandparents decided to resume their regular summer visits to Switzerland and took me with them. The train deposited us on Göschenen station, near Andermatt, and at once Granny took me to buy a walking stick. Thereafter at each place we visited I would get a metal badge fixed to it, so that by the end the stick was completely covered. It became my most treasured possession and I have it still. We travelled on to the Riffelalp Hotel at Zermatt and the days there were like a dream. The amazing spike of the Matterhorn dominated the skyline of snowy peaks. We rode up to Gornergrat on the highest railway in Europe and walked on the Gorner glacier, where Grandpa cut steps with his ice-axe. By the Riffelsee Granny made me draw the Matterhorn and the sketch survives. Even life in a grand hotel was an education, as I learnt that you could eat fruit with a knife and fork. We went on to Saas Fee, where we walked among more mountains and glaciers while Grandpa took photos; to Lucerne, where we criss-crossed the lake by steamer; and finally to Berne with its bears. I returned a total convert to foreign travel.

There were many changes affecting the family in 1947. My father, on reaching fifty, retired from the navy and found a post in the Ministry of Food, based in Birmingham. In December my other grandfather, Grandpa Bayne, died and we moved into his house in the London suburb of Beckenham, near the local golf course. I learned to hit the ball a mighty thwack, so that it vanished out of my sight, as I was short-sighted. Eventually my parents realised what was wrong and I took to wearing glasses. But Christopher declared he would no longer play with me, as he spent all his time looking for my ball. My brief golfing career was over.

In the spring of 1949 my mother took Christopher and me for a week to Amsterdam, where I loved the canals and windmills and eating cheese for breakfast. But in our absence Grandpa was struck down by a fatal heart attack and we had to hurry home. It was a sad blow for Granny, but a worse tragedy was in store for her. Her younger son Michael had had a brilliant career, with a scholarship to Eton and a first in mathematics from Magdalen College Oxford. He had worked on code-breaking at Bletchley Park and was now earning high praise at the Treasury. But in December 1949 he died of cancer, aged only twenty-nine. It took Granny a long time to get over this second cruel bereavement and she kept in touch with Michael's friends for the rest of her life.

These deaths brought my childhood to an end. I had had a carefree life and was a cheerful boy. As compared with conditions before the war, let alone with the present day, my life might have seemed deprived. I did not see my parents for long stretches. I wore Christopher's cast-off clothes and had no expensive toys. But not having known anything different, I was content with my lot. My close family came through the war unscathed, with no one killed or wounded. I had little idea of what the war had meant. I understand better now and am thankful that neither I nor my sons have had to go to war ourselves.

CHAPTER 3

# Education at Eton

B Y THE TIME I WENT TO Eton in 1949 the family had moved to the Lickey Hills near Birmingham. My parents bought a house, for the first time in their married life, and we stayed in it for eleven years. 'Heatherfield' was an unpretentious brick structure from the 1930s. But it had an acre of garden, with a hard tennis court, and commanded a wide prospect over the Severn valley to the Malvern Hills.

Life at Eton was a major change. At Stone House we were told where to go. At Eton boys had to find their own way to divisions (Etonian for classes), chapel, meals and games. Once I got the knack of it I enjoyed the freedom to organise my own life. I shared a room with Christopher, who bore it philosophically. I liked my housemaster, Denis Wilkinson, who was also my classical tutor, responsible for my academic progress. He had a friendly wife Gillian and three sons William, John and Dick. My first half (Etonian for term) went well, but this was not to last.

Just after Christmas I was struck with a painful earache, which led to a mastoid operation. While in hospital I was diagnosed with nephritis, inflammation of the kidneys. In those days the only treatment for nephritis was to avoid all exertion and follow a salt-free diet until the kidneys healed themselves. So I spent the first three months of 1950 without leaving my bed, which looked bad for my scholarship prospects. But my parents arranged tuition at home, with my father teaching me maths and my mother French. Adrian Cary, a friend of Uncle Michael's, taught me classics and my Latin and Greek improved fast. Otherwise I read a lot and listened to the radio. By May I had recovered to the point that I could go back to school, though without doing anything strenuous. I sat the scholarship exam again and the home tuition paid off. I came sixth on the list and earned a place as a King's Scholar. But the nephritis returned and I was back home in bed, missing the rest of the Summer Half and the whole of the Michaelmas. By the end of the year I was very restless, but my parents and doctors would not risk another relapse.

At last I was allowed back to school. I entered College, where the seventy King's Scholars of Henry VI's foundation lived, and enjoyed the

historic surroundings of College Chapel and Hall. The other members
of my election (Etonian for a year of Collegers) were not as intellectual
as I had feared. We all lived in Chamber, a long room divided up by
ancient wooden partitions. Stephen McWatters, the Master in College,
was a bachelor with a nervous manner. I grew to like and respect him,
but feared the draconian Matron in College, Miss Iredale Smith.

Eton preserved many traditions. We wore black tail coats as school
dress, in mourning for George III. Junior boys acted as fags (i.e. servants)
to senior ones, though the duties were seldom onerous. I fagged for
William Wilkinson, my tutor's son, and chose as my own fag his brother
John, later an MP. Discipline involved corporal punishment of a
bewildering variety. I counted six distinct ways that boys could be
beaten: by the senior boy in their house ('beaten up'), the school rowing
eight ('eight-tanned') or the self-selecting Eton Society, alias Pop
('pop-tanned'); by their housemaster, the Lower Master or the Headmaster ('swiped'). The tortures sound gruesome, but in fact they were
easily avoided. In Summer Half 1951 I was made Captain of Chamber,
responsible for keeping order among my election. I found that I too had
the power to beat boys, with a length of rubber tubing called the siphon,
and on one occasion I was forced to use it. A newly arrived Colleger
had never been to boarding school before and was persistently teased. He
reacted with furious acts of violence, for which I was obliged to beat
him. I hated doing it, as his tormentors were guiltier than he was and I
had failed to control them. I was glad to escape from Chamber into a
room of my own and from then on avoided occasions when I would have
to impose discipline.

On the face of it, my scholastic career at Eton was very successful. Up
to the point when we took O-levels (now replaced by GCSE), I would
compete with Gavin Barrie Murray, my closest friend, to be top of my
election. But in the critical half that determined our 'final order', I
dropped to third place and thus missed the chance to become Captain of
the School. I chose to become a classics specialist and progressed to A1,
the senior division. In my last year I won the Newcastle scholarship, the
most prestigious classics award, followed by the Reynolds prize,
competing against the whole school. But in fact my classics teachers
found me a disappointment. The highest scholarly achievement was to
write elegant Latin and Greek, in prose and verse. We studied Greek and
Roman authors as guides to style and vocabulary for our own

compositions. But composition did not come naturally to me. I could do it if I concentrated really hard, but otherwise I soon fell into errors.

This did not worry me unduly. I was good at translation into English because I was interested in the content of what Homer or Cicero was saying. I enjoyed essays for 'Sunday questions' in divinity, which was treated as part of classics. My marks for class work were undistinguished, but the order depended entirely on performance in trials (Etonian for exams), where I could concentrate for long enough to produce compositions of sufficient quality. My success in the Newcastle came from my strong performance in the divinity papers and Richard Martineau and David Simpson, who taught me, were not happy at this result. For my part, I found their teaching in A1 uninspiring as compared with others like Raef Payne, who was now my classical tutor. The best teaching of all was the course on Dante given by Robert Birley, the Headmaster. His command of the subject and manifest enthusiasm made Dante's unfamiliar world come alive for us and we were always sorry when his division ended. The result was that the most satisfying part of my Etonian education, in both classics and other things, took place outside the classroom and even away from the school altogether. Here Eton had a tremendous amount to offer.

At home on the Lickey Hills we lived a fairly isolated life. My parents found few congenial neighbours. My father cultivated his vegetable garden, which did not appeal to me, though I enjoyed his tennis lessons. I amused myself playing with my brother David. We equipped armies of Halma men with swords from pins, shields from tiddlywinks and helmets from halibut oil capsules – I have them still. The Penguin Classics were beginning to come out and I became fascinated by classical mythology. But archaeology soon took its place.

For Easter 1952 my grandmother took me to Rome. She was an enthusiastic sightseer and I acquired a lifelong addiction from her. We visited every ancient Roman site we could and in a short dash to Naples added Pompeii and Herculaneum; we also met the Pope. At school I joined the Archaeological Society and gave them a lecture on Pompeii. On whole holidays the society would go up to see sights in London or make bicycle expeditions to local churches. I never missed the chance to go on such excursions. I had been in Windsor Castle on my fifteenth birthday, with the rest of the school, to see the coffin of King George

VI pass by. I became a Steward of St George's Chapel, responsible for guiding visitors on Sunday afternoons. I showed off the tomb of King Henry VI and before long could identify all the stalls and banners of the Knights of the Garter. As a Steward, I could watch the annual Garter procession and was there to see Sir Winston Churchill admitted.

In 1953 Aunt Diana invited me to join her in Greece. I travelled out alone and got on the wrong train at Rome, heading for Sicily rather than Brindisi. I discovered my mistake at dawn at Paola, deep in Calabria, and spent the whole day in local trains crawling from the toe of Italy to the heel. But I reached Brindisi just too late and my ship left without me. By great good fortune another ship was sailing next day and I contrived to travel on the *Kolokotrones* without paying an extra fare. I arrived at Corfu only one day late to meet Aunt Diana, who had been burning the wires to England when I had failed to turn up.

We travelled round the Peloponnese by local bus. It was paradise for a keen classical sightseer, even better than Rome. I inspected every temple, marketplace, stadium and theatre from Olympia to Corinth, with Byzantine churches and Venetian castles for good measure. We gave the same treatment to Athens, where Granny joined us, and finally to Delphi (Plate 1). While all the classical ruins absorbed me, I was most intrigued by the prehistoric palaces and beehive tombs of Mycenae and Tiryns. I liked the idea of reconstructing a culture without the help of written sources. On my return home Aunt Diana entrusted me with a very large trunk, which I was to register through to London at Brindisi station before boarding the train for Rome. But my bad luck returned: the train left with me on it, but the trunk still on the platform. I had to stop in Rome and seek the help of the embassy, where another of Uncle Michael's friends was eventually able to retrieve the trunk. Back at Eton my lecture on 'Travels with an Aunt in Greece' went on so long that it spread over two sessions of the Archaeological Society.

I found more archaeological openings as I went up the school. I gained access to the Egyptological collection in the Myers Museum, presided over by Mr Tait. I began excavating: first from school at a Saxon palace in Old Windsor; then in the holidays at the Roman town of Viroconium, near Shrewsbury. The summer I left Eton I joined Celia Topp and her family excavating a dolmen in western Ireland. I was happy to be on a prehistoric dig in an area so rich in megalithic remains. We all shared a caravan and our finds went on display in the archaeological museum in Dublin.

Apart from archaeology my main pursuits centred on acting and creative writing. Soon after Raef Payne arrived, he directed *Henry IV Part 2* as the school play. He chose me as Falstaff, the part he had played himself in *Henry IV Part 1* as a boy eight years before. I cultivated a voice and manner 'redolent of sack and debauchery' (as one master put it) and was padded out by cushions in front and behind (Plate 2). The play went well, but I had entered so far into the spirit of Falstaff that it took me the rest of the year to shake him off.

I wrote light verse and humorous prose, which sometimes appeared in the weekly *Eton College Chronicle*. As a result, I was chosen as one of the two editors of the *Chronicle* in my last year. At first I enjoyed planning the paper, writing leaders, thinking up competitions and riding my bicycle everywhere. I achieved enough fame to be elected to Pop. But I became tired of chasing up laggard contributors to complete the 7,000 words needed each week. Two ribald leaders escaped my editorial eye and earned me reprimands from the Headmaster. When I left Eton I gave up journalism.

Though I did not shine at most sports, I enjoyed myself in the Wall Game (Plate 3). This consists of a continuous scrum played against a long brick wall. When a dominant team drives its opponents behind a white line near the end of the wall, it can score a 'shy', like a try in rugby. Collegers play throughout their time, so that with acquired skill they can match a team of boys from the rest of the school who have only played for one year. A large crowd watched the annual match on St Andrew's Day, though it is the world's worst spectator sport. In the year I took part, deep mud covered the players and prevented either side from scoring. By the end even my parents did not recognise me.

Sex had no part in my life. Homosexual passions developed between some boys, certainly, but I never observed any in my own election and no one made a pass at me. The more obvious vices were alcohol and smoking, but since most Collegers were poor, we could not really afford them. My own resistance to temptation was increased by my links with the Franciscans. The chaplain who had prepared me for confirmation asked me to look after an Anglican friar, Brother Peter, who visited the school in my last year. He was an inconspicuous man, whose brown habit looked too big for him; but when he spoke, everyone listened. I learnt from him that the service of God required a personal commitment, like the poverty and humility practised by the Franciscans.

Only a few of those I met at Eton remained part of my life afterwards. Most members of my election were going to Cambridge, while I was bound for Oxford. After my nomadic diplomatic life began, I lost track of all except Gavin Barrie Murray, who became my solicitor, though I have rediscovered others in my retirement. But I remained in touch with Raef Payne, who later did even more for my three sons than he had done for me. I had no hesitation in sending them to Eton, despite my critique of classics in my time. I enjoyed myself at the school and had opportunities I would not have found elsewhere. My sons had the same experience.

CHAPTER 4

# Oxford undergraduate

M Y ENTRY TO UNIVERSITY DID NOT go according to plan. I applied to
Magdalen College Oxford, where Christopher was already reading
history and Granny had endowed the Michael Ashcroft scholarship in
mathematics. When I sat the scholarship exam in December I thought
the omens were good. But Magdalen did not offer me an award, only a
place as a commoner. I had made a poor showing in the exam papers
and clearly had not concentrated hard enough. This was a major setback
for my confidence and for my parents' finances. But there was just time
to enter for the Christ Church scholarship in January. I banished Falstaff
for good and spent the Christmas holidays reading Cicero and Sophocles.
These efforts earned me a classical exhibition at Christ Church, to my
great relief.

Before I went up I had to decide about my National Service, then
compulsory. Christopher had already done his two years, but Christ
Church and my family wanted me to go up at once. So my service was
deferred till after my studies were over. But having been an incompetent
cadet at Eton, I wanted to join the army in optimum conditions when
the time came. I therefore joined the Officers' Training Corps (OTC) at
Oxford and did six weeks basic training in my first long vacation. For
the next three summers I spent time with artillery regiments and passed
a War Office Selection Board for officers. In fact these precautions were
not needed, as my deferment carried me beyond the end of National
Service.

My OTC experience was not wasted. I saw the great wire barrier in
the forest that divided East Germany from West, chilling evidence of the
Cold War. I learnt the gun drill for a 25-pounder gun and fired one in
the University Parks on Remembrance Sunday to mark the two-minute
silence. My best moment came when the BBC needed a dozen French
soldiers for a programme on Napoleon's return from Elba, being shot
near Oxford. The commandant of the closest regular unit decided that
he could release his men to portray British soldiers, but not French ones.
He passed the request to the university OTC and I was lucky in the

ballot. I spent a happy day shouting '*Vive l'Empereur!*' outside Waddesdon Manor, wearing a blue uniform coat and a tall black shako. It was my first and most dramatic TV appearance.

In October 1955 I went up to Christ Church. As at Eton, I was much taken with its history and architecture. It had been founded by Cardinal Wolsey, in the former priory of St Frideswide, and Henry VIII re-founded it on his deathbed as a combined college and cathedral. I enjoyed worshipping in a Romanesque cathedral, dining in a Tudor hall and studying in a Palladian library. I lived in a garret in Peckwater Quad designed by Dean Aldridge in 1705. Some of the undergraduates had a reputation for rowdiness, but I easily kept out of their way.

The first five terms of the classics course were devoted to language and literature, called 'Mods'; the remaining seven covered philosophy and ancient history, called 'Greats'. In Mods we read a wide range of Greek and Latin texts and studied 'special books' in each language in greater depth; I chose Greek tragedy and Roman comedy. Homeric archaeology, my 'special subject', alone made the course worthwhile. The lecturer, Dorothea Gray, did not warm to masculine items like arms and armour, but produced a set of Homeric Barbies to illustrate women's costume. I spent an hour each week with a Christ Church tutor and attended a few lectures. That disposed of work and left plenty of time for other things.

I got to know and like the others reading Mods in the college: Justin Banbury, who became my closest friend, Gervais Angel, who spoke Welsh, and Simon Freebairn-Smith, who sang. I made friends with classicists from elsewhere: Christoper Roberts of Magdalen, Richard Sorabji of Pembroke and Timothy Gee of Trinity. I first met Tim Gee at tea with Mr Wainwright, a retired Egyptologist who revealed himself as the 'anonymous donor' of a generous archaeological prize. I had just won this with an essay on prehistoric Malta, while Tim came second. We formed an immediate bond and together joined the university Archaeological Society. Its leading figure was David Sturdy, a historian at Christ Church, who had learnt that new student rooms would be built on a college car-park. He and I started a rescue dig in January 1956, with snow on the ground, hoping to learn what had preceded the college, or even the priory, at that spot. But we found the site hopelessly disturbed by a large brick drainage sump, part of the original plumbing for Peckwater Quad.

Tim Gee and I hankered after prehistoric excavation and gained the support of Humphrey Case, deputy keeper at the Ashmolean Museum. We persuaded the Archaeological Society to conduct a summer dig at Lyneham Iron Age camp in North Oxfordshire. A party of diggers took up residence in the youth hostel at Charlbury, travelling to the site in a Ford van lent by the museum. Lyneham was a small circular camp with a single earth rampart. We dug a section through this, revealing a low stone kerb at the back, a walkway on top, and a stout wall in front, most of which had tumbled forwards into the ditch. Soundings inside the rampart, where huts might have stood, produced a few good potsherds, a bone needle and a sling bolt. These were enough to date Lyneham to 150–200 BC, like similar camps in the eastern Cotswolds. I wrote up my report and was proud of my first published work.

In September 1956 the family planned to take a cruise to the Eastern Mediterranean. But because of the tension over Suez everyone withdrew except Christopher and me. I broadened my knowledge of classical ruins, but the prehistoric sites still excited me most – Minoans in Crete and especially Hittites in south-east Turkey. I was in a small group of enthusiasts detached to visit Karatepe in the Taurus Mountains, where the Hittite reliefs were well worth three dusty days in local buses. On our overnight stop at Ceyhan I shared a room with Oliver Gurney, author of the Pelican book *The Hittites*. Severely bitten by bed-bugs, he emerged from our room around midnight to discover that our hotel was also a brothel. Luckily I was a heavy sleeper.

I became very involved with the Franciscans again. In Holy Week 1956 I paid my first visit to the Friary, a group of converted farm buildings in Dorset. The friars followed the monastic offices and there was a full set of Easter services, with much Gregorian chant. As well as time in the chapel, guests also helped with gardening and cooking. I was asked to direct the passion plays from Dorothy Sayers' *The Man Born to be King*. Though written for radio, they proved very moving on stage and my cast did wonders. Brother Peter and other friars would come to Oxford in most terms, to hold services, meet old friends and make new ones. Peter was preparing me to take over as the Franciscans' Oxford Secretary.

Time passed cheerfully. Suddenly I realized I had only sixteen weeks left before the Mods' exam in April 1957 and I was not ready. I cut off all outside activities, even archaeology and the friars. I passed my days studying in libraries or my garret, ending after supper with a long reading from Homer or Virgil. I compiled detailed notes, finding that if I wrote things down I would remember them. The Christmas vacation was spent alone in Birmingham University library. I finished this crash course just in time before the exams and was rewarded with a first.

I looked forward to the Greek and Roman history part of the Greats course. This was familiar ground and covered archaeological evidence as well as the literary sources. Philosophy also involved the classical authors Plato and Aristotle, but even more it embraced the work of the Oxford philosophers of the day. They focused on linguistic analysis, to show what words and concepts meant. I found I could just about grasp this by breaking it down into simple propositions. But I shared my tutorials with Peter Jay, later journalist and ambassador in Washington. He and the logic tutor delighted in its complexities, so I felt even more at sea. I now had two tutorial sessions per week, with an essay required for each, and more lectures than before. My practice was to devote Tuesday to Thursday wholly to academic work, leaving the long week-end free for other things.

Archaeology now resumed in full force, stimulated by a family holiday to the painted caves of the Dordogne and the megalithic monuments of Brittany. Lascaux, the finest cave, was already shut for restoration, but Granny talked her way in. I spent the summer term cycling round Oxfordshire looking for a site for the Archaeological Society's next excavation. The choice fell on Madmarston Camp near Banbury, a large Iron Age hill-fort with a Roman settlement in the valley below. The dig was directed by Peter Fowler, who had come up to read history with a proven record as an excavator and took charge at Madmarston for three seasons. In the first year we put a section through the Iron Age banks and ditches, working in pairs.

I had led a male-dominated life for twelve years and more. I had met few girls and felt ill at ease with them. But Peter Fowler gathered a good crop of female diggers, including Joanna Close-Brooks, Edna Kilgour and Diana Wilde from Lady Margaret Hall (LMH). I was paired in the trench with Diana Wilde (known as Dee) and was taken with her from the start. She had a slender figure, a tall brow, a cheerful smile and a calm manner that disarmed my shyness. We found that digging went better to music, especially the 'Anvil Chorus' from Verdi's *Trovatore*. But I saw that she had many other admirers.

In October 1957 a set of Bronze Age ring-ditches at Eynsham became the main site for the Archaeological Society. As Excavation Secretary I would lead a party out on Saturdays, with keen newcomers like Nicolas Hawkes (son of an archaeologist) and Jeffery May (who later became one). Dee and Joanna usually came too and I was glad to see them. On our return I would invite the party back for tea and crumpets, having acquired a spacious corner room in Peckwater, normally given to a don. Later in the year we were called out to a Roman cemetery at Dorchester-on-Thames, threatened by gravel-digging. Driving back in the dark in the Ashmolean van, we were stopped by the police just below Carfax. We all held our breath, as the van's legal limit was four people. It then contained seven living souls and four Roman skeletons. But the police only pointed out that a headlight was not working.

I went back twice to the Friary for the annual Epiphany Pageant. In one year I played the prophet Isaiah, with a fine black beard, who introduced the drama. In the next I was the Evangelist, reading passages from the gospels while the Christmas story was mimed on stage. As planned, I became the Oxford Secretary for the Franciscans, responsible for organising their visits. Meanwhile Brother Peter entered Cuddesdon theological college, to emerge as Father Peter. I met the local British Council representative, Richard Frost, who was worried that overseas graduate students in Oxford were neglected by their colleges. Could resident undergraduates help to make them welcome? Using my Franciscan contacts, I set up a welcoming network for foreign scholars, which got off to a good start.

I made more classical forays abroad. One summer Justin Banbury, Tim Gee, Christopher Roberts and I drove to Sicily in Justin's sister's car, an aging Standard 10. The shock-absorbers had to be replaced in Paris, the radiator sprang a leak in Calabria and the exhaust-pipe came apart at Enna, in the middle of Sicily, but we got to where we wanted. I added to my stock of classical ruins and was dazzled by the Norman mosaics of Monreale and Cefalu. Tim and I made a detour to Malta and saw the amazing megalithic temples that had earned me the prize which financed most of my trip. Next spring the same party, with John Barron of Balliol replacing Tim, went out to Greece. We celebrated Orthodox Easter in Athens, watching Christ's coffin pass by on Good Friday. At dawn on Easter Sunday we waited on the hill of Lycabettus to join the procession with our lighted candles. We reached the island sanctuary of Apollo on

Delos and his remote temple at Bassae, lost in the cloud. We admired Nestor's Mycenean palace at Pylos, recently uncovered, and inspected the great Minoan sites on Crete more thoroughly than I could do on my cruise.

In the summer term of 1958 Dee Wilde sometimes invited me and Tim Gee to join her and her friends on adventurous expeditions. She had read how T. E. Lawrence had gone down the Trill Mill Stream, an underground river in Oxford, and suggested we might do so too. We arranged to meet at Folly Bridge, but Tim failed to appear. Dee and I set off in a canoe and tracked down the entrance near Oxford castle. It was blocked by a gate, but we hauled our canoe over the top to gain access to a brick-lined tunnel, with a good depth of water in it. Light filtered through gratings at intervals and the tunnel was surprisingly clean. After twenty minutes paddling we pushed through a curtain of foliage to emerge into Christ Church memorial gardens. Damp but triumphant, we repaired to my room to change, concealing the large tear that Dee had in the seat of her jeans.

In the vacation I began the year-long revision for my Greats exams. My father had a new job in the Ministry of Agriculture, based in Worcester. My parents left Heatherfield and rented part of Norton Grange, in a village just outside the city. There they found congenial neighbours, especially Terence Smith, a retired Gurkha brigadier, with his wife Gwen and daughters Susan and Joanna. Christopher was now working for Shell in Venezuela. David was at Eton and already a keen horologist. Norton Grange had a clock tower and he made the ancient clock work again.

Yet I could not give my mind to revising. Dee had left Oxford with a second in English and gone home to Bideford in Devon. She had got a job with ICI and I did not know when I would see her again. I found this prospect more than I could bear and realised that I had fallen in love with her. I did not dare to declare my love, for fear of rejection, but wrote poetry instead. An example follows; Sabrina, with lilies in her hair, is borrowed from Milton's *Comus*.

*Lines to be Enclosed in a Bottle and Thrown over Worcester Bridge*

Nymph of Severn, fair Sabrina,
Listen to my anguished prayer,
Where you sit with calm demeanour
Knitting lilies through your hair.

I'd resigned myself to spending
One whole year in endless toil,
Daily to the classics bending,
Nightly burning midnight oil.

I decided this; but Cupid
Had reserved a different fate –
Love. Yes, love, which drives me stupid,
Will not let me concentrate.

Blindly over Aristotle
I pursue the scholar's art;
While within this fragile bottle
I enclose my broken heart.

Take it! There! As you go gliding
On your journey to the south,
Let my message, safely riding,
Travel with you to your mouth.

When the sea attempts to mingle
Your fresh waters with his tide,
Do not let him. Nymph, stay single;
Thrust him courteously aside.

So let the unsullied Severn,
Cleaving the Atlantic flow,
Bear these verses safe to Devon
By the sands of Westward Ho!

There, untroubled, with no knowledge
Of the ache that racks my mind,
Dwells my love beside the Torridge,
A slim maiden fair and kind.

Drive your stream through the slow reaches
Where the Devon rivers meet;
Seek her on the hidden beaches,
Cast this bottle at her feet.

Your mission is completed. Turning,
Seek this city whence you start.
Leave my love alone there, learning
How she rules another's heart.

If she loves me, you'll be sharing
All the joy a lover knows.
If not . . . soon you may be bearing
Me, where now this bottle goes.

When I went back to Oxford in October I found some solace. Dee's friend Kate Taster had married Richard Sorabji, classicist and philosopher. Dee often came to spend the weekend with them and I always found an excuse to call while she was there. At last I plucked up my courage. I sent Dee a Valentine card and invited her to the theatre in London. We went to *Irma la Douce*, a light-hearted musical, and enjoyed ourselves thoroughly. From then on we met in London or Oxford as often as we could. I was no longer in doubt that she enjoyed going out with me or spending time together in her flat in Pimlico.

While we were apart, I still wrote poems and did not yet dare to send them to her. This one was written in the garden of Norton Grange.

*The Pear Tree*

The pear tree up above my head
Drops blossom on my Cicero,
Whose perorations lie unread
Beneath the drift of petal snow.

I have no energy to write
My complex notes on Rome's decay;
The spring which turns the pear tree white
Beguiles my longing heart away.

Your fresh and smiling image floats
Between me and the classics now.
The blossoms that obscure my notes
Wreathe in a garland on your brow.

And since I know you cannot share
My boundless view of changing sky,
But only glimpse a distant square
Framed by blank walls of ICI,

I bend this flower-strewn page, and hope
The petals in the fold may bring,
Imprisoned in the envelope
A message of the fragrant spring.

And as my unaccustomed pen
Achieves these verses, now I know
I must collect my thoughts again
And concentrate on Cicero.

The exams approached. With just a week to go I developed mild conjunctivitis due to eye-strain. My Oxford doctor unknowingly prescribed a drug to which I was allergic. My face swelled up with an ugly rash, which made it painful to read. I was deeply cast down, but found the strength of will to keep working. By the time the exams began I felt better and I got through all the papers in good shape. As the term ended, Dee escaped from ICI to join me at the Worcester College ball and to spend some days at Madmarston, where we dug together an untidy cutting in the Roman settlement. After a long wait the exam results came through – and again I had won a first. Even my philosophy marks showed I had absorbed much more than I had realised. Among the congratulations I received the best was a telegram from Dee. As soon as I could I went up to London and we celebrated by going to see John Wayne in *Rio Bravo* – a film that will always have romantic associations.

Our courtship now advanced apace (Plate 4). I went to Bideford to meet her parents and we took a picnic from Clovelly to Blackchurch Rock. She came to Norton Grange to meet my family and I gave her my poems at last. We spent a weekend excavating on Bredon Hill, with David as chaperone. Later we joined a party to dig in France, at a Neolithic camp called Biard near Cognac. The director was Claude Burnez, a friend of Humphrey Case from the Ashmolean. He owned a brandy firm called the Maison Prunier, but his real passion was prehistory. ICI was persuaded to give Dee an extra week's holiday as an essential member of the group. After a hard day on the site the cognac would flow freely and one night I drank to excess, with Dee as witness. But it served its purpose – I have never done so again.

My academic life had thus achieved all its targets. In my personal life I was happily in love. Dee and I knew we wanted to marry and told our parents so. But we did not yet know when that could be, because my professional life remained to be settled.

CHAPTER 5

# Archaeological research

FOR MANY YEARS I HAD intended to become an archaeologist. But as the prospect approached, I began to question this ambition. Did I really want to spend my life poring over the problems of the distant past? Should I not be thinking of a career of greater service to the community? I was moved in this direction by the example of the Franciscans and knew that many of my friends, like Justin Banbury and Gervais Angel, were bound for the Anglican ministry. I had no vocation myself and was not attracted by teaching either. But I made enquiries about the civil service, especially the Foreign Office. I liked the idea of an international career and was encouraged by my experience with welcoming foreign students. My family were also in favour and a diplomatic friend of Uncle Michael gave me valuable advice.

However, I was still keen to do some archaeological research. Entry to the civil service was highly competitive and I might not get in. Once in, I might find it did not suit me. A research degree would be my ticket back into academic life. Other friends, like Peter Fowler and Joanna Close-Brooks, were embarking on archaeological careers. I decided to ride both horses for as long as possible. I therefore applied in spring 1959 to begin a Bachelor of Letters later in the year, which was the usual transition to a doctorate. I planned to take the exam for the Foreign Office early in 1960. If successful, I would seek postponement of my entry at least till mid-1961, to give time to complete my research. If I failed, I would persist with archaeology. This complicated programme worked out according to plan. This chapter tells the full story of my research activity, continuing after I joined the Foreign Office.

To get started, I needed a good research subject. I wanted to combine classical studies with prehistoric archaeology and to work in both Greece and Turkey. Homeric archaeology met all these criteria and I turned to Dorothea Gray for help. She agreed to be my supervisor and pointed me towards my subject. The Trojan War, as treated by Homer, was thought to have happened at the end of the Late Bronze Age, around 1200 BC.

Not only Troy but many other sites down the coast of north-west Turkey were destroyed at that time. Settled occupation in the Early Iron Age, often by colonists from Greece, resumed only slowly from around 900 BC. Both the Late Bronze Age and Early Iron Age peoples used distinctive types of grey monochrome pottery. Unlike contemporary painted pottery, these grey wares had not been much studied. They could hold clues to what had happened in the missing centuries.

I was duly accepted to conduct research on: 'The Grey Wares of North-Western Anatolia in the Middle and Late Bronze Age and the Early Iron Age and Their Relation to the Early Greek Settlements'. I settled down to read up all the sources I could find in the library of the Ashmolean Museum, emerging only at midday for a pie and a pint in the Lamb and Flag across St Giles. I also prepared for a summer of fieldwork in Greece and Turkey, joining the British School of Athens and the British Institute of Archaeology at Ankara. I acquired two more mentors. Professor John Cook of Bristol, with a Turkish colleague Ekrem Akurgal, had excavated the site of ancient Smyrna, near modern Izmir, and found both prehistoric and later grey pottery. He was my guide to the evidence for Greek settlement and later became my supervisor. James Mellaart, Deputy Director at Ankara, had already shown that the prehistoric grey ware was not Greek in origin but began in Anatolia. He became my instructor in matters prehistoric. Both Cook and Mellaart were experts in identifying ancient sites from the potsherds found on their surface. I expected to do a lot of that.

The geographical scope of my research embraced the classical region called Aeolis (see Map 1). The historian Herodotus listed twelve Aeolic cities strung along the coast of Asia Minor, from Smyrna to Pitane. He placed six more cities in the island of Lesbos and referred also to settlements under Mount Ida, close to Troy. Whenever excavated, sites identified as these cities yielded 'Aeolic' grey ware during the Early Iron Age. Earlier, in the Middle and Late Bronze Age, grey ware was also found over the same region, though always mixed with red and buff wares in similar shapes. The most complete excavations were at Troy, where an American team under Carl Blegen had just published, in four large volumes, the results of work done in the 1930s. In the same period Winifred Lamb had excavated at Thermi and Antissa on Lesbos. The results from the recent dig at Smyrna were still unpublished. John Cook warned me that Akurgal seldom allowed anyone else to write about his sites.

When 1960 began, I had to interrupt research and turn my mind to the Foreign Office entry. I sat a written exam in a chilly hall in Bayswater. Then I was called to an interview board. Over two stressful days, in a group of six, I solved problems in writing, discussed them in committee and was interviewed by the three board members. I thought the other candidates did better than me and prepared for failure. But in due course I was called to a final interview with suited figures across a circular table, and stood my ground in an argument about treasure trove. Just before I left for Turkey, I learnt that the Foreign Office would accept me. I had been very lucky, because the Foreign Office, having under-recruited for years, was taking twice the usual crop of new entrants. I arranged to start work in July 1961, hoping to have done most of my research by then. A few of my Oxford and Eton friends joined the public service with me. Christopher Roberts went into the Board of Trade and Tim Gee into the British Council. Christopher Mallaby, a contemporary Eton classicist, became a colleague in the Foreign Office, while I later worked with Anthony Loehnis, Mistress Quickly to my Falstaff, in the Bank of England.

Meanwhile I went with Granny and Aunt Diana on a spring tour of Egypt, Jordan and Israel. This was my last foreign trip with Granny and we got into places that would never be accessible now. Cairo and Luxor were bliss for an archaeologist like me and I greeted as old friends monuments I had studied at Eton with Mr Tait. The Holy Land was more unsettling. In Jerusalem I was shocked by the divisions of Christendom and doubted the authenticity of the plethora of holy places. But I found I could imagine the presence of Jesus better from the Roman remains surviving in Jerusalem and Capernaum, even when they dated from later periods. Archaeology allayed my scepticism about the oral traditions.

I said goodbye to Dee and my family and started for Turkey. I landed in Istanbul late on 28 April and found a curfew was in force after a day of anti-government riots. A soldier stopped me with the word '*Yasak*' (forbidden) and a gesture, and I went indoors at once. I travelled on to Ankara and established myself at the British Institute, where James Mellaart and his Turkish wife Arlette made me welcome. Nervously, I bearded Ekrem Akurgal at the university. He readily allowed me to study the material there from Smyrna and other sites. I learnt to tell my two types of pottery apart. The prehistoric ware was clearly imitating metal and often glittered with mica. It favoured pale shades of grey and could have a soapy feel. The Aeolic ware was harder, smoother and usually darker, and the shapes were less obviously metallic.

Having made a good start in Ankara, I travelled to Izmir to take ship for Athens. On 27 May there was a coup d'état and the Turkish government was overthrown. Fortunately my ship was allowed to leave next day, escorted by a naval gunboat. I settled in Athens at the British School, but was soon diverted from my studies. Sir Edward de Stein, an old friend of Granny, on retiring from his merchant bank, was taking his three partners round the Aegean in a steam yacht. I was recruited to escort a partner's daughter of my own age. In conditions of great luxury, the cruise took me to Patmos, where St John wrote the Revelation, and Samos, where I got Sir Edward to eat octopus (he did not like it). After the cruise I flew back to England for two weeks, generously financed by Christopher, home on leave from Venezuela. I had a happy reunion with Dee, with a night at the Christ Church ball and a visit to Madmarston, now directed by Jeffery May.

Back in Greece, I sailed to Mytilene to begin my fieldwork. I studied the grey wares in the museum there and set out to trace the Aeolic cities on Lesbos. All except Mytilene itself were free from later building and most were by the sea. I would reach them by bus, followed by long treks on foot, and gather potsherds from the surface. Then I would swim and eat my lunch under an olive tree. At Antissa I found the prehistoric levels visible in a great bank exposed by the sea. From there I walked all day to Eressos, the home of Sappho the poetess, where a friendly shepherd lodged me for the night. I followed John's Cook's directions to a new prehistoric site at Perama, where again the sea was revealing a rich harvest of sherds. I took a flight to nearby Lemnos, where an Italian expedition was working. I studied their finds in the museum in Myrina, the island's capital, fortified by a delicious Lemnian breakfast called *bougatsa*. One evening I watched the town festival, with a procession of boats and fireworks just like the Fourth of June at Eton. That completed my Greek fieldwork. I sailed to Chios and crossed the narrow strait to the Turkish mainland. I settled into the Izmir museum to work on the prehistoric pottery from Smyrna kept there. But I was impatient for the arrival of Dee and her party.

We had planned that Dee would use her three weeks holiday from ICI to visit me in Turkey. She would come out with Fiona Greig, an

Oxford-based archaeologist, and her friend Robert Sandell. But Robert dropped out and Dee's friend Edna took his place. I met the three girls off the *caique* from Chios and we spent our first fortnight visiting famous classical sites – Pergamum, Ephesus, Miletus, Priene and Didyma. We wandered almost alone through this splendid series of ruins, as tourism in Turkey had not really begun. We sailed to Bodrum, where Edna's money blew into the sea and a friendly Turk dived in to save it. Near Miletus we attended a *sünnet* (circumcision) party, with gipsy music and dancing. We even did some serious archaeology, looking for a prehistoric site along the empty beach at Kuçadasì. The tall Turk in pyjamas watching us turned out to be the chief of police.

We stayed in simple hotels, often sleeping on the roof on hot nights. I wondered how the Turks would react to me and my seraglio of three. But I seemed to gain face in their eyes and they never molested the girls. As I was the Turkish speaker, I would go ahead, talking to the caretaker of that day's ruins, while the girls followed discreetly a few paces behind. In our last week we made a long bus journey north to visit Troy (Plate 5). I found the site extremely evocative. The great walls of Middle Bronze Age Troy VI still stood up high, with gateways and staircases. Inside we made out the cramped dwellings of Late Bronze Age Troy VIIA, thought to be Homer's Troy. Finally we crossed the Sea of Marmara to Istanbul. We visited churches, mosques, palaces and the bazaar by day and went by night to Western films dubbed into Turkish. In the Topkapi Museum Fiona attracted the roving eye of a professor of Islamic studies. He took us all swimming and then fed us peach jam in his flat, behaving impeccably throughout. Next day I sadly waved off the girls' ship from the Seraglio Point.

I was more in love with Dee than ever, after our happy time together, and work was the only solace. I set off north along the coast from Izmir, to complete my survey of sites on the Turkish coast. I sometimes took buses or got lifts, but was usually on foot; once a friendly Turk took me up on his horse to ford the river Hermus. The country was fertile, full of olive and fig trees, and dotted with springs and fountains very welcome to a thirsty archaeologist. Most of the ancient settlements were near the sea and I could swim after searching for pottery. I would visit villages to get guides to remote sites and stay overnight in the lodging provided free for passing travellers. I sat up late with the villagers, over glasses of tea, until I had satisfied their inexhaustible curiosity about their visitor. But I always paid for food and transport, as the local practice was. In this way I visited all the mainland Aeolic cities named by Herodotus and found several more sites from the Bronze Age. Eventually I came to Pitane, the northernmost city, to find Ekrem Akurgal excavating an early Greek cemetery. He welcomed me and allowed me to inspect his finds. But when I went round the dig taking notes, he grew angry and tore the pages from my notebook, saying I had gone too far. I apologised and he calmed down; but it took me a long time to recover my equanimity.

On the coast beyond Pitane I only found one relevant site, on an island, probably because the sea had come up farther in antiquity. Then I came out into the Edremit plain, a triangle of land in the shadow of Mount Ida. This marked the boundary of the Troad and the limit of my survey; I knew that John Cook was covering the Troad and I could draw on his findings. But the plain itself appealed to me. The Homeric city of Thebe was here, the home town of Hector's wife Andromache. Achilles had sacked it and captured Chryseis, daughter of Apollo's high priest, who called down the plague that starts the *Iliad*. I decided to conduct an intensive survey of the plain and tracked down a variety of ancient settlements, including a good candidate for Thebe. I made friends with a helpful student called Mehmet and was shown sites by the local antiquarian and a well-informed doctor with a German wife. Mehmet came back with me to Izmir to take an exam, but sadly failed it.

My time in Turkey was running short. I went to Bodrum again on the weekly bus, which left Izmir at 4 a.m. I overslept and reached the bus station just too late. I leapt into a taxi, crying 'Follow that bus!' and caught it up at the edge of town. In Bodrum I was intensely excited to see the finds from the Mycenean wreck at Burun Kale, the first harvest of underwater archaeology off Turkey: great copper ingots, bronze tools, Egyptian scarabs and a Hittite seal. Back in Izmir again, I took the night bus to Ankara. There I washed, sorted, marked and recorded my pottery collection, which took three days. I left Turkey on 12 October, bearing a sleeping bag bulging with potsherds, three *kilims* (woven rugs) bought with the help of Arlette Mellaart, and a book full of the addresses of Turks to whom I had promised to write.

I returned to Christ Church for the launch of the new Graduate Common Room, one of the first to be founded at Oxford. The idea came from Paul Kent, an enlightened chemistry don: Nicholas Grey, a chemist friend, was the first president; I was the secretary. I was just in time to be presented to the Queen when she visited the college. I remember the conversation vividly.

ER: What are you doing at present?
NB: I am doing research into early Greek archaeology.
ER: And what will you do when you leave Oxford?
NB: I have been accepted by the Foreign Office.
ER (knitting her brow): How will Greek archaeology help the Foreign Office?
NB (taken aback): Well . . . they are allowing me to finish my research.

By now I had firmly decided in favour of the diplomatic service, rather than archaeology. I was pleased with what I had done in Turkey, but I had often found it stressful and solitary. Even at Oxford I was working alone; I longed to be part of a team. I wanted company in my personal life too and so Dee and I became formally engaged in the New Year of 1961. But the wedding had to wait till I was earning a salary.

I set up another journey to Turkey in early March. In the train across Yugoslavia I met a Bulgarian tenor returning from training in Milan. Cravenly, I agreed to smuggle some watches across the border, to help him finance his Italian course. Retribution overtook me at Sofia, where my shoes were stolen. My first objective was to study the pottery in the Istanbul Museum from Troy and other sites. It was intensely cold and I huddled round a stove in the museum store. But only restored pots were visible from Troy, not the broken potsherds. A museum contact met the year before had promised me access, but he was ill and unavailable. Thus I never got to see all the finds from Troy and this had consequences later.

I moved on to fill in gaps left in last year's fieldwork. I visited Gordion, capital of Phrygia, out on the bare Anatolian plateau. The American excavators had uncovered marvellous palaces and royal tombs and found lots of grey pottery. In the Edremit Plain the almond blossom reminded me of the pear-tree at Norton Grange and I missed Dee. So the remote Aeolic site of Tisna, covered with wild flowers, stimulated another poem.

*Love among the Ruins*

No travellers to this city come,
Buried under heath and stone,
Save I – to find the threshold dumb
And walk the marketplace alone.

No challenge halts me as I pass
From bronze-clad warriors on the keep:
The hyacinths in the spring grass
Keep their watches while they sleep.

They do not fear their enemies
Might scale again the city wall,
Where crimson-stained anemones
Mark a memorial to their fall.

Alone I wander on the hill,
While vultures circle overhead,
Questing in the heather still
The bodies of the ancient dead.

Here lightly an embroidered cover
Of grass and flowers lies above
True lover parted not from lover,
Secure in an immortal love.

Sleepers, with your loves beside you,
Grant solace to my yearning heart.
Where you sleep, none may divide you;
My love and I must lie apart.

The flowers that wreathe your bones can bring
No joy, but mock us with new pain.
My love and I can find no spring
Till I am in her arms again.

Crossing to Lesbos, I trekked twenty-five miles to visit the temple site of Apotheke. There was not much pottery visible, but I found an isolated chapel open – it was Orthodox Easter. (Over Anglican Easter, a week before, I had been in the empty tomb of a Phrygian king at Gordion.) I sailed on to Athens and caught the train home.

I was deep into drafting my thesis, now intended for a doctorate. But I only had two chapters written when I joined the Foreign Office and continued working away after hours. It was incomplete when I was posted to Manila, where I finally finished it in my air-conditioned bedroom. I submitted it in May 1964, having taken nearly five years over it. Home on leave that year, I was examined by John Boardman and Vincent Desborough, two giants of early Greek archaeology, who had never felt the need for doctorates themselves. But they approved of my work and I achieved my degree, lodging my thesis in the Bodleian Library.

The conclusions of my thesis were as follows. I had developed a typology for both prehistoric and Aeolic grey wares, with regional variants. I could show which forms came latest in the prehistoric sequence and which appeared first among the Aeolic ware, so as to suggest the transition between them. I found that at Troy and on Lesbos, but not at Smyrna and neighbouring sites, shapes derived from Mycenean pottery were popular in grey ware at the end of the Late Bronze Age. When Aeolic grey ware first emerged after the transition to the Early Iron Age, it was closer to these Mycenean imitations than to the indigenous forms. The Greek settlements elsewhere in Asia Minor used painted ware brought from mainland Greece. But the Aeolic colonists adopted the monochrome pottery tradition they found on the spot; painted pottery was very rare.

The transition could now be explained. Though the Trojans had imported and imitated Mycenean pottery, this was all the result of trade. But on Lesbos the finds from Perama and the late levels at Antissa suggested they were settled by Mycenean refugees, around 1100. Cut off from their roots in Greece, these refugees merged their pottery with what the local Lesbians made. More waves of settlers came across the Aegean later. Some stayed on Lesbos, while others took the monochrome pottery on to the mainland, where the earliest Greek levels at Smyrna went back to about 1000. This archaeological conclusion fitted in well with the foundation legends for the Aeolic cities, as recorded in authors writing many centuries later.

My next task was to get my research published. I could not do this with the entire thesis, since it drew heavily on unpublished work. But John Cook invited me to publish the prehistoric finds from Smyrna. I asked Oliver Gurney, now editor of the Ankara Institute's journal *Anatolian Studies*, if he would find room for this. But he was reluctant, as Smyrna had been dug by the School at Athens. He invited me to submit something else and I worked up a piece called 'Mycenean Finds in North-West Anatolia'. But in far-off Manila I was cut off from learned publications and I suffered from not having seen all the material from Troy. Gurney refused my article, saying that my findings had been anticipated in work already published. When I got back to London late in 1966 I resumed work on Smyrna for John Cook. But I had to catch up on scholarly work done in my absence in Manila, while coping with a busy job in the Office and a growing family. My script was still not ready when I was posted to Germany in 1969 and it was clear that I would never finish it. John Cook never reproached me, but I felt bad about it. I thought it irresponsible to do research, with help from many sources, but not to make the results known.

Yet this story has a happy ending. In the 1990s an Oxford-based scholar called Nigel Spencer published an article on Lesbos, arguing that in ancient times the island was culturally part of Anatolia, rather than Greece. He had found my thesis in the Bodleian and used it extensively to support this view. This article caught the eye of two German archaeologists, Dieter Hertel and Andreas Schachner, who read my thesis too and thought my findings were still valid. They wrote to ask if they could publish it and I enthusiastically agreed. I had the text put on a computer disc, checked the references as best I could and resurrected my original drawings from a trunk in the attic. The British Institute at Ankara gave me generous support and the British School at Athens chipped in too. In 2000 my original thesis appeared as Volume 37 of *Asia Minor Studien*, supplemented by an 'afterword' by Hertel and Schachner. I remain deeply grateful to them and to Nigel Spencer, who brought my work to light. At long last my research was published and my conscience was clear.

# CHAPTER 6

# Novice diplomat: UN Department

THE WORLD WAS IN A TURBULENT state when I joined the Foreign Office in July 1961. The Royal Navy was deployed in the Gulf, to deter Iraq from invading Kuwait. The East Germans, with Russian blessing, were about to build the Berlin Wall. A civil war was raging in the Congo. I learnt about these and other crises from the folders of telegrams that crossed my desk three times a day. I had been appointed the desk officer for economic questions in United Nations Department and learnt the job by doing it. Alan Horn, the assistant head of department, was my mentor. I rarely saw the head, John Tahourdin, while the Olympian under-secretaries were invisible to me. As I arrived, the department was preparing for the UN General Assembly in New York in September. I was due to be sent there as a reporting officer on the United Kingdom delegation. But before that happened I married Dee – the best thing I did in my whole life.

As our wedding approached I got to know Dee's family better. The Wildes had originated in Derbyshire and made their name in the legal profession in nineteenth century London, one of them becoming Lord Chancellor. A younger son, however, chose to join the Indian Army: he fought in the Mutiny, commanded the Punjab Frontier Force and ended as General Sir Alfred Wilde KCB. His youngest son Charles, Dee's grandfather, was educated at the United Service College in North Devon, the model for Kipling's *Stalky and Co*. Charles Wilde spent his working life abroad, but never forgot seeing Alicia Scott in church at Westward Ho, and in due course he married her. Dee's father Thomas Wilde was born in the Bahamas, where Charles and Alicia had created a sisal plantation. But this was ruined by hurricanes and young Tom Wilde grew up in Dutch Caribbean colonies, where his father worked as engineer or plantation manager.

Tom Wilde made his career as an instructor at the Merchant Navy College for wireless operators. During World War II he worked on secret radio transmissions to occupied Europe. After the war, the sale of the

Wilde family's legal offices at College Hill in the City brought him enough capital to make him independent. He moved to Bideford, where his mother still lived, and bought the run-down Gaiety Cinema in nearby Appledore. He restored the cinema and ran it with his wife for several years. But it could not compete with the advance of television, so that he had sold up shortly before I met the family. Tom Wilde was good with his hands, as carpenter and interior decorator; he was also widely read, especially in history. Like Dee, he was adventurous and always ready to make expeditions along the splendid scenic coast of North Devon. His wife Renée, however, gained greatest pleasure from being at home, looking after her family and providing delicious meals.

We were married on 16 September in the village church at Abbotsham near Bideford, which had monuments to Dee's family on the walls and in the churchyard (Plate 6). The vicar gave a free run to Father Peter, who took the service, and Justin Banbury, my best man. The local bell-ringers, at odds with the vicar, happily agreed to ring a peal for us. They were meant to stop when the bride arrived, but in their enthusiasm ignored all my signals. So Dee and her father marched up the nave with organ and bells in competition. At the altar we made our vows to each other directly, without any prompting from Father Peter, to show that we really meant them.

Less than a week later we flew off to New York. The other members of the visiting delegation, unaccompanied by their wives, were lodged in hotels. But the admirable Betty Wallis, who looked after accommodation in the resident mission, found a flat for us and a job for Dee as social secretary to the wife of Sir Patrick Dean, our Permanent Representative at the UN. The flat, near the Metropolitan Museum, contained all we could need. It was large enough for us to do some modest entertaining and Betty Wallis was our first guest. Dee could walk to the Deans' appartment, where she found Patricia Dean very easy to work for. She learnt many skills useful for a diplomatic wife and earned more than enough to cover her airfare.

The work of the UN General Assembly got under way slowly, being overshadowed by the death of Dag Hammarskjöld, the Secretary General, in an air crash. Dee and I had time to absorb the stimulating atmosphere of New York. We went to diplomatic parties and were entertained by Granny's American friends, who took us to Coney Island to eat lobster. But we enjoyed our own company best of all. We went up the Empire State Building, thoroughly explored the Metropolitan and became very attached to the Frick Collection. The first three months of our married life were a happy extended honeymoon.

I divided my working days between the UN building and the UK mission. In the first week I listened to speeches from President Kennedy, Soviet Foreign Minister Gromyko and Lord Home, the British Foreign Secretary. Then I settled into taking notes and writing reports on the general debate in the Economic Committee. I sat behind Barbara Salt and Michael Errock, the economic team from the mission. Barbara Salt was a formidable operator, able to range from persuasive feminine charm to rudeness that would never be tolerated in a man. But most often the front seat was occupied by Michael Errock, an independent-minded first secretary who taught me a lot. I built up my knowledge of the world economy by listening to the speeches, though in the duller passages Michael and I exchanged limericks. I chatted warily to Sergei Prokhorov, a Russian of my own age in the seat alongside. I distrusted him and was not surprised to learn later that he had been expelled for spying. Sometimes I helped out in the Social Committee, where there were many women delegates. I was there when the elegant black ladies representing Senegal and the Ivory Coast were reduced to incoherent fury as Nigeria's Foreign Minister, Jaja Wachuku, held forth in praise of polygamy.

The dominant political issue was decolonisation, on which Britain was on the defensive. Our West African colonies were now independent, but those in East and Southern Africa were not. We were strongly attacked not only by the Soviet Union and its allies, but also by new Commonwealth members, like India. We got little help from the United States or even from France, which had now freed all its African colonies. These attacks surprised me, as I had thought of the British Empire as a force for good. They taught me that countries will always prefer what they do themselves to anything imposed from outside – one of my first lessons in diplomacy.

We tried to prevent the venom of anti-colonialism from infecting the economic debates, but could not escape the Cold War. Western states made much of the financial support they provided to developing countries. Britain and France were generous aid-givers, mainly to ex-colonies, and so was the United States, encouraged by the success of the Marshall Plan. In 1961 all three countries were providing over 0.5

per cent of their national income in official aid, much more than in later years. We were also the main contributors to UN technical assistance programmes. The communist countries had fewer resources to offer. But their centrally planned economic system looked attractive to developing countries that had achieved independence under autocratic leaders. So the developing countries tried to get as much as they could out of both sides. They were also beginning to see the United Nations as a vehicle for their own ambitions, since they now had a built-in majority.

In November the Economic Committee turned to drafting resolutions. I graduated to writing speeches and even to occupying the UK seat in the committee, as Barbara and Michael were busy negotiating texts behind the scenes. The key resolution declared the 1960s to be the United Nations Decade of Development. The developing countries were pressing for a target of 5 per cent in annual economic growth, on which our instructions were sceptical. But Michael Errock, realising that it would be voted through anyway, decided to gain credit by welcoming it outright. This enabled him to head off an unwelcome proposal for a UN trade conference. Even so, the conference proposal was adopted a year later, and the UN Conference on Trade and Development (UNCTAD) became a permanent institution. The first UN Development Decade proved a success and more than met its 5 per cent growth objective.

The Economic Committee, working late into the night, wound up its work on 19 December and Dee and I flew home. I was reunited with Barbara Salt and Michael Errock in Geneva for the UN Economic and Social Council in July 1962. Dee came with me again, though seven months pregnant, and we found a small flat with a view of Mont Blanc. During the session, the UN Secretariat asked for Britain's help in getting authority for their land reform programme. Michael Errock put me in charge of getting the necessary draft resolution through. I had to brief myself rapidly on land reform issues, introduce the draft (Dee was in the public gallery) and respond to proposals for amendment. I fought off a Russian attack and finally got the resolution adopted unanimously. I also had to organise Barbara Salt's farewell reception, which involved smuggling large quantities of liquor over the border into France. She was due to go as ambassador to Israel, the first woman to head a British diplomatic mission. But tragically she got blood clots in both legs, which had to be amputated, and was unable take up her post.

★   ★   ★

Back in London from New York, Dee tracked down a flat for us in Cornwall Gardens, off Gloucester Road. It was on the ground floor and had a spacious living-room for which we borrowed furniture from our families. To the front we looked over the private gardens, to which we had access. At the back we could hear the rumble of the Underground, as we were close to where the body is put on the roof of a train in the Sherlock Holmes story *The Bruce-Partington Plans*. For the first time we could unpack all our wedding presents. We had to live frugally, as my annual salary was under £800, but Dee was an excellent manager. After the excitements of New York we settled to a more mundane life as a couple. This required more effort and forethought than I had expected, but was always rewarding and instructive. I learnt that there are many similarities between marriage and diplomacy.

Dee took a part-time job with the UN Association off Oxford Street until her baby was due. She became impatient as the date passed, but a night out at the film *Caesar and Cleopatra* induced the child to appear. Thomas Bayne was born on 14 September 1962, two days before our first anniversary. He lived out his early weeks in the shadow of the Cuban missile crisis and we wondered what his future might be. But the tension eased and the Cold War never became so dangerous again. Tom was an alert, active baby, given to waking in the night to demand food and entertainment. Dee provided the first, while I was responsible for the second. If he still cried, Woodward's Gripe Water was a regular standby. Once he began to yell as we were expecting guests to dinner. I reached into the kitchen for the familiar cloudy bottle and Dee poured a spoonful down his throat. But he yelled louder and began to blow bubbles; we had dosed him with shampoo instead.

In UN Department I settled to a routine. I worked in the main Foreign Office building, looking out over Downing Street. Though monumental outside, this was surprisingly shabby inside, with corridors cluttered with filing cabinets and pneumatic tubes for carrying messages. The technology was primitive. Telephone calls outside the Office had to go through an operator. We had no fax machines or photo-copiers, let alone computers. Documents for wide distribution were typed on a stencil and then printed off rather smudgily. I was responsible for producing the briefs on economic issues for use at the Economic and Social Council and the General Assembly. I learnt the techniques of inter-departmental consultation and developed good links with the Commonwealth Relations Office and Colonial Office, still separate ministries, and the new Department for Technical Cooperation, our embryo aid ministry. It was harder work dealing with the Treasury and Board of Trade, because they did not take UN activities very seriously. They were content to leave the Foreign Office in the lead, but reluctant to back any initiatives we might propose. They worried that these might interfere with their own preferred institutions, the International Monetary Fund (IMF), the World Bank and the General Agreement on Tariffs and Trade (GATT).

I found it easy to adapt to this work and enjoyed the intellectual challenge of mastering different economic issues. My training in logic proved very valuable, as I could easily tell valid arguments from spurious ones. Ancient history was less useful, though I recalled the Athenians' problems with the Delian League against the Persians when asked how to get the Russians to pay their UN contributions. But I was frustrated that the consultation process led to negative briefing, mainly telling the delegation what they could not do and discouraging initiative. It needed a strong-minded delegate like Michael Errock, who would risk going beyond his instructions, to make progress.

During the 1962 General Assembly I regularly responded to requests from New York for instructions on draft resolutions. Their telegrams, sent overnight, would be on my desk as I arrived and I had the morning in which to consult other departments concerned. If my reply got off by 2 p.m. London time, the delegation would have it by the start of their working day in New York. One morning I found a telegram with a message in red ink objecting to the phrase 'remunerative commodity prices' in a draft resolution. I thought little of it, having forgotten that red ink was only used by ministers. Later in the day Alan Horn summoned me to see Ted Heath. He was then the Foreign Office minister negotiating our entry into the European Community (EC), a process of which I knew little. He told me angrily that the appearance of this phrase in a UN resolution would undermine his efforts to resist high agricultural prices in Europe; it must be struck out. I tried to explain that there were no grounds for objecting to this phrase in UN contexts and in the end Alan Horn and I persuaded him that 'equitable and remunerative prices' would be acceptable. But this encounter rather shook my nerve. I was not sorry to learn that I would be posted in spring 1963 as third secretary (political) in the British Embassy in Manila.

Quite by chance, I had begun my Foreign Office career in economic diplomacy, with no inkling of how much time I would spend on it later. But as economic desk officer in UN Department I had a very limited perspective. The United Nations' economic role was only vaguely defined in its charter. It was largely limited to non-binding resolutions. It could set targets but could not ensure they were met, nor could it be sure of funding for its programmes. The UN only dealt with the problems of developing countries. It was becoming their favoured arena because their growing majority gave them power to control what happened. Yet many ex-colonial countries, having had to fight for their political independence, took a similarly combative approach to economic relations. They argued that the existing international system was created for the benefit of the industrial rich and was loaded against them. These factors made for a frustrating and confrontational form of diplomacy, where political manoeuvring took priority over calculations of economic benefit. I had been introduced to the process of economic diplomacy, both in London and in multilateral contexts, but I still had a lot to learn.

CHAPTER 7

# First posting: Manila

THE WINTER OF 1963 WAS intensely cold. The round pond in Kensington Gardens was solid ice and we wheeled Tom across it in his pram. The snow piled up on the flat roof of our kitchen and water dripped through the ceiling. But none of this distracted us from preparing for our posting to the tropical Philippines. We pored over the post report on local conditions and got good advice from Derek Thomas, a lively colleague who had recently served there. Armed with outfit allowance and car loan, we bought in lightweight clothes and ordered a car to be shipped out. We gave up our flat in March and got ready to travel out by sea – rather nervously, as Tom was starting to crawl. But then Tom Wilde brought his wife up to see a specialist. The news was not good and I had to break it to Dee that her mother had terminal cancer. She and Tom at once joined her parents in Devon. I flew out to Manila alone.

Manila was hot and humid and full of exotic vegetation. It had been the capital of a Spanish colony for over three hundred years. The main survivals from this period were the Roman Catholic Church, the San Miguel Brewery Company and a fine embroidered shirt, the *barong tagalog*. The Americans had taken over early in the twentieth century and brought the country to independence in 1946, despite its wartime occupation by Japan. They introduced universal education, which used English from the secondary level. They bequeathed a lively press and a buoyant economy, so that the Philippines was then the most prosperous country in South-East Asia. Other legacies were less successful. The Americans had transplanted their political system, with Liberals and Nacionalistas instead of Democrats and Republicans. While this might work in its country of origin, it proved inefficient and corrupt when imposed from outside. However, with American help, the Philippine government under President Magsaysay had put down a dangerous communist insurgency.

Magsaysay and his successor Garcia were Nacionalistas and kept close to the United States. But when the Liberal President Macapagal took office in 1961, he favoured a more independent foreign policy. He decided to pursue the Philippine claim to North Borneo (locally called Sabah), which brought him into direct conflict with Britain. Before the Spanish colonists arrived in Manila, Muslim sultans had established their rule over the Sulu archipelago, in the south-western Philippines, together with neighbouring Sabah in Borneo (Map 2). For centuries the sultans of Sulu had kept the Spanish at bay. When he could hold out no longer, Sultan Jamalul Kiram I in 1878 granted Sabah to the British North Borneo Company, rather than yield it to Spain; it later became a British crown colony. Soon afterwards the sultan conceded Spanish control over Sulu itself, though he and his successors still claimed sovereignty. In due course Spain's rights passed to the United States and in 1936 the last sultan of Sulu died. In his will he ceded sovereignty over his possessions to the Philippine government, which by then had internal autonomy, though not full independence.

In the early 1960s Britain agreed with Malaya and Singapore that the Borneo colonies of Sabah and Sarawak would be absorbed into the Federation of Malaysia. The plan was for Malaysia to come into being in September 1963, but this provoked vigorous objections from the new country's neighbours. President Sukarno insisted that Sabah and Sarawak were integral parts of the Indonesian province of Kalimantan. The heirs of the last Sultan of Sulu, led by his strong-minded niece, Princess Tarhata, stirred up the Philippine government to claim Sabah, on the grounds that the 1878 transfer had been only a lease, not a cession. Macapagal hoped that by joining forces with Sukarno he could force Malaya to give way. But the Malayan Prime Minister, Tunku Abdul Rahman, stood his ground and Britain promised to back him. This was the position when I reached Manila in May. It was my responsibility to keep track of the dispute, guided by Theo Peters, who was in charge of the mission until a new ambassador arrived.

Macapagal invited Sukarno and the Tunku to Manila for a summit in early August. But the Tunku refused to delay the launch of Malaysia. The most he would concede was that Indonesian and Philippine observers could join the UN teams that were checking the state of opinion in Sabah and Sarawak. Sukarno then outflanked Macapagal by seeking to take over the whole of Borneo, including Sabah. He launched a strategy of armed 'confrontation' along the Malaysian frontier, while a mob burnt down the British Embassy in Jakarta. Happily, we knew the Philippines would never go this far. Macapagal did not formally abandon his claim, but he was in no position to enforce it. Meanwhile so many telegrams poured in from London, Jakarta and Kuala Lumpur that embassy wives were called in to help decipher them.

On arrival I took over a handsome wooden house of traditional design in a small compound. There I lived a monastic life for three months till Dee could join me, resisting the temptations of Manila's steamy night-life. Once, as duty officer, I took a taxi home late at night after checking the office was secure. As we drove along the waterfront, the taxi driver offered me a sequence of attractions at very economical prices: 'blue movies'; striptease; massage by a lovely girl, or a boy if I preferred; and a beautiful Filipina for the whole night. I declined each in turn and he fell silent for a while. Then he asked, 'Are you American?' and I replied, 'No, English'. 'Ah,' he said, 'I could get you a *genuine British subject*. She is in the Manila Hotel, but she is very expensive' – and he quoted a figure equivalent to 5 per cent of my salary. My curiosity was aroused, I confess, but fortunately we reached home just at that moment. To distract me, I took to writing poetry again – an example follows.

*Endymion – to My Dear Absent Wife*

Let me recall how, long ago,
Your namesake, goddess of the night,
Looked where a shepherd, far below,
Lay sleeping on the Carian height.

She kissed his forehead with her beams
And in his sleeping heart she shone;
Diana stepped into the dreams
Of her beloved Endymion.

So shall I, in the tropic noon,
Wait restless through the lingering day,
Till, cool and quiet, the rising moon
Brings in your love from far away.

And I shall greet, with arms spread wide,
The image that your love will send.
Dreaming, I'll clasp you to my side
And wish the night would never end.

Now sets the moon for me – to rise
Half round the world and there to spread,
Amid the softer Devon skies,
The light of love about your head.

Low, stooping to your window-sill,
Her beams will scatter from above
My world-encircling thoughts, to fill
Your longing heart with all my love.

Dee and Tom finally arrived. Her mother had died soon after I left, but she had stayed to comfort her father and see him established in the house in Bideford where her grandmother was already living. With the family reunited, we could settle properly into our house in Wilson Compound. Our quarters on the first floor were grouped round a spacious *sala*, with a ceiling fan and massive teak floorboards. Our staff lived on the ground floor: Ana, the cook who also looked after Tom, and Chris, the maid and laundress. Ana was experienced, but sometimes moody. Chris was quiet and thrifty, saving her wages to pay for a niece's education. Our part-time gardener Aquino looked after a fine stretch of lawn, shaded by two great rubber trees. When our second son Charlie was born we added a nanny, Anastasia. We did not live in such style again till I became an ambassador twenty years later.

Two weeks after Dee the ambassador, John Addis, arrived. Rather reserved in manner and a great expert on China, I found him an excellent chief, who never left me in any doubt of what he expected. He lost no time in sending me off on a tour of the Muslim areas of the southern Philippines and allowed Dee to accompany me. The aim was to test opinion among the Muslims, to see if they were keen on the Philippine claim to Sabah. We flew in ancient DC3 aircraft to Cotobato in Mindanao and then to Jolo, capital of Sulu province. In both places we made contact with the Oblate Fathers, long established among the Muslims as educators, not evangelists. Thanks to their protection all doors were open to us. We wandered round Jolo, looking warily at the locals hung about with guns and machetes. The old town consisted of wooden houses built out over the water and reached by narrow gangways of split bamboo; the largest belonged to Princess Tarhata. Where the houses ended were the houseboats of the Badjaos, sea-gypsies who seldom came on shore.

Father Holland flew us on to Sibutu in the Oblates' four-seater amphibian, with pusher airscrew, keeping low over the sea to avoid tropical storms (Plate 8). Borneo was clearly visible across a narrow strait and we met a few people who supported the Philippine claim because they had relatives in Sabah. But everywhere else we found strong opposition, since it would ruin the smuggling operations that enriched the province. Most of the imported cigarettes smoked in the Philippines were in fact smuggled from Sandakan in Sabah into ports in Sulu, using fast boats called *kumpits*. No one attempted to conceal this and we easily identified the luxurious houses of the smugglers, with *kumpits* moored outside. On return to Manila I reported these findings. I added that the Muslim communities everywhere seemed calm, because they controlled local politics and Manila left them alone.

London gradually lost interest in the Philippines politically. In early 1964 Rab Butler, now Foreign Secretary, paid a brief visit and Denis Healey also came through as his Labour shadow. Healey was not impressed, except when I took him into the countryside. Elsewhere the region was in turmoil: 'confrontation' between Indonesia and Malaysia persisted until Sukarno fell; the war in Vietnam was getting hotter; and the Cultural Revolution was starting in China. But the worst that happened in the Philippines was the violent election campaign in which Ferdinand Marcos defeated Macapagal to become president in late 1965. (A prescient journalist told me that, once elected, Marcos would never give up power willingly.) Marcos promised to crack down on smuggling and in July 1996 Dee and I went back to Sulu to check if this was happening. The Oblates told us that nothing had changed and we saw evidence of smuggling still blatantly on display. Later, however, Marcos' policies provoked a Muslim insurgency that took years to bring under control.

As politics went down, culture, my second responsibility, rose strongly. There was no British Council office in the Philippines, so that I looked after the library and lecture-room of the Philippine-British Centre. I took care of visiting lecturers, like Robert McKenzie the psephologist and Anthony Powell the novelist. When the British Council launched a programme to mark the 400th anniversary of Shakespeare's birth the Filipinos responded enthusiastically. The foreign minister came to the first showing of a film of *Macbeth* and thereafter we put it on so often that the soundtrack wore out. Dee and I, with others from the embassy, staged Shakespeare readings in Manila and the provinces: our Orlando and Rosalind from *As You Like It* was much admired. Encouraged by Father Donelan, who had also studied English at Oxford, Dee taught a course on Shakespearean tragedy at the Ateneo de Manila, the Jesuit university. This was the first of several literature courses she taught there, earning her a place in the academic procession when Dr Oakeshott, lately Vice-Chancellor of Oxford, came for the inauguration of Father Donelan as the Ateneo's new president.

The high point came when the British Council sent the New Shakespeare Company, who usually performed in Regent's Park, to put on *The Taming of the Shrew* and *The Tempest* in January 1965. This was the first time a professional stage company had ever played in Manila. It generated tremendous excitement and a great deal of work for me. The only theatre that could accommodate their elaborate scenery was in the private Far Eastern University. The admirable Sarah Joaquin, Head of Drama there, had the stage in good technical order, and her students worked like Trojans to prepare it for the company. But the auditorium was very shabby and I asked the British business community if they could help to smarten it up. The local head of Unilever revealed that he had 45,000 pink plastic roses in store, for a promotion of Palmolive soap. He handed these, on loan, to the best florists in Manila, who made the theatre into an earthly paradise. The two productions were a revelation to the Filipino audiences. The *Shrew* was brisk and lively and the *Tempest* haunting and imaginative, though Prospero, tired after a long tour, was hard to hear. After the company left, however, I found that only 30,000 plastic roses remained. I had to compensate Unilever from the ticket sales and disguised this as 'advertising' in the accounts I submitted.

The success of these plays encouraged the British Council to send us more, while a local impresario, Ralph Zulueta, took much of the burden off me. Within a year we had Emlyn Williams as Charles Dickens and the Nottingham Playhouse with *As You Like It* and *A Man for All Seasons*. Though all were very successful, *A Man for All Seasons* was outstanding and introduced Manila to modern British drama. Our visitors invariably found the Filipinos were excellent audiences. The visit of Charles Dickens encouraged Charles Bayne to appear, three weeks early, on 15 June 1965. I was present for his birth in the Manila Sanitarium, wearing a surgical cap and gown that were much too small for me. The hospital was run by Seventh-Day Adventists, who fed Dee vegetarian meals, sang hymns round her bed and provided the best maternity services in town. Charlie grew into a sturdy child with a round beaming face and a great liking for beer, which Dee and I also drank copiously.

Against my cultural successes I have to set one resounding failure. In July 1966 the Beatles stopped off to give a concert in Manila. The embassy left all the arrangements to their local impresarios, not realising the excitement they would cause. Unknown to us, President Marcos and his wife Imelda had invited the Beatles to the palace to sing for their ten-year-old son 'Bong-Bong'. Arriving late at night, the Beatles found the yacht where they were lodged to be intolerably noisy and escaped to the Manila Hotel. In the confusion the invitation from the President and First Lady never reached them. When finally told of it, they flatly refused to go. Leslie Minford, then in charge of the embassy, pleaded with Brian Epstein, the Beatles' manager. He remained adamant that they would neither go to the palace nor send an apology. The news did not break until after the Beatles' concert, but next morning the press was incandescent over their snub to the presidential family. The media raged against Britain in general, believing that the Queen, by giving MBEs to the Beatles, had made them 'British knights'. The Marcoses were philosophical, but their supporters wanted to punish the Beatles. All security was withdrawn at the airport as they left and they had to board the plane through an angry mob. The Beatles themselves were unscathed, but Epstein was badly knocked about. We did not feel very sorry for him.

There were not many opportunities for economic diplomacy. Only a few British firms were present in the country, as Philippine trade was mainly with the United States. Domestically, the key economic issue was land reform. A few large landowners, many of them politicians, owned the bulk of the arable land, which was farmed by poor tenants paying a share of their crop as rent. The reform of this system, which had provoked the earlier communist uprising, was a main plank of Macapagal's original election campaign. I took an interest in the government's plans, drawing on my UN experience, but they made little headway. Macapagal's administration did not have the power to break up the big estates or the resources to support small farmers on new holdings. His failures in domestic as well as foreign policy led to his defeat by Marcos. Yet even now, in 2010, the problems of land reform are unresolved.

Britain supported Philippine economic development through its technical assistance programme under the Colombo Plan. I was responsible for this programme, which mainly consisted of one-year training courses in Britain for over a hundred Filipino officials each year. I worked on the selection and briefing of candidates with Luz Pagaduan from the Civil Service Commission, who had been on a course herself, and Hilde Manoloto of the Foreign Ministry – two very congenial colleagues. This enabled me to appreciate the dedication of Philippine public servants, in contrast to the venality of politics. I thought they had little to learn from outside experts, though these could help local reformers to overcome resistance to change.

The first large diplomatic reception that Dee and I hosted was for returning Colombo Plan scholars (Plate 7). We were nervous, but our guests visibly enjoyed themselves, and from then on we entertained with growing confidence. Manila was the easiest place in the world to give a party. I just rang up Special Events at the San Miguel Brewery Company and gave them date, place and numbers. On the day a truck would appear with beer, soda, tonic, soft drinks, ice, glasses and napkins, plus a collapsible bar with barman for every fifty guests. The only charge was for the drink consumed, though the barmen got good tips, which they deserved. We simply had to provide the hard liquor and the food (prepared by Ana), and have the garden fumigated against mosquitoes. If rain drove us indoors we held our breath, as the *sala* floor was riddled by termites; but it always held out. Filipino guests rarely answered invitations and often arrived late, but they usually turned up and always liked a party. After Manila diplomatic entertaining could only go downhill.

Dee and I took every opportunity to travel outside Manila. Keith Lightfoot the defence attaché (who became a life-long friend) lent us his Land-Rover and driver Carlos for a trip into the Mountain Province. This rugged country north of Manila was never penetrated by the Spanish. The Bontoc and Ifugao tribes living there retained many of their animist beliefs, though American Episcopal missionaries were now at work. So after taking part in a rain dance in Bontoc on a Saturday night, we went to a service next day in the cathedral at Sagada, which we supported through the church we attended in Manila. We drove on to the much photographed rice terraces at Banawe, which filled an entire valley and impressed me not by their great antiquity (which was disputed) but because new ones were being created all the time. Next day we visited the remote Ifugao village of Batad. We climbed up and up on a zig-zag path and Carlos whispered to Dee: 'Never have I known such hardship.' At the top we met a man wearing a g-string and carrying a spear, as an Ifugao should, though his t-shirt and baseball cap rather spoilt the effect. Over the pass a vast theatre of rice terraces opened out, with women at work on them; the men were said to be out hunting. At the bottom we found a village of houses on stilts, with steep thatched roofs. Pigs were rooting about underneath and a smith was making axe-heads of a type I thought had gone out in the Early Bronze Age.

Tony Quintos, who helped me with the New Shakespeare Company, invited us to his home town of Bolinao on the coast facing China. We drove there in our own car, with Tom and Chris, but chose the wrong route. The road got so bad that our exhaust pipe fell off and broke in two, on a stretch notorious for bandits. But some kindly Filipinos stopped for us and mended it with a beer can. We arrived in time for the Bolinao fiesta, where I helped to crown the carnival queen. Next day we visited an archaeological site: a pre-Spanish cemetery, where the skulls had teeth inlaid with gold studs and the grave goods included Chinese ceramics of the Sung dynasty. We also saw the ruins of the first cable station in the country, which had linked the Philippines to Hong Kong in 1890. An early British telegrapher was buried there, while there was a British-built lighthouse just down the coast.

I joined a small party to climb the 8,000-foot Mount Mayon, a perfectly conical volcano far to the east of Manila (Plate 9). On our first day we scrambled up a dry watercourse through thick forest, to emerge onto a bare slope about halfway up. There we camped for the night, on a slope of 30 degrees, and set off at dawn for the summit. At first we climbed on a scree of lava, which was sharp to the hands but stable underfoot. By the end we were struggling through shifting dust and pebbles on a slope of 45 degrees. At the top we admired the magnificent view, keeping upwind of the sulphurous smoke pouring from the crater, as Mayon was still active. I then found that while coming up had been hard work, going down was frightening. The ground underfoot was treacherous and there was nothing to stop me if I slipped. I came down much more slowly than the rest of the party. They were all bachelors, while I had a pregnant wife waiting in Manila.

Our next volcanic excursion seemed tame by comparison. We had often taken visitors, like Denis Healey, to the viewpoint of Tagaytay above the great caldera filled by Lake Taal. An island in the middle was all that remained of a volcano that had been dormant since 1911. During Dr Oakeshott's visit we offered to take him, as a memorable excursion, across the lake to the island. We drove down to the lake edge, chartered a boat and landed at a fishing village. A path inland led us to another miniature lake that marked the most recent crater. It was an intense pale blue and too hot to approach closely. We retraced our steps safely all the way home. Two weeks later the volcano erupted. The villagers we met fled over the lake and not all of them survived. The shape of the central island was permanently changed and the volcano remained active for many months, provoking severe earth tremors that were felt in Manila. Thus we had our fair share of natural phenomena, as we had also lived through a typhoon. In a night of terrific wind and rain, suddenly everything went quiet as the eye of the storm passed over Manila. When the gales began again, a big rubber tree in our garden blew over, luckily away from our house.

We took advantage of two home leaves for some international sightseeing. We travelled home in August 1964 by way of Angkor. Tom, nearly two, chatted away in his own version of English, saying 'pim' for swim. As we flew into Kai Tak airport in Hong Kong he looked out at the sea beside the runway and enquired 'Airplane pim?' Later he rode into Angkor Wat with Dee on an elephant, giving ecstatic cries of 'Emphalant pim!' as it waded across the moat. We had the temples almost to ourselves, especially those deep in the jungle. Coiling tree-roots seemed to throttle the masonry, like great snakes, and I found it most uncanny. On our way back to Manila we visited New Delhi, where Tim Gee was posted with the British Council. He gave us a two-day tour of Mogul monuments – Humayun's Tomb, Delhi Red Fort, Akbar's Tomb, Agra Red Fort and the Taj Mahal – that took our breath away. At sunset, in Akbar's great red sandstone city of Fatehpur Sikri, we heard the muezzin called from the white marble mosque, before we drove back to Delhi in the dark.

In England we first stayed with my parents at the Malt House in Long Compton, under the scarp of the Cotswolds, where they had lived since my father retired. We saw the entire *Wars of the Roses* sequence of Shakespeare plays at Stratford, where Peggy Ashcroft, a distant cousin, took us backstage. We visited Justin Banbury, Tom's godfather, at King's Lynn where he was now curate at St Margaret's church. We moved on to Devon, where Dee's father had taken a cottage at Peppercombe by the sea. Tom would sit on the shore as the waves rolled in, crying, 'Go away pimming!', much as I had done at Woolacombe a generation before. For our second home leave, in midwinter, we went first to a rented house in Devon. Unaccustomed to the cold, we stoked up the night-burning stove too high and started a fire. At Long Compton we found Christopher, now back from Venezuela for good, with his fiancée, whom the boys called 'Aunt-to-be Anne'. But there was no visit to King's Lynn, as Justin had died in a car crash. His parishioners erected a moving memorial to him in the tower of St Margaret's, which we saw nearly fifty years later.

On our way home in 1965 Joanna Smith, our friend from Norton and Charlie's godmother, invited us to visit her in Rangoon, where she was at the embassy. She took us all round the city, from the terrace of the golden Shwe Dagon pagoda to the decaying Edwardian buildings left over from British rule. I looked in vain for the house where my father was born, which had been obliterated by a vast Chinese embassy. We drove through green rice fields to Pegu, which had another great golden pagoda. We liked the way the Burmese treated us white foreigners with dignified reserve, in contrast to the ever-curious Filipinos. I was so taken with Burma that I made a second trip alone, while Dee heroically took the boys back to Manila without me. Joanna and I, with her Burmese friend Marjolaine, travelled by the night train to Mandalay and then took a jeep to the ancient capital at Pagan, dating from the eleventh century. The city had prospered for 200 years, with kings and nobles competing in the construction of Buddhist temples. A vast plain along the River Irrawaddy was still covered with monuments, great and small. Some shrines were in use, with whitewashed walls and gilded spires, but most were crumbling brick ruins romantically overgrown with creepers. I was deeply impressed by the two ancient cities of Angkor and Pagan. I had also hoped to see the great Buddhist temple of Borobodur, but Indonesia was off-limits.

We finally left Manila in October 1966, shortly after our fifth wedding anniversary. On the way to the airport we found that Dee's passport had expired, as it was dated from our marriage; we hauled the vice-consul out of a children's party to get it extended. In those five years, in New

York, London and Manila, we laid the foundations for a marriage that has lasted happily for nearly fifty. We learnt how to be diplomats in the most favourable conditions. The Filipinos were a cheerful and friendly people, who liked foreigners. There was no language barrier. Being British, we provided a welcome change from the ever-present Americans. The country was politically stable, unlike the rest of the region. There were no missions from communist countries to threaten our security. We had an enlightened ambassador in John Addis, who allowed Dee to teach at local universities and be paid for it. Dee and I were able to operate as a team, in travels, play-reading and entertaining at home. It would seem quixotic to want to give up so congenial a life, but I was restless. I always had plenty to do, but it became repetitive. I looked for work with more policy content. I had also been away from England too long, as the Beatles' fiasco revealed. So even though it meant cold weather and washing up, we were glad to be going home. I could look forward to a six months economics course, followed by a new post on promotion to first secretary.

CHAPTER 8

# Information research in the Cold War

A s soon as i got back to England in October 1966, I started my economics course at the Treasury Centre for Administrative Studies, the precursor to the Civil Service College. There were fifteen or so participants, nearly all from the home civil service. But I was happy to find that Tim Gee was on it. Since I had visited him in New Delhi, he had successfully transferred to the Foreign Office.

The course packed a great deal into five months. First, it aimed to teach us all the theoretical economics covered in an undergraduate degree. We unravelled the mysteries of supply and demand curves, perfect competition, marginal cost and marginal revenue. We advanced to macroeconomics and the components of gross domestic product (GDP). We learnt how to interpret statistical tables. I could grasp all these subjects fairly well, but was thoroughly baffled by finance. Peter Oppenheimer, who taught this subject, warned me never to speculate on the stock exchange; I have always followed his advice. Then we moved on to the application of theory: how to conduct government business and manage public expenditure. We analysed recent economic policy decisions, and especially why the National Plan of 1964 had not worked. All this was more relevant to those from home departments than to me as a diplomat, but I learnt what their priorities were and how they took decisions. I found my home civil service colleagues very congenial and one of them, Tony Hutton of the Board of Trade, became a good friend.

The course included expeditions outside London, to inform ourselves about the British private sector, and even to Paris for a week, to examine French agriculture. We learnt about advertising from a large food retailer and made a special study of the telecommunications industry. In Paris, officials explained how they were trying to encourage farmers off the land and make those who remained more productive. They were very open about their problems, given that Britain was again locked in negotiations to join the European Community, and I warmed to them. We finished with a happy day at the Paris agricultural show, tasting wine and cheese and admiring huge Charolais cattle. By the end of the course I had acquired many new skills and was keen to practise them. But Personnel Department was famous for not sending people where they expected to go. My next three posts had virtually no economic content. I did not wholly forget what I had learnt, but I soon had other priorities.

Dee and I and the boys settled into a rented flat near Holland Park. As soon as we knew we would be staying in London, Dee suggested that we should buy a house, to provide a firm base for the family whenever we were in England. My salary as a first secretary would enable us to raise a decent mortgage and we began hunting for houses costing around £8,000. We were much taken with a Gothic cottage in Battersea, but withdrew when we learnt that a new road would go across its front garden (in fact it was never built). Then we found a promising house in Arlington Square in Islington, owned by an insurance company that readily offered us a mortgage.

But when I gave the news to my family, Granny was strongly opposed. She did not think Islington was suitable: it was too far from the Foreign Office and there was not enough green space for the children. I did not want a family row over our first house, especially as Granny, while she lived, had control over the Fleischmann fortune. I gave way and did not pursue it, though Dee was very unhappy. To console her, we went to look at a house at Hampton Court that she had spotted in *The Times*. As we walked into the sitting-room of Clarence Cottage, a deer walked by outside the french window and I knew it was the house for us. Our offer of £8,000 was accepted, but we despaired of getting a mortgage. The back of the house was built directly on the wall of Bushy Park and therefore belonged to the Crown, who could, in theory, require us to demolish it. London-based mortgage lenders recoiled from this risk in horror. But Dee's father saved us through his links to a building society based in Bideford. They were used to dealing with shared ownership and readily advanced us what we needed. In April 1967 we all moved in, with Tom and Charlie happily playing in the cardboard boxes as we unpacked our possessions from Manila.

Clarence Cottage dated from the early 1800s, with low ceilings but big windows and plenty of floor space. It had four good bedrooms and a large basement, which became the boys' playroom. The front looked towards the gardens of Hampton Court Palace, while at the back we had direct, though unauthorised, access to the wide expanse of Bushy Park. The boys were soon making friends with the children next-door. The house was shabby and neglected and we began a complete redecoration. Instructed by Dee and Tom Wilde, I became a competent paper-hanger, house-painter and electrician.

It was a very happy chance that brought us to Hampton Court. The historical associations of the palace and the green spaces of the parks attracted us so much that we never wanted to live anywhere else. We left it reluctantly to go overseas and were always glad to return. Communications were good too. We were well placed to drive to Tom Wilde at Bideford or to my parents in the Cotswolds. The train that started from Hampton Court station took me to the office on weekdays. At weekends we explored every corner of Hampton Court Palace and took the boys into the remoter reaches of Bushy and Home Parks, full of deer, rabbits, squirrels and ornamental waterfowl. We had access to the garden of Hampton Court House, an old people's home nearby. This contained a shell grotto, where Charlie claimed a dragon lived.

In June 1968 our third son Richard was born. Like Charlie, he decided to arrive early, while we were entertaining Richard and Kate Sorabji to Sunday lunch. Dee endured the contractions long enough to cook and eat the meal. Then we left the Sorabjis to wash up and mind the boys and walked across Hampton Court Green to the Bearstead maternity hospital. Next day I delivered Tom and Charlie to my parents and prepared to welcome Dee and the baby home. In the fine summer evenings we walked with the infant Dick in the woodland gardens in Bushy Park. This marked him for life: he grew up a keen gardener and a most enthusiastic walker.

Long before this I had begun my new job in the Foreign and Commonwealth Office (FCO), as it had now become. I was made the head of Soviet and East European section in Information Research Department (IRD). This was an unusual department, created in response to the Cold War. Its aim was to counter false and misleading propaganda put about by communist states. IRD compiled and issued accurate accounts of what was actually going on in these countries, which the authorities tried to conceal. But because anything openly attributed to the British government could be regarded as biased, IRD material was wholly anonymous. The department occupied its own building at the end of Vauxhall Bridge. My Soviet and East European section was the largest geographical division and also covered Germany and the Sino-Soviet dispute. I had a team of regional experts under my direction, some being exiles from our target countries. Others were academics: I had met my Hungarian expert before as a classics don at Oxford.

Our task was to research and write up stories that revealed communist deception or injustice anywhere in the region. The basic rules were that we had to be strictly accurate and we could only use open, published evidence, not classified sources. IRD's editorial section would then convert the material produced by the researchers into articles that would appeal to the media. This process caused a lot of friction. My experts grumbled that their careful research was being mangled and distorted by the editors. As head of section, I had to keep the peace, mainly by exhorting my team to improve their writing style, so that the editors had less reason to make changes.

We had three basic methods of identifying suitable stories. The first was what the Reuters correspondent in Berlin described to me as the 'however technique'. Communist public statements always began with long passages extolling the success of their policies. But towards the end, as people's attention flagged, they would slip in sentences, beginning with 'however', which admitted that not everything had gone according to plan. The second method was exhaustive research in all sorts of communist sources. While major organs like *Pravda* and *Izvestia* revealed nothing, there was not such rigid control over specialist or local publications and broadcasts, which sometimes gave the game away. As I spoke none of the languages, I relied on the daily output from the BBC monitoring centre at Caversham. But my experts read extremely widely in search of true accounts, often in the most obscure publications. A third method was to show where other communist countries were trying to be different from the Soviet Union. Hungary sought greater freedom in economic policy, as political easing would not be tolerated. Romania pursued an independent foreign policy, but domestically was the most repressive of all. The Polish government had to respect the Catholic Church, but four Soviet divisions served to deter unrest. In Czecho-slovakia economic failures aroused protests against the regime. Only Bulgaria and East Germany seemed content to toe the Soviet line.

During 1967 our main target was the Soviet Union itself, as November would mark the fiftieth anniversary of the Bolshevik

Revolution. The Soviet authorities wanted this occasion to demonstrate the triumphs of communism. IRD aimed to show it was now undermined by failure and disunity. We had a stroke of luck with the defection of Stalin's daughter, Svetlana Allilueva. Though she settled in the United States, we got her revealing autobiography published in London. We exploited the growing unrest among writers and other intellectuals in Russia. While Khrushchev was in power, works critical of the Soviet regime were published by Solzhenitsyn and others. But Brezhnev and Kosygin decided to crack down again, with the show trial of Andrei Sinyavsky and Yuri Daniel. Other authors had to fall back on underground publication, or *samizdat*; IRD helped to get such works out into the open. Finally, we documented the growing tension between the Soviet Union and China, which a well-informed Russian in my section had been tracking over the years. She was able to show that the confrontation was getting much worse. Red Guards attacked the Soviet embassy in Beijing; Russian troops were massed along the Chinese frontier; and in 1969 there were armed clashes across the Ussuri River. All this revealed the deep divisions at the heart of communism.

In January 1968 Alexander Dubček took over as party leader in Czechoslovakia. Though a convinced communist, he wanted the party to regain popular support, as Gorbachev would later try to achieve in the Soviet Union. Dubček introduced a programme of 'socialism with a human face', which allowed greater freedom of expression and tolerance of opposition. He also moved to reduce economic controls. Dubček's policies aroused great enthusiasm in Czechoslovakia and attracted favourable attention in Western media, without any effort from IRD. Our concern was with the Soviet reaction, as we could not believe the Russians could tolerate the openness of the 'Prague spring'. We set out to document all the pressure exerted on the Czech government by the Soviet Union, first in negotiations and then through threatening military manoeuvres just over the border. We had the slender hope that by making Soviet intentions public we might induce the Russians to hold their hand. The *Economist* produced a series of hard-hitting articles using our briefing, but to no avail. Soviet tanks rolled into Czechoslovakia on 20 August 1968 and the Prague spring was over. But we still had plenty of work to do, as we tracked down and publicised Soviet statements justifying the invasion. We used these to show how the 'Brezhnev doctrine' now imposed complete submission on Russia's client states.

I supported IRD's objectives but had increasing doubts about its methods. The practice of anonymity had more drawbacks than advantages. The best use of our products was made by close contacts, who knew they came from official British sources but were prepared to keep this secret. Otherwise I did not believe serious journalists would trust material where they could not check its origins. Maintaining anonymity obliged us to practise a degree of concealment that left us at constant risk of exposure. I enjoyed the research aspects of the job and acquired a wide, if superficial, knowledge of the Soviet Union and Eastern Europe. I kept in touch with the policy departments in the FCO that covered the region, though they worried that IRD's activities might complicate their diplomatic task. But I could not visit these countries from IRD and what I learnt at my desk did not make me want to be posted to any of them.

The position was different, however, with Germany. This was a rather neglected part of my empire, as it provided few openings for IRD. The East Germans were kept loyal to Moscow by the massive presence of Soviet troops, while they enjoyed a more prosperous economy than any other communist country. However, I did make two visits to Germany, which had a critical influence on my later career. I went to West Berlin to be briefed by Julian Hartland-Swann, who covered East Germany from his desk in the British Military Government. Julian had not only extensive knowledge but also valuable contacts in East Berlin. He took me through Checkpoint Charlie to meet one, on the only day I ever spent behind the Iron Curtain. I seemed to have stepped back in time. Everything in East Berlin – the buildings, the cars, the shops and the goods in them, the clothes and expressions of the people – seemed to belong to the 1950s, not the late 1960s. After meeting Julian's friend I had an afternoon off and spent it in the Pergamon Museum, going even further back in time. The altar of Zeus from Pergamum, the Roman library from Miletus and the Ishtar Gate from Babylon made me nostalgic for my days as an archaeologist.

Separately I took part in Anglo-German information talks held near Düsseldorf. These were co-chaired by Sir Frank Roberts, our short but energetic ambassador in Bonn, and a senior West German official. I prepared a presentation on East Germany, based on what I had learnt in Berlin and briefing from my London experts. This was the last item on a long agenda and I waited nervously for my turn. But once I got started, I sensed a buzz go round the room. The West Germans plied me with questions and I realised that IRD could tell them things about East Germany that they did not know themselves. I could see this was making its mark on Sir Frank Roberts too. Not long afterwards I was told that my next posting would be to the embassy in Bonn and I believe Sir Frank asked for me, though he had gone when I arrived. So far my posts in UN Department, Manila and IRD had been on the fringes of diplomatic activity. At the embassy to the Federal Republic of Germany I would move into the inner circle of British foreign policy.

CHAPTER 9

# European politics: Bonn and Planning Staff

I N JUNE 1969 WE CROSSED THE Channel, heading for Germany. Our new car was laden down with Dee and myself, the three boys (rising seven, four and one), our mother's help Julie and as much luggage as we could fit in. We reached Bonn very early and a sleepy colleague threw down our house keys from his bedroom window. Then we unloaded ourselves at No 5A Körnerstrasse, an unpretentious house with garden in a leafy cul-de-sac in Bad Godesberg. For three years we lived very happily there. Most of the 150-odd British staff were housed together in flats near the embassy, called the ghetto. Senior figures were clustered in Im Etzental, a street known as the golden ghetto. As a first secretary, I was one of the few that lived among the locals.

Bad Godesberg was a pleasant spa just south of Bonn, then the capital of the Federal Republic of Germany (FRG). Bonn itself, the birthplace of Beethoven, had been a quiet university town by the Rhine before Konrad Adenauer chose it to be the seat of government. Sir Roger Jackling had succeeded Sir Frank Roberts as ambassador. He was habitually calm and conciliatory as a diplomat, but could dig his toes in when he had to. I formed part of the embassy's political section, headed by Richard Hanbury-Tenison, elder brother of the explorer. I looked after Germany's relations facing eastwards, called *Ostpolitik*.

By now Federal Germany was fully integrated into the western world, as a leading member of NATO and the European Economic Community. But its relations with the communist bloc still harked back to the arrangements made between the four wartime allies – the United States, Britain, France and the Soviet Union – as the hostilities ended. Germany had been divided into four zones of occupation, intended to be reunited in due course. Britain, France and the US kept their promises and combined their zones into the FRG. But the Soviet Union made its zone into a separate communist state, the German Democratic Republic (GDR). Berlin, isolated in the Soviet zone, was likewise divided into

British, French, American and Russian sectors. Detailed arrangements were agreed between the four powers linking the western sectors, by road, rail and air, with their respective zones. These were only meant to be temporary. But ever since the Berlin airlift of 1948–9, maintaining these rights of access had been essential to the city's survival, so that it was not swallowed up by the GDR.

Issues concerning 'Berlin and Germany as a whole' would dominate my professional life in Bonn, to the exclusion of everything else. Responsibility for these issues was vested in the 'Bonn Group', composed of the political counsellors from the American, French and British embassies (Jock Dean, René Lustig and Richard Hanbury-Tenison) and a senior German official (Günther van Well) from the Foreign Ministry (MFA). I was Richard's deputy; my counterparts were Mike Boerner, François Plaisant and Hanno Bräutigam. We met every week on Tuesdays and Wednesdays and more often if necessary, always operating in English. I spent more of my waking hours with this group than with anyone else, even in my own embassy and sometimes, it seemed, in my family. A very strong bond grew up between us.

When I first arrived the issues were routine, but still taxing. Berlin questions were almost always about the access routes. Access by air was along three air corridors, served by British Airways, Air France and Panam. Traffic was handled by the Berlin Air Services Centre manned by controllers from the four powers, including the Russians. Since the East Germans had no hand in it, Berliners considered air travel the most reliable. Rail access, starting from Brunswick, was reliable too, but slow and inconvenient. Road access was by three dedicated routes across the GDR, but these were poorly maintained and traffic was liable to harassment. Just before I arrived the East Germans had closed the access roads for several days, in disapproval of some activity in West Berlin.

Both Russians and East Germans were always testing our determination to keep these routes open. One day the Russians suddenly announced they would close the air corridors for a time during the coming night. Though there would not be any flights then, unilateral closures were outside the rules. The Bonn Group recommended British, French and US air force flights down the corridors to assert our rights. These required authority at head of government level and President Nixon had to be tracked down on an aircraft carrier. But eventually we got the American and British flights off, though we sat up all night doing it; the French aircrew got tired of waiting and disappeared to a local bar, so that they never flew. Another time the GDR tried to insist that allied military traffic on the roads should receive a movement ticket (*Laufzettel*) from the East German police. We could not accept that the East Germans had any control over this traffic. At once we sent probing jeeps down the roads in both directions and the GDR backed off. We interpreted these Russian and East German actions as the first slices in unacceptable salami tactics and reacted sharply.

Questions concerning 'Germany as a whole' centred on the international status of East Germany. The West Germans, following what was called the Hallstein doctrine, refused to admit that the GDR existed, since this would compromise their ultimate aim of reunification. The three western allies supported them. The FRG would cut off diplomatic relations with any country that recognised the GDR as a state, just as China has always done over Taiwan. At first only other communist countries had recognised the GDR, but in my first year in Bonn ten non-aligned countries did so. It became increasingly hard to hold the line.

This was the position till the West German elections in October 1969, where the Christian Democrats (CDU), who had ruled the FRG since its creation, were defeated. The Social Democrats (SPD) formed a government for the first time, in coalition with the liberal Free Democrats (FDP): Willy Brandt became Chancellor, with the FDP leader Walter Scheel as Foreign Minister. Just after the elections I went off for a month to Karlsruhe, in Baden, to improve my German, but after three weeks the ambassador called me back. Brandt had announced an ambitious new *Ostpolitik*, which reversed all that had gone before. His aim was complete reconciliation with Germany's communist neighbours, especially Poland and the Soviet Union, leading to the full recognition of the GDR and the simultaneous admission of East and West Germany to the United Nations.

Brandt argued that the existing policy of ostracising the GDR was in fact making ultimate reunification less likely. The German people could only begin to come together as a result of regular contact between the two halves of the country, on conditions both could accept. It was also essential to overcome the suspicion about West German intentions elsewhere in Eastern Europe. So Brandt's first initiative was to negotiate treaties with the Soviet Union and Poland, which recognised Germany's present frontiers and undertook that these could only be changed by mutual agreement. Brandt went to Warsaw to sign the Polish treaty and knelt in penitence before the memorial to those who had died in World War II, a gesture that aroused great international admiration. He was also making informal moves to meet his East German counterpart, Willi Stoph, and charged Egon Bahr, State Secretary in the Chancellor's Office, to begin negotiations for a general treaty with the GDR.

The western allies welcomed these moves as regards Germany as a whole. But we worried about their impact on Berlin. We did not believe that the West Germans, on their own, could guarantee access to the city of Berlin, and prevent encroachment and ultimate absorption by the East Germans. If that should happen, Brandt's *Ostpolitik* would have turned into a disaster for Germany. Many Germans thought the same way, including the Berliners themselves and the CDU opposition in the FRG, who still had a majority in the *Bundesrat*, the upper house of parliament. The *Ostpolitik* as a whole was highly controversial, so that a joke circulated:

> *First German*: Have you heard? Brandt, Scheel and Bahr went for a cruise on the Rhine. The boat sank and they were all drowned.
> *Second German*: What a disaster! Were any saved?
> *First German*: Yes: the Federal Republic.

It was clear that Brandt would never get his treaties with the Soviet Union, Poland and the GDR ratified in the *Bundesrat* and brought into effect, without a parallel agreement to reinforce the position of Berlin.

It was therefore decided to revive four-power negotiations on Berlin that had been abeyance since the 1950s. The three western ambassadors in Bonn sought a meeting with the Soviet ambassador in East Berlin. In March 1970 Roger Jackling joined Ken Rush, a former businessman with a direct line to Nixon, and Jean Sauvagnargues, a diplomat with much German experience, and they flew to Berlin in the US Air Force plane at Rush's disposal. There they met Piotr Abrasimov, a Soviet official of the old school, in the post-war Allied Control Commission building, and all four made formal statements of position. I drafted Sir Roger's speech and was there in his delegation, with Richard Hanbury-Tenison and Teddy Jackson, the political adviser at our mission in Berlin (Plate 10). Allies and Russians disagreed on almost everything, except to meet again in the same format and a monthly rhythm.

That was enough to get the negotiations started. For the next eighteen months, I worked harder than I have done in all my life. Every allied move, great or small, had first to be agreed in the Bonn Group. The combative Dean, thoughtful Lustig and cerebral van Well all held strong views, which could only be reconciled by long debate. Yet once they reached a consensus, they stuck to it. Richard Hanbury-Tenison, in contrast, seemed oddly distrait and often left me wondering what I should be doing. But he left after the first four-power meeting and was replaced by Christopher Audland, a very different character. Christopher was forthright, decisive and a skilled negotiator. He made me responsible for all detailed briefing and reporting, while he handled overall strategy. The British team was reinforced by two ex-soldiers: Nigel Broomfield, a gifted diplomat who was later ambassador to the GDR and then to the reunited Germany; and the patient, industrious Alex Mineeff. Finally there was David Anderson, the embassy legal adviser, whose ingenious lawyer's mind would find elegant solutions to the most intractable problems.

Any deal struck in the Bonn Group had to be endorsed by the four capitals. Christopher Audland arranged early on that John Drinkall, the head of West European Department in the FCO, and David Bendall, the responsible under-secretary, should come out to Bonn to meet the Germans concerned and agree a general strategy. London then allowed us to proceed, provided we checked with them at every stage. Thereafter my comprehensive reporting and Christopher's skilful advocacy always carried the day. The French and American governments were less flexible and less predictable. Sometimes we had to ask our embassies to intervene in Paris or Washington to move things along. At other times Henry Kissinger or President Pompidou seemed to be pursuing their own agenda with the Russians. The Germans were divided. Scheel, the Foreign Minister, was a strong supporter and had no axe to grind. But Brandt's approach was more complex. He was emotionally committed to Berlin, where he had been Governing Mayor for a decade. But he had often clashed with the allies there and regarded us as part of the old dispensation, which he was trying to replace. He was much under the influence of Egon Bahr, his *eminence grise*, who was all too ready to make concessions so as to get the East Germans to the table. The allied ambassadors at times had to rein back Bahr from undermining their negotiating position. The Berliners also distrusted Bahr and had more faith in the allies, though they doubted whether we could succeed.

Much later I wrote a Bonn Group song for the embassy Christmas revue, based on a poem from A. A. Milne's *When We Were Very Young*. The first two verses summarise the position reached so far.

Rush, Rush,
Sauvagnargues, Sauvagnargues,
Jackling, KCMG,
Took great
Care of the Chancellor,
Though they were only three.
Rush, Rush,
Jackling and Sauvagnargues
Said to Herr Brandt: 'Don't fuss;
But you'll never get far
With the GDR
Without consulting us.

Brandt, Brandt,
Federal Chancellor,
Needed a pact on Berlin.
Rush, Rush,
Jackling and Sauvagnargues
Hardly knew where to begin.
Rush, Rush,
Jackling and Sauvagnargues
Said to the Bonn Group: 'You
Must leave your wives
And devote your lives
To telling us what to do.'

The monthly exchanges with Abrasimov did not make much progress until the FRG signed its treaty with the Soviet Union. Then the Russians indicated that they could promise some improvements in access to Berlin and movement within the city, in return for West German undertakings not to treat West Berlin as part of the FRG. This looked hopeful, so that quadripartite meetings began at counsellor level between Dean, Lustig and Audland, with their deputies, and Yuri Kvitsinski from Moscow, supported by Abrasimov's political adviser Khotulev. (Kvitsinski later became famous as an arms control negotiator.) But an exchange of draft agreements in spring 1971 showed how far apart we were. The allies wanted to stress four-power responsibilities, but the Russians insisted that they had delegated all theirs to the East Germans, who would have to take any action that might be agreed.

However, the allies were convinced that, whatever they might have conceded in public, the Russians would secretly welcome any chance to increase their hold over the East Germans. We had to find an approach that would take advantage of that. We proposed a three-stage structure for an agreement: first the four powers would lay down some guidelines; next the two German sides would agree practical measures; then the four powers would bring the whole package into effect. This idea found favour with Kvitskinski. Then we laboriously built up the text of an agreement in a way the Russians could not object to. We began by writing phrases on a blackboard, for the Russians to amend and endorse before they went down on paper. Next we converted these to sentences, with any disputed wording replaced by dots: for example 'Traffic by road and rail shall be . . . on the access routes from the FRG.' We constructed a complete agreement, full of dots, covering: general principles; access; movement within Berlin; limits on West German activity; external relations of West Berlin (a late addition at FRG request); and final provisions for signature. Then we went back over this again, replacing the dots by agreed language where possible or by alternative allied and Russian proposals in brackets.

In their early exchanges the counsellors used German, which tested my linguistic ability to its limits. I was relieved when we moved to drafting, which was done in English. We would spend long days in Berlin negotiating texts, ending when the counsellors (Audland and Teddy Jackson for the UK) broke for dinner. I would return to the house of Peter Swain, our economic counsellor in Berlin, to work far into the night on reporting telegrams or texts for use next day. Outside the nightingales would be singing *fortissimo* in his lakeside garden. Then we would head back to Bonn to brief the West Germans and work out our future moves with them, before returning to Berlin for another round. Teddy Jackson and his allied peers would update the West Berlin authorities, the *Senat*. The Russians, as we suspected, had an easier time. They never consulted the East Germans in advance, but told them later what they had agreed. The next two verses of my song summarise this phase.

Dean, Dean,
Lustig and Audland,
And van Well of the MFA,
Went and
Told the ambassadors
All that they had to say.
Rush, Rush,
Jackling and Sauvagnargues
Weren't in the least impressed.
They said: 'You next
Must produce a text
And then we'll tackle the rest.'

Dean, Dean,
Lustig and Audland,
Sat with the Russians all night.
They wrote
A Berlin agreement
But couldn't get everything right.
Dean, Dean,
Lustig and Audland
Showed their ambassadors: 'See!
We just put in lots
Of convenient dots,
Whenever we couldn't agree.'

By the end of July 1971, with both counsellors and ambassadors now meeting frequently, the four-power agreement was nearly complete. Christopher Audland and I hoped for a break in August, to take some leave. But Ken Rush pressed for the ambassadors' meetings to continue and Abrasimov agreed. We suspected this was due to secret contacts between Kissinger and Gromyko, as was later confirmed. Roger Jackling insisted that Christopher should take his leave, as he was exhausted. I was charged to take his place for this critical final stage, while Dee took the family back to England without me.

The first August meeting was quite short and ended with the ambassadors going off into East Berlin for lunch with Abrasimov. Sir Roger was staying on in Berlin, so I arranged to fly back to Bonn in the American plane. But I spent too long writing up my report before leaving for Tempelhof airport. As our diplomatic car drove onto the tarmac, I could see the plane's engines were running and it was just moving away for take-off. I leapt out and flagged down the plane with the traditional hitch-hiker's gesture. It stopped, the steps came down and I gratefully scrambled aboard with my party. I went to apologise to Ken Rush and found him in great good humour. During the lunch with Abrasimov, his chauffeur had kept his car's air-conditioning running. When Rush was ready to leave, the battery was flat and he was stranded. Sir Roger had rescued him in his Daimler, so that he was happy to repay a debt to the British.

The three allied ambassadors reconvened with Abrasimov on Monday 16 August, intending to meet for as long as was needed. Teddy Jackson and I flanked Sir Roger. Günther van Well, with a West German team, and a Berlin *Senat* party led by the laconic, level-headed Günther Meichsner, lurked in the basement, out of sight of the Russians, and we briefed them whenever we could. The ambassadors worked steadily through the agreement for three days, settling outstanding points. Twice Abrasimov tried to weaken the commitments on access; Rush and Sauvagnargues seemed to waver; but Sir Roger stood firm and the original Russian promise of *unimpeded* access remained. Late on Wednesday night the last open issues, on West Berlin's external relations, were resolved. The ambassadors agreed the entire text *ad referendum* to their capitals and decided to meet on 3 September to sign the agreement formally on behalf of their governments. It fell to me to bring this news to the waiting West German and Berlin representatives. They were delighted and impressed; we had secured far more than they had ever expected.

I spent Thursday writing up the detailed assessment of the agreement needed for London. The opening principles had some blemishes, reflecting different legal views. The Russians would only speak of 'the Western Sectors of Berlin', so that we had to use the awkward phrase 'the relevant area' to mean Berlin as a whole. Even so, all four powers agreed to respect their rights and responsibilities, which could not be changed unilaterally. The practical provisions were solid. The Russians undertook, after heavy pressure, that road, rail and waterway access to Berlin would be unimpeded and get preferential treatment. There were detailed arrangements for goods traffic, non-stop trains and buses, and travel by car. The Russians also offered improvements for West Berliners visiting East Berlin and the GDR. The three allies undertook that the West Germans would not make West Berlin part of the FRG or conduct political activities there. The Russians accepted that the FRG could represent West Berlin in international contexts and provide consular services for its citizens. West Berliners could travel on FRG passports, provided these were stamped 'issued in accordance with the Quadripartite Agreement'. In return the allies allowed the Russians to open a consulate and trade office in West Berlin. Altogether the agreement met all our objectives.

Sir Roger decided that David Anderson and I should fly back to London to explain the agreement and seek approval for it. I had to confess to the FCO that I had no passport, as I had not needed it to go from Bonn to Berlin. Early on Friday morning we flew into Heathrow and I approached the immigration officers nervously. But they had been warned and averted their eyes as I went through. David and I were grilled all morning in West European Department, but kept our end up. Then the assistant, Peter Unwin (bless him), took us off for a restorative lunch and produced a travel document for me. After lunch we went through the text meticulously with Tom Brimelow, the senior under-secretary concerned, who had deep experience of dealing with the Russians. At length he was satisfied and sent me along to the Foreign Secretary's office. This final stage proved unexpectedly easy. Sir Alec Douglas-Home was not there, as it was now late on Friday. The private secretary spoke to him on the phone, checked one point and then secured his blessing. My task was done.

Exhausted, I caught a train from Paddington into the Cotswolds, to be reunited with my family and recover over the weekend before returning to Bonn. Sir Roger now insisted that I should take my leave, once I had briefed Nigel Broomfield to hold the fort. So I missed the signing ceremony, though Christopher Audland was back in time for it. The final verses of my song bring the story to a close.

Rush, Rush,
Jackling and Sauvagnargues
Thought it was time for the crunch.
Rush, Rush,
Jackling and Sauvagnargues
Wanted to finish by lunch.
Rush, Rush,
Jackling and Sauvagnargues
Whispered to Abrasimov:
'Just get the word go
From old Gromyko
And we'll soon polish this off.'

Rush, Rush,
Jackling and Sauvagnargues
Settled with Abrasimov.
They then
Said to the Chancellor:
'Now you can talk to Herr Stoph.
You may
Think our agreement
Hardly deserves all the fuss.
But you'll never get far
With the GDR
Without consulting us.'

Thereafter the FRG and GDR worked out the detailed measures required; the FRG's treaties with Poland and the USSR were ratified; and the four-power and inner-German agreements on Berlin were brought into force in June 1972, after I had left Bonn. No one then foresaw that within twenty years the Berlin Wall would come down, Germany would be reunified and the Cold War would be over. Brandt's *Ostpolitik* looked like a bold gamble which could easily go wrong. But the four-power agreement acted like a tonic on the Berliners and soon brought them visible improvements. This moved the West Germans to rally behind the *Ostpolitik* and helped the East Germans to believe that communism would not last for ever. Though it is now history, the Berlin agreement served an essential purpose. It offered the first hope of an end to the division of Europe.

My time in Bonn was nearly over. Late in 1971 I was called back to London to meet Sir Alec Douglas-Home, as I was one of two candidates to be a private secretary. We had a pleasant chat, but he chose Michael Alexander, whom he already knew, rather than me. This did not worry me at the time, as I had not raised my hopes. But I now see it was a missed opportunity. As a private secretary I might have developed the political instincts that did not come naturally to me. The opportunity never recurred, so that later in my career I always found it harder to deal with ministers than with my fellow officials. As it was, I was soon given a new posting to the FCO Planning Staff, to begin in May 1972.

Unlike our lavish lifestyle in Manila, Dee and I lived a quieter domestic life in Bonn. I worked extremely long hours in the office: usually till late in the evening, sometimes all night, regularly on Saturdays and often absent altogether in Berlin. Dee ran the household and brought up the family without much help from me. She was supported by a sequence of mother's helps, who usually got on well with the boys. The competent Julie got us started, but soon left to marry her German boyfriend. Gentle Frances stayed the longest, but eventually went off to train as a nurse. Kathryn from New Zealand covered our final summer efficiently, though she and Tom argued. But Tom, like the others, responded well to Hilary, the last and most intellectual. She also married a German, who later taught at the LSE.

As they grew up, the boys became excellent company for us, as well as for each other. Even on our shortened weekends we made many rewarding outings, especially to the ruined castles that abounded in the region. Many of them were open and unattended, so that we could wander at will round the battlements and up the towers. We inspected the spectacular Roman remains at Trier and Charlemagne's great church at Aachen. The boys enjoyed an early theme park called Fantasialand, a favoured site for birthday parties. We had plenty of visitors from England, which was only a long day's drive away: Dee's father; my parents and Granny; my brother Christopher and his family; and friends like Joanna Smith, Christopher Roberts and the Sorabjis. John Addis passed through and we took him to the baroque chateau of Schloss Brühl, site of the annual diplomatic ball. We returned to England for one summer leave and two Christmases, as well as for my brother David's wedding to Felicity Wethered, where Charlie was a page.

Our sons gave us great delight but some anxieties too. Tom cut his arm badly on some spiked railings; Charlie fell out of a tree-house that I had insecurely put together. Charlie and Dick went into the excellent RAF hospital at Wegberg for minor operations and behaved very gallantly. Charlie took much comfort from a stuffed tiger given long ago to Tom; thereafter he and Tigger were inseparable. Dick's operation was to correct a squint; though he had to wear glasses and see orthoptists for some years afterwards, eventually it cleared completely. Tom and Charlie went to the British Embassy Prep School and impressed everyone with their large vocabulary. But when he was nine we decided to send Tom back to boarding school, for which the FCO would pay. This seemed natural to me, as I had done it too, but it was a serious wrench for Dee to be parted from him. Fortunately Tom readily took to Swanbourne House and was soon making his mark not only in class but on the cricket, rugby and athletics fields. We were lucky that all three boys enjoyed boarding school and that we were not far away during their schooldays.

We did our best to contribute to embassy life, despite my workload. Dee found herself chairing the International Ladies Group and enjoyed their meetings, though most of the other diplomatic wives involved were senior to her. She had trouble in getting her chosen successor accepted, but carried the day in the end. I became a lay assistant and then vicar's warden at the local Anglican church, just as a new chaplain arrived. He was a good pastor, but wanted more financial backing than our small community could afford. He decided to resign and I was unable to extract a successor from the diocese of Fulham and Gibraltar before we too left for England. I have been wary of church administration since then.

We returned to England in April 1972 and decided to move out of Clarence Cottage. Though we liked the house very much, it was on a busy main road. We had long envied a pair of elegant Georgian houses nearby: these also backed onto Bushy Park, but faced across Hampton Court Green, which was ringed by trees that screened the traffic. As we got back, we learnt that one was up for sale. The asking price of £45,000 seemed quite unreasonable, until we realised that Clarence Cottage could fetch £25,000, as house prices had shot up in our absence. We embarked on long and nail-biting negotiations, almost as tense as the four-power talks. In January 1973 we became the owners of No 2 Chetwynd House at just over £40,000, thanks to a larger loan from our building society and a generous subsidy from Tom Wilde. We live in the house to this day. We sold Clarence Cottage to Colin and Kathy White. They too are still there, our oldest friends in the area.

Chetwynd House had a simple, elegant façade, as if transplanted from Bloomsbury, and large sash windows which filled the rooms with light.

A well-proportioned drawing-room looked over the park, with a similar bedroom above for Dee and me. Tom had a bedroom of his own, which he filled with model aeroplanes. Charlie and Dick shared the room above it, where Charlie, a keen author and artist, created exciting stories featuring Tigger, himself, Dick and Dick's familiar, Sleepy Dog. In due course Charlie followed Tom to Swanbourne. The boys were always happy to have holidays at Bideford, as Tom Wilde had constructed a tree-house in the woods, called the 'gorilla house'. But we also spent our first summer in France, near Toulon, in the house that Keith Lightfoot had bought on retiring from Manila. This was a great success, but strained the family exchequer; first secretaries in London were not well paid. We got to know our neighbours well: John Gandy, an engineer, had the twin house to ours; the actor Marius Goring was on the other side.

My personal life was thus going on happily; my professional life was not. I was sure that I would do well in Planning Staff. I looked forward to work of high intellectual content, for which my experience of complex problems in Germany would be a good preparation. I was part of a team of only four and found Leslie Fielding and John Goulden very congenial colleagues. Though James Cable, the head, was rather withdrawn, we got on well enough. But my over-confidence duly attracted its nemesis. My time in Planning Staff was the least successful of my whole career and I have wiped most of it from my memory.

At long last Britain was about to enter the European Community. James Cable decided that we should produce a trio of planning papers explaining what this would mean for British foreign policy towards the West, the communist bloc and the Third World. He put me in charge of drafting these and I went around the FCO gathering material. I soon found that, as a planner, I was not expected to go deeply into complex problems; the line departments could do that more thoroughly than I could. Instead, after a rapid survey of an issue, I should be able to produce new and original insights to challenge the conventional wisdom. I proved no good at this. My drafts were pedestrian and unconvincing, and in the end James Cable completely rewrote all the papers. We disagreed on the substance too. I thought that, as we had finally got into Europe, we should make the most of any advantages that gave us. He, as an early eurosceptic, worried about our loss of influence with traditional allies like the United States.

1. *In the ruins of Delphi (page 18)*

2. *As Falstaff in the Eton school play (page 19)*

3. *After the Eton wall game (page 19)*

4. *Courting Dee by the Cherwell (page 29)*

*5. At the site of Troy (page 34); Dee took the picture*

*6. At our wedding in Abbotsham (page 41)*

7. *Manila: presenting diplomas to Colombo Plan scholars (page 54); Dee and John Addis below*

8. *Father Holland (in white shirt) and the plane in which he flew us round the Sulu archipelago (page 51)*

9. *After climbing Mayon volcano (page 55)*

10. *First session of Berlin negotiations (page 69); Soviet Ambassador Abrasimov seated on right*

11. *Paris: as Father Christmas, between Sir Nicholas and Lady Henderson (page 92); Charlie and Dick (in glasses) on extreme right*

12. *Meeting President Mobutu of Zaire (page 121)*

13. *Family on the residence veranda, Kinshasa (page 120); Tom, Charlie and Dick in front, with Pamela Wallis*

14. *Cutting the ribbon at the new British embassy in Brazzaville (page 123), watched by Auriol Almond, Joyce Milner and Mary McGoran*

My later efforts at mainstream planning work had no better success. I only prospered in subsidiary activities, such as when John Goulden and I wrote a speech at short notice for Sir Alec Douglas-Home, so that he could respond to misguided remarks by Henry Kissinger. I welcomed the opportunity given to Planning Staff to interact with outside bodies, like the Royal Institute of International Affairs at Chatham House. In general, however, I did not do well and did not enjoy myself. When Leslie Fielding left to join the European Commission, I became James Cable's deputy and felt even more exposed. So I was not sorry, late in 1973, to receive a summons to Personnel Department to discuss my future. This was to be the turning-point of my career.

CHAPTER 10

# Economic diplomacy begins: the Treasury and Paris

'HOW WOULD YOU LIKE TO BE financial counsellor in Paris?' asked the desk officer in Personnel Department. My jaw dropped. Promotion to counsellor under forty was very rare and I was only thirty-six. 'Are you serious?' I asked: 'I haven't had a proper economic post and I don't speak French.' He waved this away: 'You did the economics course, remember. You will be seconded to the Treasury for a year to prepare yourself. That will give you plenty of time to bring your French up to scratch.' Harold Wilson had first proposed posting a Treasury official to Paris when he met General de Gaulle during Britain's second attempt to enter the European Community. The General agreed to the post, but still vetoed our entry. The initial incumbent had a difficult time and no one from the Treasury wanted to follow him. So the FCO was asked to supply someone, who could be prepared by a Treasury secondment in advance. Derek Thomas, who had briefed me before Manila, was the first FCO holder of the post and was very well regarded by the Treasury. I would succeed him. Though it seemed too good to be true, I found the work suited me admirably and one economic post followed another. From now on these memoirs will be full of international economic activities.

I was introduced to economic diplomacy at a time of great upheaval. The world economy had grown steadily in the 1950s and 1960s, while the international monetary system was based on fixed but adjustable exchange rates. But in August 1971 the United States had abruptly abandoned the dollar's link with gold, the foundation of the system. Many countries lost confidence in the dollar and adopted floating exchange rates, including Britain. The six members of the European Community (EC), however, maintained fixed rates between their currencies, in a narrow band called the snake. When Britain at last entered the EC in January 1973, we came under strong pressure to join. The Treasury hesitated, but finally put sterling into the snake in June.

The financial markets were not convinced and within a week the pound was forced out again. The Treasury's attitude to European monetary integration was permanently marked by this unhappy experience.

In September 1973 another economic disaster struck. After Israel emerged victorious from a short, bitter war with Egypt, the Arab oil producers tried to cut off oil supplies to Israel's allies, notably the United States. As a result the world price of oil tripled, from $4 a barrel to $12, and the members of the Organization of Petroleum Exporting Countries (OPEC) were only too happy to enjoy this windfall. The western industrial economies were heavily dependent on imported oil and this sudden price increase damaged their prospects for growth, inflation and balance of payments equilibrium. Britain was more vulnerable than most, as Ted Heath's government had over-stimulated the economy while battling with the trades unions. The 'dash for growth' ground to a halt and energy shortages led to a three-day working week.

Just as I joined the Treasury early in 1974, Heath's government fell. Labour returned under Harold Wilson, with Denis Healey as Chancellor of the Exchequer. Healey later calculated that within a year the higher oil price added £2.5 billion to Britain's external deficit and 10 per cent to inflation, while reducing national income by 5 per cent. His strategy was to give priority to restoring growth and preserving jobs, while relying on wage restraint by the unions to keep inflation in check. He was encouraged when other industrial states also promised to keep up economic activity, since this would help Britain to export its way out of trouble. But in practice the US and Germany did the opposite, giving priority to cutting inflation and reducing imports. The unions failed to control wages. So Britain's economic position got much worse and inflation soared out of control.

On arrival, I found the Treasury to be much more compact than the FCO and much less hierarchical. From being an FCO first secretary I converted to a principal, and became responsible for European monetary matters. I was part of the international finance branch, headed by Geoffrey Littler as under-secretary and Sir Derek Mitchell as second permanent secretary. I got used to a different style and rhythm of work. I had always imagined the Treasury to be a monolithic, internally disciplined institution. But I found this to be only a façade, maintained for purposes of Whitehall infighting. Inside the Treasury there was intense debate between different schools of thought. While supporting growth was the government's favoured strategy, there were plenty of people who argued for tougher measures to hold down prices instead. There were even some who believed that putting the pound back into the snake had merit. However, most officials held that Britain needed the flexibility of a floating exchange rate and I did not dispute this view. I therefore found myself running a largely defensive policy towards European monetary integration.

The Treasury released me for six weeks in the autumn of 1974 to go on a course for British officials at the École Nationale d'Administration (ENA) in Paris. The ENA was the forcing-house for senior grades of the French civil service and most public figures, including the president himself, were *énarques*. The British group numbered about twenty, a quarter being diplomats and the rest from the home civil service. Each day began with language tuition, followed by lectures on aspects of French public administration or visits to institutions like the National Assembly. We broke for lunch at a local restaurant, with a generous supply of wine, so that my colleagues, perhaps less motivated than me, found it hard to stay awake in the afternoon lecture. Once, when our speaker on French industrial policy had paused for questions, I saw that almost everyone was asleep and distracted him by a series of eager enquiries. He commended me afterwards on my interest and invited me to call when I took up my post. That was how Georges Dominjon and his family became our closest French friends. The course ended with a provincial tour to Lyon, including a bibulous day in the Beaujolais vineyards, and a week in which the members of the course pursued their individual projects. I spent my time visiting as much of the Ministry of Finance as I could. I knew this would both interest my Treasury colleagues, who were curious about French procedures, and serve me in good stead when I took up my Paris post.

Back in London I was plunged into a totally different activity. Denis Healey was not a fan of European monetary integration. But he saw merit in working with his EC colleagues on international financial issues. He supported the action taken by the International Monetary Fund (IMF) to help countries unable to pay for their oil imports. When the IMF wanted to increase the funds available, Healey concluded that a common European front could win over the Americans, who were dragging their feet. He therefore invited his fellow finance ministers to a meeting in Lancaster House in early January 1975 and put me in charge of organising it. This was no easy task, as the European institutions took a long Christmas holiday. But the conference went well and served its purpose, so that I made my mark with the Chancellor. He remembered meeting me in Manila, while I could observe the penetrating mind at work behind the rather combative manner. Sadly, however, while I was tied up with the conference, my grandmother's life was ebbing away. She died in that January, just short of her ninety-fifth birthday.

My short secondment was nearly over and I had thoroughly enjoyed it. Though I was known to be a native of the FCO, the Treasury welcomed me as an adopted son. I was regarded as part of the Treasury team not only while I was there, but for the remaining twenty-odd years of my career and even beyond. It was not just that I had worked with many rising stars who would be key contacts in my later posts. More generally, my previous secondment entitled me, in the eyes of Treasury officials, to criticise their policies in ways that would never be tolerated from other diplomats. These fifteen months proved the most valuable professional investment I ever made.

In April 1975 I packed up the family and drove off to take up my new post. We took over Derek Thomas' flat, close to the Place de l'Étoile and an easy walk to the embassy down the Champs Élysées. The flat was L-shaped, with rooms for entertaining in the longer arm. The shorter arm had more basic quarters for the boys and Gisèle, our shy but faithful Breton mother's help. We found it hard to occupy three active boys, aged twelve, nine and six, who were used to ranging over Bushy Park. There was little open space in central Paris and no grass that could be walked on. After we had gone up every available monument – Eiffel Tower, Notre Dame, Arc de Triomphe, Sacré Coeur – the boys resorted to passage cricket in the flat. Intervening at the wrong moment, Dee got a conspicuous black eye, which provoked lively speculation among the embassy staff: 'Have you seen Diana? Is everything all right between her and Nicholas . . .?'

Thus during school holidays we took the boys out of Paris as often as we could. The rocks in the forest of Fontainebleau were much favoured, while the park at Versailles was acceptable. Every summer we spent as long as possible in a rented holiday house, always in a different region. The houses we found in Normandy and northern Burgundy were close enough to Paris that I could commute by train in July before going on holiday in August. We also went south to Provence, with a return visit to the Lightfoot house, and to Perigord, where a French friend from the ENA course got Dee and me into Lascaux. One high spot was a journey to Brittany for Gisèle's wedding, where Dick was a page at the nuptial mass. After a marathon lunch, we took the boys off to clamber over the megalithic alignments at Carnac. They came to regard prehistoric monuments, ancient abbeys and World War II fortifications as acceptable alternatives to ruined castles, though France proved as rich in these as Germany.

By now Tom towered over his brothers and was the tallest boy at Swanbourne. At short notice, he was called on to play Portia in *The Merchant of Venice* and performed with great dignity. He did 'very respectably' in the Eton scholarship, but not quite well enough, and instead started in the house headed by Raef Payne, who had been my classical tutor. Under Raef's guidance he came high on the scholarship list at his second attempt and so moved into College. Charlie, with his friend Douglas Westbury, gained fame at Swanbourne from a lavishly illustrated tale of adventure on the Spanish Main. Dick stayed with us in Paris at first and went daily to the École Active Bilingue. He adapted very well and developed an exchange programme with a fellow-pupil, Jean-Raphael Heckly. Partly because Jean-Raphael resolutely refused to speak English, Dick became truly bilingual.

The embassy in Paris represented Britain in a style suitable to a great historic capital. The ambassador's residence had been bought by the Duke of Wellington from Napoleon's dashing sister Pauline Borghese in 1814. It had come complete with all its furniture, including Pauline's state bed, whose latest occupants were Sir Nicholas Henderson and his wife Mary. The offices next door on the Rue du Faubourg St Honoré were slightly less grand, but the ambassador's room still had frescoes on the ceiling. On my first visit to him I was waved in – 'the ambassador is expecting you' – but found the room empty except for a large Dalmatian dog. I was wondering whether the ambassador was a shape-shifter when he emerged from a concealed door to the residence.

The rest of the staff made up a galaxy of talent, with many gifted diplomats destined for the highest posts, like Robin Renwick, later ambassador in Washington. As counsellor (financial) I worked to the economic minister, the forthright Ronald Arculus, and my closest colleague was David Ratford, counsellor (agriculture and economic). My supporting team included Anthony Goodenough and Ivor Rawlinson, both of whom would later reappear in Canada. I soon concluded that, although the political section carried greater prestige, mine was the best job in the embassy.

One reason was that Nicko Henderson was passionately interested in politics and gave his political team a hard time. His morning meetings were marked by vigorous arguments, in which he was quick to exploit any hesitation in those answering his questions. Fortunately, he was less engaged with economics. If he asked me a question, he did not know the answer in advance. I learned to reply promptly and confidently, whether I was sure of my ground or not, and to correct any errors privately afterwards. Nicko relished having someone on his staff with a direct line to the Treasury and allowed me a free hand.

A second reason was that the political section had mainly to deal with the foreign ministry, the Quai d'Orsay. This was unrewarding. The Quai considered that the best way of promoting the interests of France was to reveal as little as possible, particularly to countries like Britain. If they told us nothing, we could not oppose their plans or embark on rival initiatives to steal their thunder. The Quai was also engaged in a power struggle within the French administration. They sought to be the only channel for conducting France's external relations. In politics they could largely carry this off, but in economics their claims were anathema to the finance ministry. So I found that my contacts there were all too ready to spill the beans on the details of French policy, to score off their rivals in the Quai d'Orsay.

The third reason was that the finance ministry, to which I had privileged access, was the most powerful institution in the state by a wide margin. It covered a wider range of policy than the British Treasury, including prices, insurance and external trade. It oversaw a large group of public financial institutions, like the Caisse des Depôts and the Credit National, which steered funds into both government and private investment. It controlled the three largest commercial banks, which were owned by the state, and closely supervised the private banks. More than all this, the ministry had its own unconcealed mafia in the form of the *inspecteurs des finances*, a super-elite drawn from those who passed out high on the list from the École Nationale d'Administration.

*Inspecteurs des finances* would begin their careers in the ministry itself, but would not stay there for long. In their mid-forties at latest, they would move on to other influential positions in or out of the public service. *Inspecteurs* provided the heads of public financial bodies and not only of nationalised banks but of private banks too. They filled the private offices of ministers or became political figures, like President Valéry Giscard d'Estaing himself. They secured prestigious international posts, like Managing Director of the IMF. Wherever the *inspecteurs des finances* appeared, they were a visible reminder of the power of the French Finance Ministry.

My closest professional contacts were with the Direction du Trésor, which handled finance (I use the French term to avoid confusion with the British Treasury). I would call on the austere *directeur*, Jacques de Larosière, and his deputies, approachable Michel Camdessus and saturnine Jean-Yves Haberer. (Larosière went on to head the IMF, where Camdessus followed him. Haberer became chief executive of the Credit Lyonnais and caused a scandal from which the bank never recovered.) I cultivated Jean-Michel Bloch-Lainé, the genial *sous-directeur*, who called me 'the white wolf of the British Treasury', and the bureau chiefs under him. I regularly visited their offices on the Rue de Rivoli or took them to lunch in restaurants nearby. At first I thought French officials would have no interest in talking to me, when the British economy was so weak. But I realised that finance ministries have no friends in their own administration; other departments fear them and even hate them. So they are forced to seek friends among the finance ministries of other countries. The links between the French Trésor and their British counterparts were close and there was much mutual curiosity.

As soon as I began asking questions about French policy, I would get reciprocal queries about British policy. At first I asked the Treasury for guidance on what I should say. When London proved reluctant to help me, I took to writing my own instructions. From the information available to me I would construct what I thought British policy was, expound it to my French contacts and carefully report to my colleagues in London what I had said in their name. This practice did not pass unnoticed in the Treasury, but I was never criticised for it; I think it suited them as much as me. Thereafter in my diplomatic career I made a point of anticipating instructions from London whenever I could. I thought I knew what British policy was just as well as the home team did, while I could judge better what approach would be most persuasive with my foreign interlocutors. This never did me any harm that I could tell.

I did not limit my attentions to the finance ministry. We gave small dinners at home for local and expatriate bankers, so as to understand the private financial scene. I cultivated the Banque de France, which had a pleasing reflective style; Gabriel Lefort, a sympathetic deputy governor, invited Dee and me to his flat in the attics of the Palais Royal. I kept close to the SGCI (always known by its initials) that matched the European secretariat of the Cabinet Office in London. There Bertrand Schneiter (another *inspecteur)* would happily reveal what the Quai d'Orsay would not tell me about French policies in the European Community. I found informative colleagues at the Commissariat au Plan. In preparing the national plan they gathered a wealth of assessments of French economic performance, which they readily shared with anyone who took an interest. In this way I was able to penetrate the domestic policy of the country more deeply than in a conventional diplomatic post.

President Giscard enjoyed greater direct power than any other European head of government. As a former finance minister, he resolved to exert his personal influence in overcoming the economic crisis created by the oil price shock. With this aim, he launched an initiative in 1975 for an informal summit between the world's major economies. This concerned me directly at the time and has occupied me ever since.

While he was finance minister, Giscard had joined his American, Japanese, German and British counterparts for informal meetings in the library of the White House, on the margin of IMF gatherings. He was much taken with the unbuttoned exchanges in this Library Group, which later became known as the G5. When he became President of France he decided to replicate the Library Group at his own level. He found eager support from his friend Helmut Schmidt, who had made a parallel transition from finance minister to Federal German Chancellor. In July 1975 the American and French Presidents, German Chancellor and British Prime Minister, meeting in Helsinki, agreed in principle to hold an economic summit on Giscard's model and to co-opt Japan as well. But this was unwelcome to Bill Simon, the US Treasury Secretary, who feared that President Gerald Ford would be outmanoeuvred by his more expert European peers. Giscard had to agree that the leaders could be supported by their foreign and finance ministers. He reluctantly invited Italy, to fortify its government against the communists, but refused to add Canada, which only joined when the summit met again next year.

The first economic summit was held in the chateau of Rambouillet outside Paris over a rainy weekend in November 1975. The constant passage of helicopters stirred up the fallen leaves in the park and stripped the trees of those that remained. The British delegation office was in Napoleon's bathroom, complete with a zinc tub and scenes from his victories painted on the ceiling. From the embassy Robin Renwick was attached to Harold Wilson, while I supported Denis Healey. On the first evening everyone gathered in a hall opening off the private wing of the chateau, waiting for their host to emerge. Giscard made a theatrical entrance, wearing a cashmere pullover and holding his wolfhound Jugurtha on a leash. He expected to greet his fellow heads of government alone. He was not pleased to find the room packed with Ford's security men.

When work began, Giscard sprang a surprise. Ever since 1971 the IMF had debated how to accommodate floating rates in its international regime. Most members, led by the United States, argued that floating should be as legitimate as fixed exchange rates. But France insisted that fixed rates should have preference, with floating only allowed in emergencies. At the last IMF meeting the other members had urged France and the US to reach agreement among themselves. Giscard instructed Larosière, the Directeur du Trésor, to negotiate a bilateral deal in secret with his counterpart in the US Treasury, Ed Yeo. The two officials struck a bargain, under which France would lift its reservations on floating. In return the Americans and other financial centres would intervene to counter erratic fluctuations in the foreign exchange markets that were not justified by underlying economic trends. This agreement was now unveiled.

The substance of this deal was welcome to Britain and the rest, but the Franco–American paper that expressed it was very sketchy. While the leaders worked through the rest of the economic agenda, Denis Healey, Derek Mitchell and I had a lot of work to do. The documents from the summit had to be robust enough to form the basis for amending the IMF's Articles of Agreement so as to legitimise floating. They also had to provide sufficient guidance for central banks to determine whether market pressures were merely 'erratic fluctuations' or a sign of more serious imbalances. The first half of this requirement worked out very well. The IMF Articles were successfully amended in January 1976 and the new regime has survived to this day. This achievement enhanced

Giscard's reputation as a world leader and encouraged those present to establish the summit as a regular annual event.

But at the time Giscard attached greater importance to the second half of the Rambouillet deal. Before he became president, the pressures of the oil crisis had forced the French franc to float. Giscard was determined to revert to a fixed rate and in May 1975 he abruptly put the franc back into the snake, without informing his finance minister in advance. The Rambouillet agreement on coordinated intervention was intended to help the franc stay in the snake. But it broke down almost at once because of the troubles of sterling. British inflation reached 26 per cent in January 1976. Though the figures improved thereafter, as Wilson and Healey finally got the unions to hold down wages, the markets were sceptical. Mistakes by the Bank of England in early March led to a ten-day run on the pound. Then the markets looked for other vulnerable currencies and put the franc under intense pressure. Transferring of money out of France into Swiss bank accounts was a favourite bolt-hole in times of trouble. These transfers shot up and I warned the Treasury to expect a move. Over the mid-March weekend the franc dropped out of the snake and floated once more. Soon afterwards Haberer summoned me to the Trésor late at night and angrily accused the British authorities of provoking the currency crisis. He claimed that our negligent management of sterling had turned the markets against the franc and implied we had done it on purpose. It was one of the most unpleasant interviews of my career.

For once I asked Derek Mitchell for instructions on how to respond. He wisely advised saying nothing and French anger cooled. But the crisis in the British economy grew worse and the government was forced to apply for a massive loan from the IMF. The Fund attached unwelcome conditions, some of which were negotiated in Paris out of the eye of the British media; I provided shelter and moral support to the Treasury officials concerned. The final agreement with the IMF was linked to arrangements to neutralise the sterling balances held overseas. The French proved helpful over these when Jim Callaghan (now Prime Minister) and Healey met Giscard at an Anglo-French summit in November 1976.

Once the IMF loan was in place, the British economy improved fast. The crisis atmosphere eased and I was able to give more time to other activities. Dee and I met the Queen Mother, whose programme in Paris included a drink with French captains of industry in Ronald Arculus' flat.

Neither party seemed sure why they were there, but she gripped her dry martini and charmed the businessmen with her fluent French. With other members of St George's Anglican church, we met the Archbishop of Canterbury at the abbey of Bec in Normandy, the mother house of his great predecessors Lanfranc and Anselm. I was asked to brief Margaret Thatcher on the French economy, as she passed through Paris. But I barely got a word in as she told me at length what the French should be doing, pausing at times to give me a dazzling smile.

I looked after Joel Barnett, Chief Secretary of the Treasury, when he came over for a day of talks. The IMF had insisted on deep cuts in Britain's public sector borrowing requirement and the Treasury wanted to know how the French kept theirs so low. I explained that the French kept almost all capital spending off the budget, but Barnett was keen to hear it at first hand. I arranged a programme that included the junior minister for the budget, the head of the Caisse des Depôts, the president of the Audit Court and finally the acting finance minister himself. For each successive call we went up a grander staircase and met in a more opulent office, but Barnett was not at all abashed. I found him a most congenial visitor and enjoyed taking him and his wife to Chartres at the weekend.

Back in July 1976 I had persuaded François Heilbronner, an elusive member of Prime Minister Jacques Chirac's office, to lunch with me. I asked him about French economic policy over the turbot and Sancerre, but found him strangely detached: 'M. Chirac has got other things on his mind.' A week later Chirac abruptly resigned as prime minister. To succeed him Giscard chose Raymond Barre, an economics professor and former European Commissioner. Barre was both prime minister and finance minister and thus became a member of the G5. Meetings of the G5 were secret, to keep out of the limelight and prevent the Italians turning up uninvited. But as prime minister, Barre could not leave France unobtrusively. He therefore invited the G5 finance ministers to hold their quarterly meetings at La Lanterne, his official country residence near Versailles. I would brief Denis Healey, Derek Mitchell and Gordon Richardson, the Governor of the Bank of England, over lunch at the residence before these meetings. Sometimes the ambassador was there too, but I preferred it when I had them on their own.

It was not easy to keep Denis Healey, a conspicuous figure, out of the public eye. Once he and his wife Edna flew in by economy class, pretending to be tourists, and this worked perfectly. Edna Healey was writing a biography of Angela Burdett-Coutts, the Victorian philanthropist, who had briefly rented the chateau of Chantilly. Dee escorted Edna on a visit there, while Denis went to the G5. A midwinter meeting was more eventful. I had arranged for Chancellor and Governor to land unobtrusively at the military airport of Villacoublay, but it was closed by a freak snowstorm. They had to fly on to Orly, where the press spotted them. The G5 meeting ended with a dinner for ministers only at the Louvre. The ambassador's Rolls-Royce was sent to bring Healey home, but he preferred to walk and vanished down a one-way street to avoid being tailed by the car. The chauffeur returned, crestfallen, to say that he had lost the Chancellor; but Healey soon turned up, much restored by his bracing walk.

Healey also came out for ministerial meetings of the Organisation for Economic Cooperation and Development (OECD). This was a forum for policy consultation among western economies, originating from the Marshall Plan. Each year the OECD would review the prospects for the British and the French economies and I made a point of attending these sessions; Arthur Maddocks, our ambassador, welcomed my interest. The OECD favoured using all the available macroeconomic instruments, both fiscal and monetary, for treating the current crisis. It argued for policy coordination that would enable weaker countries to benefit from the advances made by stronger ones. These ideas were backed by the new US administration of President Jimmy Carter and naturally appealed to the British government in its economic troubles. As a result the economic summits of 1977 and 1978 achieved a level of policy coordination that has never been matched since, with linked commitments in macroeconomics, trade and energy. Exposure to the OECD strongly influenced the way I thought about economic diplomacy and I remained involved with the institution for the rest of my career.

Halfway through our time Dee and I moved into a new flat, on two floors. There were decent bedrooms above and an elegant drawing-room below, opening into a dining-room hung with dark blue velvet. Five tall windows and a balcony looked across the Jardin de Ranelagh towards the Bois de Boulogne, where the boys could let off steam. The flat was further from Dick's school, so that Dee drove round the Place de l'Etoile four times a day until Dick went off to join Charlie at Swanbourne. All three boys were getting more out of life in France now. Two winter visits to the Loire valley added Renaissance chateaux to the acceptable forms of culture: great log fires blazed in Chambord and the floods rushed under the arches of Chenonceaux. We also made a day trip to the field of Waterloo, for Charlie's sake. While Tom was still devoted to model aeroplanes, Charlie painted miniature Napoleonic soldiers and was expert on the wars of the period. Like Dick, Charlie developed a French exchange with Hervé Gisserot, whose parents were professional colleagues. Pierre Gisserot was *inspecteur des finances* and mayor of a rural commune north of Paris, while Helène became a junior minister.

Paris was a marvellous city for the cinema and we saw the first two *Star Wars* films, Ridley Scott's debut *The Duellists*, Kubrick's *Barry Lyndon* and John Huston's stirring *The Man Who Would Be King*. There were good parties around Christmas-time and I established a role as bilingual Father Christmas (or Père Noel) at the one held at the residence. I would don the costume in my office and walk with my sack of toys to the residence next door, turning heads in the fashionable street. One year it was the Hendersons' silver wedding and Father Christmas awarded them the Order of the Silver Reindeer, made from a Christmas tree ornament (Plate 11).

I came home from an OECD meeting one day in 1977, to find a message from my brother Christopher that my father had had a bad stroke. He recovered enough physically to come home from hospital sometimes and appeared his usual courteous self. But his mind was confused and he was easily distressed when he could not do familiar things, like signing his name. Eighteen months later he died from a second stroke, aged eighty-one, just before I left Paris. His ashes were scattered in the churchyard of Long Compton church, whose finances he had managed for many years. My mother stayed on alone at the Malt House.

President Giscard still yearned to put the franc back into the snake, but worried whether it could keep pace with the Deutschmark (DM). His chance came in 1978 when Helmut Schmidt, picking up an idea from Roy Jenkins, the President of the Commission, proposed a new European Monetary System. This would consist of a stronger institutional structure, overseen by the EC Monetary Committee, and an Exchange Rate Mechanism (ERM) to determine currency levels. Giscard believed that the ERM could be designed so as to oblige strong currencies like the DM to revalue, instead of weak ones, like the franc or the pound, always having to devalue. On his instructions, Larosière invited Ken Couzens, Derek Mitchell's successor at the Treasury, for tripartite talks with Manfred Lahnstein of Germany. The French hoped that the prospect of getting the British on board would make the Germans more flexible, which would benefit both Britain and France.

Nicko Henderson believed that we should become full members of the new system for political reasons, to show our commitment to Europe. I was convinced of the economic case and put this to the Treasury. I argued that incomes policy was too weak to keep down prices, which were rising again as union discipline crumbled. If we had to defend sterling against other European currencies, that would oblige us to bear down on inflation. Others in the Treasury and Bank of England shared this view. But Couzens doubted whether the Germans were ready to see the DM appreciate, whatever the French hoped. He believed that the arrival of North Sea oil would distort the value of sterling and make it very hard to pick the right central rate. So Ken Couzens declined to commit sterling to the ERM and for a time it looked as if Britain might torpedo the new system altogether. But fortunately Schmidt and Giscard agreed that Britain could be in the European Monetary System without sterling having to join the Exchange Rate Mechanism. This formula was endorsed at a harmonious Anglo-French summit in November 1978, which concluded with a lavish banquet at the Elysée Palace for all participants, including me.

After the summit I hitched a lift on the official aircraft back to London. On that journey Michael Butler, the Economic Director at the FCO, told me I would come back to London early in 1979, to replace Humphrey Maud as Head of Financial Relations Department. This was welcome news, as I needed to re-establish my allegiance to the FCO. I had had four good years in Paris and my successor, Len Appleyard, was already in training in the Treasury. Dee and I had never expected to be posted to Paris, such a vibrant and high-pressure city. But we had come to feel at home there and were determined to keep up our links with France.

I spent my final weeks providing Nicko Henderson with the economic data underpinning his valedictory dispatch, which contrasted the dynamism of France with the decline of Britain. My researches showed that

France had steadily overhauled Britain since the late 1950s. In 1957 the French economy was a third smaller than the British; twenty years later it was a third bigger. Nicko's despatch was leaked to the *Economist* and made a great stir. It caught the eye of the new Conservative government and influenced his appointment to ambassador to Washington. Yet ironically we had both mistaken the trend. The interventionist policies that had helped France hitherto had exhausted their value. The long-term economic performance of the two countries was reversed, so that Britain in 2007 was once again well ahead of France. By then the power of the *énarques* and the *inspecteurs des finances* was deeply eroded. President Nicolas Sarkozy set the tone, as he had never been through ENA himself.

CHAPTER 11

# Head of Economic Relations Department

M Y RETURN TO THE FCO EARLY in 1979 seemed like a repeat of my move to the Treasury five years before. The world economy was plunged into turmoil again, by a new surge in oil prices. The British government fell, as Labour's relations with the trade unions had broken down completely. The resulting 'winter of discontent' made electoral defeat inevitable. The Conservatives came in and a major shift took place. I was now halfway through my diplomatic career and in that time the government had changed four times. But I would serve out the rest of my career under a Conservative government, led by Margaret Thatcher or John Major.

The industrial economies eventually recovered from the first oil crisis. External imbalances were corrected, growth revived and unemployment began coming down, though inflation remained stubbornly high. But then the Shah of Iran was overthrown and Iranian oil exports collapsed. This was enough to provoke another tripling of the oil price, from $13 a barrel in October 1978 to around $36 in June 1979. The negative impact on growth, inflation and the balance of payments was just the same as the first time. But the policy reaction was completely different. The strategy of sustaining growth by coordinated macroeconomic measures, promoted at the OECD and the Bonn economic summit, was abandoned. The US economy was overheated, while Germany and Japan regretted their earlier stimulus measures. There was a consensus to give top priority to inflation and not to accommodate the oil price increase. Governments should use monetary policy to fight inflation, but leave it to the private sector to revive activity.

This shift in international opinion matched exactly the strategy deployed by Margaret Thatcher and her Chancellor of the Exchequer, Geoffrey Howe, to rescue the British economy. Inflation was to be squeezed out by limiting the supply of money in circulation. Incomes policy was abandoned and the trade unions were treated as enemies. Public spending was cut back sharply. The cure was painful while it lasted and provoked strong resistance, but it was eventually successful.

Not all the Cabinet agreed with the strategy. Peter Carrington, the Foreign Secretary, kept quiet, but Ian Gilmour, who spoke on foreign affairs in the Commons, thought it would be politically fatal. He used to call me in, together with Simon Broadbent, an FCO economic adviser, to ask us for arguments to counter Margaret Thatcher's policies. This made me deeply uneasy. I was sceptical about money supply targets and thought the government too harsh to the unemployed. But I was sure that fighting inflation was the right priority and hesitated to criticise the Prime Minister. So I was relieved when Gilmour left the government.

I returned to form part of the economic team in the FCO, led by Michael Butler and Derek Thomas as under-secretaries (later succeeded by Tom Bridges and Richard Evans). I found Financial Relations Department, responsible for finance, investment and aid issues, in the hands of two experienced assistants, David Gore-Booth and Veronica Beckett (later Sutherland). But they soon left me as the department was transformed. Under Labour there had been an independent Overseas Development Ministry (ODM) with its own Cabinet minister. The Conservatives downgraded it to the Overseas Development Administration (ODA), headed by a junior minister reporting to the Foreign Secretary. The FCO and the ODA were meant to work closely together and two joint departments, one of them mine, were created to encourage this. My aid team was absorbed into a new Aid Policy Department, while I received in exchange the ODA officials concerned with North-South relations – easily identified, as they all had beards. I was blessed with a team of excellent quality in the new Economic Relations Department (ERD) and the ODA members soon completely absorbed the ethos of the FCO. (The opposite happened to the diplomats in Aid Policy Department, co-located with the ODA.) But in general I had no faith in this reform, which demoralised the staff of the ODA. They remained in the home civil service, worked in a separate building, and were not properly integrated with the FCO.

Life as Head of ERD had none of the glamour of my time in Paris, but gave me a wide perspective on international policy-making. I was in regular touch with other economic departments around Whitehall, like the Treasury and Department of Trade, and spent long hours in inter-departmental meetings. I handled many issues where the FCO was not the lead ministry and I had to persuade a home department to give due weight to international concerns. But I did not mind that. I believed

home departments should take their international responsibilities themselves, rather than passing them over to the FCO, which many of my
diplomatic colleagues favoured.

My staff in ERD divided into two teams. Andrew Green as assistant,
supported by Mike Reilly and David Lyscom, looked after relations with
industrial countries, including economic summits. The other team dealt
with relations with developing countries: Bob Stone was assistant, backed
by Richard Escritt and Kevin O'Sullivan, who even shaved his beard off.
We dealt with a variety of international institutions: the summits,
OECD, International Monetary Fund, European Community and
United Nations.

The economic summit had become much more of an institution. Each
head of government nominated a personal representative, called a sherpa,
who was supported by two sous-sherpas, one each from the foreign and
finance ministries. The sherpas would hold four or five preparatory
meetings and sit behind their leader at the summit itself. They would
complete the summit declaration in a joint drafting session, often far into
the night, before it was blessed and issued by the leaders themselves. John
Hunt, the Secretary of the Cabinet, had been the British sherpa from the
outset: Ken Couzens was finance sous-sherpa; Michael Palliser, Permanent Under-Secretary at the FCO, was foreign affairs sous-sherpa until
Tom Bridges took over in 1982.

My department was responsible for coordinating the briefing for the
sherpa meetings and the summit itself, even on subjects outside my direct
responsibility. I had regular sessions with John Hunt and his successor
Robert Armstrong and became very familiar with the summit process. In
1981, as Ronald Reagan took over as US President, the sherpas decided
to conduct a review of the summits' usefulness. Robert Armstrong was
asked to take the lead and charged me with drafting it. My work was not
very profound, as I recall, but it was well received and the sherpas
decided the summits should go on. But I never attended any of the
summits or sherpa meetings, as delegations were kept extremely small; I
made my impact from a distance.

The 1979 and 1980 summits focused on the response to the oil price
increase. Margaret Thatcher was delighted to find all her summit
colleagues were also giving priority to controlling inflation. Even Jimmy
Carter had abandoned policies of fiscal stimulus, while Paul Volcker at

the Federal Reserve tightened US monetary policy. But in consequence the world economy went into a deep recession. Carter meanwhile became obsessed by the hostages trapped in the US embassy in Tehran and urged us to freeze Iranian assets in London. Fearing the impact on the City of London, we claimed at first to have no legal powers. But in the end we enacted new legislation, which proved a useful foreign policy instrument.

The Ottawa summit of 1981 saw Ronald Reagan at the White House, while François Mitterrand had replaced Giscard at the Elysée. Reagan's economic team introduced deep tax cuts to encourage the private sector, believing that stronger growth would sustain government revenue. But 'Reaganomics' proved to be quite wrong and the US budget deficit ballooned. Volcker squeezed monetary policy even harder, so that American interest rates went up to 20 per cent and the dollar rose by 30 per cent. This put the other summit members in a painful dilemma: if they let their currencies fall against the dollar, they imported inflation; but if they raised interest rates to support their currencies, they stifled growth. Schmidt and Mitterrand bitterly criticised Reagan, but Margaret Thatcher did not, because of their close political links.

The 1982 summit was hosted by Mitterrand in the palace of Versailles and master-minded by his gifted but arrogant sherpa, Jacques Attali. There was even sharper friction between Americans and Europeans, this time over East-West economic relations. The Europeans, including Britain, had for years promoted such relations, as a means of reducing tension with the Warsaw Pact. A fat communist, it was said, was less dangerous than a thin communist. But the Reagan administration wanted to punish the Russians economically, to oblige them to cut back on military spending. The Europeans looked for supplies of gas from a trans-Siberian pipeline, whose pumping stations depended on US technology. The Reagan administration threatened to cut off this technology unless the Europeans reduced their export credit for communist countries. The Versailles summit appeared to find a compromise, but it fell apart at once, and the US carried out their threat. The ensuing uproar caused the departure of Al Haig, the US Secretary of State. His successor, the level-headed George Shultz, defused the issue by quiet diplomacy.

The summit ended with a grand banquet, opera and fireworks. The Falklands war was still raging and Margaret Thatcher abruptly decided to leave after dinner. She took the other ministers and Robert Armstrong with her, but the rest of her team were abandoned. Tom Bridges, Ken Couzens and Julian Bullard (FCO Political Director) chased her helicopter to Orly airport, only to see her plane take off with their luggage on board. They had to take the first commercial flight back next morning, still in their dinner-jackets.

My department also had the lead in Whitehall for the OECD, familiar from Paris. Its macroeconomic work had fallen out of favour with the Treasury, who now leaned towards the IMF. When the OECD forecast (accurately) that British unemployment would reach three million, Geoffrey Howe angrily threatened to leave it, though mercifully he relented. The OECD had a high reputation elsewhere in Whitehall for its work on other aspects of economic and social policy. However, each ministry wanted to preserve those OECD programmes that gave it direct benefit and did not care about the rest. So it was a struggle to get support for the OECD's budget, which was the FCO's responsibility.

I found it instructive to attend OECD meetings, especially the annual session attended by finance, foreign and trade ministers. This was widely regarded as a rehearsal for the economic summit and I could meet the sherpa teams from the other summit members. From the summit and the OECD I learnt more about international trade policy, to which I had not been exposed before. The key institution was the General Agreement on Tariffs and Trade (GATT), which conducted periodic rounds of negotiations in which countries undertook to lower trade barriers, principally tariffs. Thanks to agreements reached at earlier summits, the Tokyo Round had been completed in 1979, just before the world economy went into recession. With the pressure of negotiations removed, there were growing demands for measures of trade protection on both sides of the Atlantic. The OECD acted as a major bulwark against protectionism, through its programme called 'standstill and rollback'. In this, members encouraged each other to take unilateral action to keep their markets open.

While I had a clear entrée into summit and OECD matters, the IMF was harder to crack. I had easy access to the Treasury, as ERD's offices were actually in their building, but they jealously protected their IMF turf. I had a stroke of luck in that the annual conference of the IMF and World Bank in 1980 was threatened by a political problem. The Palestine Liberation Organization (PLO) sought observer status at these meetings.

Most members supported this, but it was anathema to the US and threatened to wreck the whole meeting. Mary Hedley-Miller of the Treasury asked me to join the delegation to give political advice, though I was no expert on the PLO.

We began at the Commonwealth Finance Ministers meeting, which always precedes the IMF/World Bank annual conference. This took place in Bermuda, where I enjoyed the island architecture. The white roofs of the houses, painted with a special solution to catch rainwater, contrasted with the walls in bright pastel colours. But the meeting was rather tense, as British policies were unwelcome to developing Commonwealth countries. I supported Peter Mountfield of the Treasury in the late night session to draft the communiqué, where we had a hard time. The IMF/World Bank conference was held in a vast hotel in Washington. All the world's finance ministers and central bank governors were there and most of the world's private financiers, pursuing profitable deals in the corridors. The PLO problem was quickly solved by having no observers invited at all. The meetings I attended were not very interesting, as the real business was done in restricted groups like the G5. But I circulated freely and observed how the Fund and Bank operated.

The chief problem for the IMF was debt. After the first oil crisis the industrial states were aware that oil-importing developing countries were suffering even more than they were. With IMF backing, they promoted a scheme whereby the surplus funds deposited by rich oil-exporters with western banks were lent on to poor oil-importing countries. This recycling process enabled developing countries to continue growing, provided they could earn enough from their exports to service their debts. But after the second oil crisis struck, the industrial countries, to counter inflation, cut back their imports and put their interest rates up. Many developing countries could no longer meet their debt obligations and were forced to reschedule them. This was largely done through a creditors' group called the Paris Club. The creditors first required the debtor to negotiate a programme with the IMF, to restore its solvency. Then they would decide how much debt they would reschedule and at what interest rate, repeating the process every year. The Paris Club process was painful and often humiliating for the debtors.

The Treasury demanded that the IMF impose strict conditions on debtor countries, requiring them, for example, to bring their budget into balance. They always consulted the FCO and would respond if we could produce foreign policy reasons for a milder attitude. They were more resistant if I invoked economic reasons, for example arguing that deep public spending cuts would create such hardship as to delay the return to economic health. I sat through many meetings on large debtors like Brazil, Egypt and Poland. In fact I worried more about the poor countries in the Commonwealth that could neither service their debts nor survive tough IMF programmes. But my efforts to get more generous IMF treatment made little progress. The Americans were known to be opposed and the Treasury were not inclined to argue with them. This part of my work played across into its second main component, economic relations with developing countries. I return to that later in the chapter.

While we were in Paris, Dee and I had worked as a team and she became a skilled and successful diplomatic hostess. This no longer applied. I would leave the house early for a long day in the office, hoping that the trains were not on strike. But I always aimed to get back in time to spend some hours with her, and with the boys if they were at home. I usually got the weekends free and could take leave for part at least of school holidays, so that family life did not suffer.

Tom moved steadily through Eton, ending in the Sixth Form as Captain of the School. During his time in this office the Headmaster, Michael McCrum, retired. Tom gave him a rousing farewell speech, which he drafted himself with minimal help from me. He delivered it from the steps of College Chapel and a photo appeared in *The Times*. He was most proud of being in the Rugby XV for three years, in the last of which they were unbeaten. On leaving Eton he took a short service limited commission in the Royal Artillery, before going up to read engineering at Oxford. His nine months in the army in fact put him off. He had brief moments of excitement, like firing live missiles in Canada, between long periods of boredom when he had nothing to do.

Charlie took the Eton scholarship exam before we left Paris and came within two places of getting into College. But he could not try again and so went cheerfully to Raef Payne's house as an Oppidan Scholar. There he formed an enduring friendship with an Indian boy called Uday Khemka. In due course he too reached Sixth Form and in the speeches on the Fourth of June gave a memorable rendering of Charles Darwin's account of the great Galapagos tortoises. Dick matched his brothers' performance in class at Swanbourne but was most famous for being calm and well-organised. This caused the Headmaster, Mr Jamieson, to make him Captain of the School a year before he expected it. Dick had no better success than Charlie with the Eton scholarship and followed him into Payne's house.

Dee returned to the teaching she had left when we got married. She joined an establishment in Victoria Street called 'Miss Dixon and Miss Wolf, Tutors'. This was efficiently run by Pauline Daly, the founders having long retired. The tutors prepared girls who had been unhappy or unsuccessful in school to pass their O-Level exams, the predecessor to GCSE. Dee taught English Literature and her girls had a good pass rate. She found it very rewarding when her pupils came to understand from her what writers like Dickens or Jane Austen had to offer. In the evenings we sometimes found time for the theatre. We saw Jonathan Pryce in a striking *Hamlet*, where the ghost spoke through him, and *The Duchess of Malfi* with Helen Mirren and Bob Hoskins; while we laughed till we cried at Michael Frayn's *Noises Off*.

Dee set her mind to upgrading No 2 Chetwynd House, which we had not been able to afford before. She enlisted the expert help of her father, Tom Wilde, and conducted two major campaigns in 1979 and 1980. Originally the house only had four bedrooms. Charlie and Dick shared one very amicably, playing complicated Napoleonic war-games, but we thought each deserved some privacy. The rooms on the top floor included the main bathroom and a large walk-in linen cupboard. Tom Wilde, with the help of a local plumber, shifted the bathroom into the linen cupboard. He then created a cabin-like bedroom for Dick in the ex-bathroom. Next year Dee and her father attacked the first floor. They tore out the existing shower room and replaced it with a much larger, proper bathroom. Tom Wilde created elegant dado panelling, to match the original woodwork in our bedroom, and an arched doorway with fanlight to spread light within the house.

Every summer we took a family holiday in France, often including my mother, though Tom went off with his own friends after he left Eton. In 1979 we borrowed the Gisserots' flat in Tignes, high in the French Alps. Next year our journey to the Jura involved a three-way rendezvous at Orly airport with Charlie returning from Gisserots in Brittany and Dick coming from Hecklys in Provence. But Dee and I got stuck on our ferry in mid-Channel, as French fishermen blocked the ports. The boys were rescued by Len Appleyard and we found them in our old Paris flat.

We then had two particularly successful holidays at St Martin de Londres, in wild country north of Montpellier. We developed an alternating programme, to everyone's satisfaction. On one day we would visit a cultural site, like the Roman monuments at Arles and Nîmes or the fortified town of Carcassonne. The next day would be devoted to swimming and boating in the river Herault or tracking down ruined castles abandoned in the bush. One year we took a river cruiser from St Gilles on the Rhône, past Aigues-Mortes to the Canal du Midi and back. There seemed to be no rule preventing Charlie and Dick, aged sixteen and thirteen, from driving the boat. So they did that in turn, very happily, while Dee sunbathed and I watched the passing flamingos. These were welcome diversions in a hard-working professional life.

When the Prince of Wales came to the FCO on an official tour, ERD was one of only two departments he visited. We gave the Prince a full account of what the department did in the twenty minutes he spent with us and he asked many thoughtful questions. He was most interested in relations with poor countries and politely implied that our policies could be more generous. I defended the government's position as best I could, but in fact I largely agreed with him.

The FCO was the lead Whitehall department for the North-South Dialogue in the United Nations generally, though the Department of Trade led on the UN Conference on Trade and Development (UNCTAD). I found myself back in the frustrating exchanges that I had seen emerging during my very first posting. The developing countries were trying to establish a 'New International Economic Order' (NIEO), to gain a better deal from industrial states. The NIEO would give them more control over foreign investment and natural resources; higher prices for commodity exports; better access to foreign markets; more generous financial flows; and more influence over decision-making in institutions like the IMF and World Bank. The proponents of the NIEO had increased the pressure after the first oil crisis,, believing that this would improve their bargaining leverage. In response, President Giscard launched the Conference on International Economic Cooperation, between selected industrial countries, OPEC members and developing oil-importers, but it achieved nothing. After the second oil crisis the NIEO's advocates tried again. They now demanded 'global negotiations' in the United Nations covering all the issues of concern to them.

The British government was fully taken up with correcting its own economy and had no time for global negotiations. We had cut back our aid programme, arguing that we must 'put its own house in order'. I thought this was wrong, as developing countries faced much greater hardship than we did. I also wanted us to adopt a more forthcoming approach to developing countries, instead of being on the defensive. I therefore followed closely the work of the Brandt Commission on International Development, which had Ted Heath, the last Conservative Prime Minister, among its members. Heath's staff briefed me on the final stages of preparing the Commission's report, called *North-South: a Programme for Survival*.

When the report appeared, I took it upon myself to draft the government's response and tried to make this as positive as possible. I built up Britain's strong record in development policies and our support for many practical proposals in the report on food and energy issues, hoping that this would offset our inability to increase our aid. But my approach had no success: the government's policy was publicly regarded as grudging and tight-fisted. I realised that I was not very good at promoting policies with which I disagreed myself and wondered if I ought to leave the FCO for this reason. I decided to soldier on, but became more cautious. In future I kept away from posts where I was out of sympathy with the government's approach, for example on European policy.

Meanwhile, work on global negotiations continued in the UN. Unlike the OECD or IMF, policy on the North-South Dialogue was co-ordinated in the European Community and an agreed position was presented by the member state holding the Presidency, which rotated every six months. This involved me in regular trips to Brussels, where I was hospitably lodged first by John Coles and later by Charles Powell, counsellors at the UK mission. The other EC members, except occasionally the Germans, professed strong support for global negotiations, so that I was hard put to defend the sceptical British position. A special session of the UN General Assembly in August 1980, while I was on holiday, was intended to launch the negotiations. But Britain and Germany broke ranks in the EC, and joined the US in voting against the key resolution: we could not accept the IMF and World Bank being dependent on the UN. So the issue went back to the drawing-board.

The Brandt Commission had recommended holding a North-South summit to break the deadlock on outstanding issues. Accordingly

President Lopez Portillo of Mexico invited twenty heads of government to meet at Cancun in August 1981. Margaret Thatcher and the newly elected Reagan hesitated over accepting, but in the end both did so. I accompanied Peter Carrington on a preparatory foreign ministers' meeting on site. He was very cross and hardly spoke to me, because he was missing a rare chance to get to a test match. For the summit itself I flew out with the Prime Minister in her dedicated VC10. As the senior diplomat on board, she made much of me, inviting me to lunch and making sure my plate was full. She fascinated me, but as a snake fascinates a rabbit, so that I was intimidated in her presence.

The Cancun summit was held in the Sheraton Hotel, which was then by far the largest building on the seafront. Warships of the Mexican navy patrolled offshore. Some delegations appeared in slacks and tee-shirts, but not the British, after the Prime Minister told us: 'You are not here to enjoy yourselves.' The meeting began late, because American security men had blocked all the lifts to protect Reagan. Then the leaders had a lively debate, with good rapport between Margaret Thatcher and Indira Gandhi, but did not decide anything. When Pierre Trudeau of Canada, as co-chairman, summarised the discussion for the press, he used a pre-negotiated formula on global negotiations that was wholly ambiguous. So the issue returned to the UN General Assembly.

Britain held the EC Presidency for the second half of 1981, which made me the European spokesman. I had a narrow line to tread, between the enthusiasts for global negotiations in the EC and my own government's doubts, shared by the Americans. The western position was debated at an OECD meeting, at which my proposals for the EC approach were fortunately endorsed by France and the Commission, the keenest advocates. I then flew to New York, played for time at my first UN meeting, and settled down to forge an alliance with the Americans, helped by a sensible Dutchman from the Commission. John Boyd, the economic counsellor at the UK mission, gave me valuable moral support. We would lunch at the Grand Central Station oyster bar and he took me home to meet his wife Julia and three small girls. It was my first return to New York since my long honeymoon with Dee and I found the romantic associations as strong as ever. I brought home a blue faience hippo from the Metropolitan Museum that we had coveted but could not afford on our first visit.

Having finally squared the US, I went with Anthony Parsons, our highly respected UN ambassador, to call on his Algerian colleague, who chaired the group of developing countries. He was a strange toad-like figure, heavily made up, but extremely alert. He thought our approach could be the basis for agreement on global negotiations and undertook to put it to his members. The other Europeans were pleased at the progress made and we broke for the weekend. Stuck inside my hotel by a snowstorm on Sunday, I turned on the TV to see Soviet tanks rolling into Warsaw. That issue monopolised the attention of the UN, so that any decision on global negotiations was postponed. I went home much relieved, as I doubted my fragile compromise could survive. (In fact agreement was never reached and the project ran into the sand.) Meanwhile Dee, writing Christmas cards as snow fell on Chetwynd House, had got a nasty shock to find water pouring through the roof.

In 1982 I began my fourth year in ERD with a memorable commodity crisis. The International Tin Agreement, to which Britain had always belonged, came up for renewal. The Department of Industry led on this issue and the strong-minded Enid Jones decided that we should oppose renewing the agreement. She argued that the agreement was economically damaging. It kept the price of tin artificially high, which hurt British tin users and reduced demand for the output of our tin mines. She forecast that the agreement would soon collapse. I was obliged to oppose her. I countered her economic arguments, pointing out that the agreement had worked well for twenty years, and advanced political arguments for its renewal. The European Community had just decided to agree its policy on commodity issues jointly. If Britain blocked a consensus, the EC as a whole could not join and the new agreement would collapse without this large block of tin consumers. This would alienate both our EC partners, who wanted to join, and developing countries, who valued commodity agreements as part of the NIEO. It would especially alienate Malaysia, then the largest tin producer, with whom we were having a series of rows. Peter Carrington told me firmly he did not want another.

Enid and I looked for allies in Whitehall. Treasury and Agriculture, who disliked commodity agreements, supported her, but Trade, as sponsors of UNCTAD, backed me. With officials divided, the matter went to a Cabinet Committee of ministers. The Defence Secretary came in on my side, as he hoped for arms contracts from Malaysia, but the deadlock persisted. The problem had to be submitted to the Prime

Minister for her to arbitrate, which looked bad for me. Before she took a decision, she and Peter Carrington went to a bilateral summit with the Germans, the only other EC members with doubts about the agreement. This could have made matters even worse for me. But Carrington, in a brilliant manoeuvre, persuaded his colleague Hans-Dietrich Genscher it was right to join; Genscher persuaded Helmut Schmidt; and Schmidt persuaded Margaret Thatcher. Britain and Germany agreed that the EC could join the new International Tin Agreement, which duly entered into force. Within three years it went bankrupt, so that I have to admit that Enid won the economic argument. But Britain was not blamed for the collapse and thus avoided a lot of political damage.

At the end of March 1982 I sent the family down to Devon for the Easter holidays. I intended to join them a week later, but I never did. On Friday 4 April Argentina invaded the Falkland Islands. Whatever else happened, I could see that we should respond with the toughest economic sanctions possible. I caught Tom Bridges just before a key meeting, to remind him we now had powers to freeze Argentine assets in London. This was done over the weekend. On Monday I drafted and cleared instructions to our mission in Brussels to seek a complete embargo on Argentine exports to EC countries. I sent these over to No 10, hoping that they were ambitious enough, and was surprised when John Coles, now on the Prime Minister's staff, rang me to tone them down a bit. Through skilful diplomacy, the mission got our proposal accepted and the whole EC banned imports from Argentina.

This was the high point of our achievement in sanctions. We never persuaded the US or Japanese governments to take action in either finance or trade. But we had done enough to discourage all western banks from advancing Argentina any credit while the crisis lasted. We did not expect economic pressure to make the Argentines withdraw, but it showed them the drawbacks of their rash invasion. I sat in on meetings in the FCO emergency centre and gave shelter in ERD to our economic counsellor expelled from Buenos Aires. But I gradually dropped out, having nothing to contribute to the diplomatic exchanges or the military decisions. I was glad to do so, as I did not agree with the military option and thought the risks were too great. Even now I do not believe that keeping the Falklands British justifies the casualties at the time or the resources expended since.

Helmut Schmidt had been a co-founder, with Giscard, of the

economic summit. At Versailles, his last appearance, he warned his fellow leaders that the pressures of external debt were becoming intolerable for many countries – but no one listened. His words came true in August 1982, when Mexico threatened to default on its debts of nearly $65 billion, and Brazil and Argentina soon followed suit. What had been a nagging problem became a full-blown debt crisis, the greatest threat to the solvency of western banks between the Great Depression and the financial collapse of the early 2000s. It would take seven years to bring the crisis under control and resolve it satisfactorily. But for the moment I was only too happy to hand it over to Len Appleyard, who moved from Paris to take over my seat in ERD. In September 1982, to my great relief, I was released to take a year's sabbatical outside the FCO.

# CHAPTER 12

# First summit book

THE FCO HAD AN ENLIGHTENED practice whereby selected officers in mid-career could take a sabbatical for about a year, to do research at a recognised place of study and publish the results. Several colleagues had been to Harvard and written highly influential works there. Crispin Tickell, for example, produced a ground-breaking study of climate change as an international issue, before joining Roy Jenkins' *cabinet* and becoming Commission sherpa. I was keen to go on sabbatical too, but preferred to stay at home. So I got myself appointed FCO fellow at Chatham House, where I had kept up my links with William Wallace, the Director of Studies, since my time in Planning Staff. There I spent the most agreeable and rewarding year of my entire diplomatic career, and in the process William and his wife Helen, also a scholar of note, became close friends.

In a busy department like ERD I had lurched from crisis to crisis, with no time to reflect more deeply. Now I wanted to stand back and identify underlying trends in economic diplomacy. I decided to make the economic summits the subject of my research, as I had been involved with them since they began and there had not been any serious academic studies of them. I proposed to look at the impact of the summits on the policy issues they treated and their interaction with wider international institutions. My subject found approval in the FCO and the Treasury, while I got a green light from Robert Armstrong as sherpa. William Wallace was also strongly in favour, since he was interested in the summits' role in foreign policy. He introduced me to Professor Robert Putnam from Harvard, who was spending the summer at Chatham House. Bob Putnam was also researching the economic summits, focusing on their effect on domestic policy-making. We got on famously together and agreed we had a lot to offer each other, without any conflict of interest.

Early in September 1982 I cleared my desk in the FCO and moved to Chatham House. The Royal Institute of International Affairs occupied the town house in St James's Square used by William Pitt, Earl of Chatham, when British Prime Minister in the eighteenth century, and by two more prime ministers in the nineteenth. I settled happily into a cosy office in the attics. The permanent staff were friendly and knowledgeable, especially the librarians. It was a delightful sensation to be my own master, free from the demands of international crises and the constraints of Whitehall consultations. But I was not idle. I did not know how long this enviable life would last, so I buckled down to my research without delay.

My first task was to work through all the written sources on summitry. The library occupied the former grand reception rooms and I had it almost to myself. As I read, I was beguiled by someone playing the flute melodiously in the building and asked the staff who the flautist might be. But no one could explain it, until somebody said that the Earl himself had been no mean performer on the flute. I was charmed by the thought that he had welcomed me to his house in this way. Since then I have often read in Chatham House library, but I have never heard the flute again.

The most important sources for me were not in books and journals but the institute's rich collection of press-cuttings. From these I built up a full dossier of what was in the public record on the eight summits held so far, as a direct foundation for my published research. It also served an indirect purpose. From my time in Paris and ERD, I knew the inside story of the summits, but I could not make explicit use of confidential material. So I used the technique I had learnt long before in Information Research Department. I looked through the press reports until I found articles that matched what I knew to be true from my own experience. I then made those articles the quoted source of what I wrote. This technique worked very well. Unlike the secretive meetings of G5 finance ministers, summit meetings of heads of government took place in a glare of publicity. It was hard for the leaders to keep their activities secret and often they did not try.

In November William Wallace carried me off to an international seminar on summitry in Maastricht, where he and Bob Putnam presented papers. On the margins of the seminar Bob and I compared notes on our work. Late one night he proposed that we should join forces. He pointed out that our two approaches were complementary and, if combined, would provide a comprehensive analysis of summitry. Jointly we could produce a full-length book, while neither had time to achieve this on our own. I agreed enthusiastically, but wondered how we could get this collaboration accepted by the FCO. I was obliged to have what I wrote vetted by the FCO, while he would clearly not accept this sort of censorship. We decided that each of us would write separate chapters of our book and make it clear in our preface that neither was bound by what the other wrote. Back in London I put this idea to the FCO Librarian, Eileen Blayney, who was the source of authority on the matter. Early in 1983, to my great relief, the FCO accepted my proposal completely, while adding that they would like to see Bob's chapters too, for information. At once I arranged to visit Bob Putnam at his home in Lexington, close to Harvard. I spent a very fruitful week there, meeting his wife Rosemary and teenage children Lara and Jonathan. I took part in some Harvard seminars and went sightseeing with the family, but most of the time was spent in planning the book.

We envisaged a book of twelve chapters, six by him and six by me, alternating narrative and broader analysis. My narrative chapters would include the first summit at Rambouillet, which I had attended. His would include the summit due to be held in 1983 at Williamsburg, Virginia. I would analyse the impact of the second oil crisis, drawing on my time in ERD. He would examine the role of President Carter, since he had worked for him in the White House. Bob's concluding chapter would review academic theories of summitry, while mine would offer ideas for future summits. Each of us would draft our own chapters, but we would agree all of them between ourselves. If I wanted to say something especially controversial, we would put it into one of his chapters. As we worked this out I became increasingly aware of my good fortune to have Bob as my collaborator. I found him lucid in explaining the most complex and unfamiliar concepts and full of original ideas. He also knew government circles well, both from his time in the White House and from his earlier research, published as *Bureaucrats and Politicians in Western Democracies*.

Our book would make extensive use of interviews with those directly concerned with summitry. Bob briefed me on the technique that he had developed in his earlier academic work. We would ask to make free use of everything our contacts told us, including direct quotations, but promise not to reveal the source. He found that almost everyone would talk openly on this basis and I had the same experience. I undertook to cover France, where he had few contacts, and relevant international institutions. I would talk to officials in other countries, while leaving political figures to him. Accordingly, after leaving Bob I conducted a round of interviews in Washington (including the IMF and World Bank), New York (for the UN) and Ottawa, greatly helped by my diplomatic colleagues in all three posts. In New York Julia Boyd took me to the opera. Washington was immobilised by a rare blizzard while I was there. I marched around the city, leaving my tracks in the snow and marvelling that the American Republic was so attached to the architecture of the Roman Empire.

Back in London William Wallace and his colleague in charge of publishing, Pauline Wickham, convinced David Hill at Heinemann Educational Books to publish Putnam and Bayne on summitry. The book was timed to appear in April 1984, shortly before that year's economic summit in London. We would have to submit our text no later than mid-November 1983. It was time to start writing in earnest, and between March and June I sent over to Bob drafts of all my chapters. Meanwhile I conducted more rounds of foreign interviews, with two trips to Paris, one to Bonn and sessions at the OECD, the UN in Geneva and the European Commission in Brussels. Once again I had tremendous help from the British missions in these places and met old friends in the process; Peter Marshall, who had been on the interview board when I entered the Diplomatic Service, was now our ambassador in Geneva. By the end of this sequence I had talked to a hundred people involved in the summits, including ten present or former sherpas. Bob had seen over two hundred people and generously shared his notes with me.

During July and August I revised all my chapters in the light of Bob's constructive comments. He was less advanced with writing than I was, but I had to allow for the FCO's vetting process. He had thought up an excellent title: *Hanging Together*, based on Benjamin Franklin's remark on signing the Declaration of Independence: 'We must indeed all hang together or, most assuredly, we shall all hang separately.' Michael Palliser, now retired from the FCO, and Bob's Harvard colleague I. M. Destler agreed to read our draft and offer comments. On 16 August, just under a year after I joined Chatham House, I submitted my six chapters to Eileen Blayney. Then I took the family off on holiday.

During my year's research I was able to do many things not open to me when I was tied to a desk in the FCO. Dee and I were active members of the Hampton Court Association, composed of local residents. Our neighbours Marius Goring and John Gandy were chairman and secretary.

On the other side of Hampton Court Green lived the treasurer Harold Edwards, a genial neurologist, and the local MP Toby Jessel, who was a keen supporter. We already knew him from his visits to Paris in the company of my cousin Percy Grieve, also an MP. As I now had more time to spare, I volunteered to take over as secretary of the association for a year.

One early task was to organise the association's Christmas concert, held in Hampton Court Palace. The music-hall songs performed by Eira Jessel, Toby's wife, were a great attraction, but she needed a good quality piano. So the committee found themselves heaving Marius Goring's grand piano onto the lorry belonging to the local market garden and driving it under the palace gatehouse, as snow was falling. I mobilised the association to oppose the grant of a licence to a new local restaurant. The licensing magistrate in Richmond (who ran a local travel agency I often used) overruled our arguments – but the new restaurant folded very soon, just as we had forecast. Finally I laid on the association's summer excursion to Cliveden Manor, where we picnicked in the gardens and ended the day at an open-air performance of *She Stoops to Conquer*.

Dee and I found time for three holidays in France. In November 1982 Charlie and Dick climbed out of Eton before dawn, to join us on a memorable jaunt to Brittany during Long Leave. We enjoyed three days as warm as high summer, beginning at the Mont St-Michel. The second day was spent at St Malo exploring forts built by Vauban, accessible only when the tide was out. On the third we discovered the Fort de la Latte, an amazing ruined castle on a rocky spit jutting into the sea, which we recognised at once from the film *The Vikings*. In April 1983 Dee and I visited our friends Christopher and Marguerite Lush, who had moved from Paris to Strasbourg. We made the most of the ruined castles of Alsace, perched on crags among the pine forests, and then travelled to Paris via the elegant architecture of Nancy and the grim wartime monuments of Verdun, seen in unrelenting rain. In August we headed for a converted barn in the Dordogne with all three boys, plus Tom's girl-friend Pamela Wallis. Tom and Pamela soon moved on, but Charlie's friend Uday Khemka appeared unannounced. From there we made a long diagonal across France to Brittany and took a motor-cruiser up the river Ourcq, as far as the riverside castle of Josselin. As before, Charlie and Dick were at the controls, while Dee and I looked out for the otters and kingfishers along the bank.

All this time I was trying to learn what my next post would be. I knew that I was due for promotion and that Personnel Department thought I should 'get my knees brown' as ambassador to a developing country. The prospects were limited to the posts then falling vacant. For an anxious month I thought it would be Havana, but luckily a Spanish speaker was found. That left the four Ks: Kathmandu, Kingston, Kinshasa and Kampala. In midsummer I was chosen to go as ambassador in Kinshasa, capital of what was then called Zaire and is now the Democratic Republic of the Congo (DRC). Fortunately Zairean bureaucracy moved slowly and did not grant *agrément* until I had finished writing. At last they gave the green light and my departure was fixed for late November.

The last two months of my sabbatical passed in mounting suspense. My chapters had disappeared into the upper reaches of the FCO, Treasury and Cabinet Office. Bob Putnam at last began producing his chapters, but I feared he would run out of time. In mid-October our readers Palliser and Destler produced a very favourable report, but strongly advised some re-organisation. I crossed to Lexington for a further session with Bob: I agreed to split one chapter into two and we thrashed out a number of discrepancies between our texts. We always ended in agreement, despite a fundamental difference of approach. As a bureaucrat, I looked for language that could reflect what both of us thought; as an academic, Bob wanted to debate the point until one of our views prevailed. I left him to finish the book, writing at top speed on his new computer. He later said he had never worked so hard before.

Everything fell into place at the last possible moment. Early in November I passed Bob's chapters to the FCO, plus the ones I had re-written. The FCO formally cleared my chapters on Monday 14 November, with only a few minor corrections. The complete book was passed to David Hill of Heinemann on Tuesday 15 November, right on our deadline. Dee and I packed up in a tearing hurry and left for Kinshasa on Sunday 20 November. Thereafter Heinemann moved with remarkable speed, so that proofs reached me in mid-December and advance copies were in my hand in February. In April 1984, well before the second London summit, the book was in the shops.

In October 1983 I had given a talk at Chatham House, later published in *The World Today*, summarising the main findings of the book and especially my chapters in it. Bob Putnam and I saw three fundamental reasons for the emergence of summitry. Growing economic interdependence required more effective action to *reconcile domestic and external pressures* on policy-making. The relative rise of Europe, Japan and Canada called for a system of *collective management* of the world economy, replacing American hegemony. Heads of government, by virtue of their authority and wide responsibility, could exercise *political leadership* to resolve policy blockages at lower levels. The summit as first envisaged by Giscard and Schmidt was a personal, anti-bureaucratic instrument. But the Americans, first Henry Kissinger and then Jimmy Carter, wanted to make it an institution. These two concepts persisted side-by-side.

The first four summits were intended to promote economic recovery after the first oil crisis and adopted increasingly ambitious undertakings. Rambouillet (1975) concentrated on monetary issues; Bonn (1978) embraced linked commitments on fiscal stimulus by Germany and Japan, energy-saving measures by the US and action by all to conclude the trade negotiations in the GATT. The next quartet of summits, from 1979 to 1982, followed the outbreak of the second oil crisis and adopted a quite different strategy. They gave absolute priority to bringing down inflation, leading to a long recession; recovery was not visible till Williamsburg in 1983.

Certain lessons emerged from the first quartet and still held good in the second. When all summit countries did the same thing, the cumulative effect was stronger than they expected. When one country followed policies at variance with others', this either ended in failure or caused grave problems to its partners, as Reaganomics did. Macroeconomic strategy needed to be consistent with policies adopted in other areas: the economic recession rendered superfluous the energy restraints adopted after the second oil crisis and made it harder to pursue trade liberalisation. In addition, these later summits saw the advance of foreign policy alongside economics, as former finance ministers disappeared among the heads of government; there were six at Bonn, but none at all at Williamsburg. Looking into the future, we wanted more attention to 'structural' economic policies, like labour, investment and competition, as well as to the problems of developing countries. We advocated more systematic treatment of foreign policy issues. Few of our wishes were in fact granted, at least for many years to come.

★　★　★

When *Hanging Together* came out in April 1984, the initial reception was good. The book received favourable reviews, notably from two former sherpas, John Hunt and Henry Owen, in *International Affairs*. But the marketing was unsatisfactory, as Heinemann had been taken over and David Hill had moved to Sage, a new academic publisher. Bob Putnam's contacts, however, led to a series of foreign language editions. Karl Kaiser, head of the German equivalent of Chatham House, sponsored a German-language edition, called *Weltwirtschaftsgipfel in Wandel*, before the second Bonn summit in 1985. One year later Bob was approached by a publisher wanting a Japanese edition, to appear before the second Tokyo summit in 1986. Bob had excellent contacts in Italy, so that it was no surprise when we were asked to prepare an Italian edition, called *Sovrani ma Interdipendenti*, in time for the second Venice summit of 1987. I joined Bob in Milan for a conference to present it, held in a room with splendid Tiepolo frescoes.

Each successive edition was updated to cover the summit of the year just past. We shared out the writing between us, though Bob conducted most of the interviews. But we really wanted a new English edition in paperback. Eventually we struck a deal with David Hill that Sage would publish this in late 1987, leaving a decent interval after the Italian version. David Hill wanted it to be more explicitly directed at the academic market and Bob undertook to expand the theoretical material in his introductory and concluding chapters. I re-wrote my own final chapter so as to compare the recent summits, from Williamsburg (1983) onwards, with what had gone before. I found that the latest round of summits had increasingly delegated economic issues to their finance ministers. The leaders had focused instead on foreign policy problems, though in a fragmented and episodic way. I assessed the summits' achievements over the whole cycle against their original objectives of political leadership, collective management and reconciling interdependence. I concluded that their performance had weakened over the years, but they were still essential instruments of cooperation.

Bob Putnam had already outlined in the first edition a metaphor of policy-making as a two-level game, with linked international and domestic boards. Backing from the domestic board was essential for a player to make progress on the international board. But skilful players could also make use of the international level to advance their domestic objectives. Throughout the 1980s Bob elaborated and refined his thinking and we had a series of lively debates. I was able to cite episodes from my own experience that illustrated his theory, such as the battle over the International Tin Agreement. Bob incorporated his revised theory in his chapters of the new edition of *Hanging Together*. He then expounded it in a more detailed article called 'Diplomacy and Domestic Politics: the Logic of Two-Level Games', and applied his metaphor to summitry in 'The Bonn Summit of 1978: a Case Study in Coordination'. These works established his reputation as one of the most innovative scholars in international relations. This time *Hanging Together* reached a wide readership and remained in print for many years.

As time passed I had greater difficulty in getting FCO clearance for my contributions. When the second English edition appeared I held a senior economic post, as UK Representative to the OECD. I had written the chapters relating to the most recent summits and these had covered controversial foreign policy issues, where I had less expertise. But I was able to negotiate amendments to my text that satisfied everyone. In retrospect, I am amazed at the patience shown by my hard-pressed colleagues, who found time to read successive versions of my book and offer constructive comment. The FCO continued to treat me well, in that I could go on writing for publication on issues related to my professional work. I produced another article when at the OECD, two when Economic Director at the FCO and three during my time in Canada. I was thus able to keep my hand in for more sustained writing after I left the diplomatic service.

Bob Putnam himself moved on to yet greater distinction from his analysis of the concept of social capital, first in his book about Italy, *Making Democracy Work*, and then in his immensely influential *Bowling Alone*, on conditions in the United States. I did not know during the time we worked together that he would become one of the most famous academics of his time. But I was not surprised when it happened. I observed in him all the gifts that make a really great scholar, not only of intellect but also of character. He had a most engaging and sympathetic personality. He radiated a genuine interest and curiosity in other people's experiences, which made them want to talk to him. He was intellectually open and honest, ready to confront counter-arguments fairly. He was far from an ivory tower thinker, but wanted to see his ideas in action and was prepared to put them into practice himself. Working with him on our book made my sabbatical a very happy experience.

# CHAPTER 13

# Ambassador in Africa

H IGH ABOVE THE SAHARA DESERT, Dee and I tucked into caviar, turbot and pheasant with chestnuts. The rules then in force enabled British diplomats taking up their first post as ambassador to fly there first class and we were making the most of it. In fact I was taking up four such posts. I would live in Kinshasa as ambassador to Zaire, the name then given to the Democratic Republic of the Congo. But I would also be non-resident ambassador to three other countries: to ex-French Congo, whose capital Brazzaville was just across the river from Kinshasa; and to Rwanda and Burundi, on the far eastern fringes of Zaire (Map 3). I had read up about the grim colonial past of this region, starting with the Casement Report on atrocities sanctioned by King Leopold of Belgium. I remembered that civil war was raging in the Congo when I joined UN Department back in 1961 and I knew that the country had gone downhill since. I expected to find evidence of poverty and misgovernment. But I did not know that my stay in this unhappy part of Africa would be also marked by family tragedy.

The FCO classified Kinshasa as a 'hardship post', but living conditions, at least for expatriates, were better than we expected,. Food was plentiful, at a price. The local beer was excellent and we drank it thirstily. Electricity was reliable, generated from the river, though the telephone service was highly erratic. The worst drawback was the lack of medical services, so that serious hospital cases had to be flown out. There were no restrictions on travel and, though theft was endemic, security was reasonably good. Kinshasa was full of greenery that distracted from the crumbling, neglected buildings and the potholes in the roads. Days would begin with hot sun and end in torrential cooling rain.

The ambassador's residence was very attractive. The well planned house, all on one floor, opened onto a broad veranda. This looked over a spacious garden full of flame trees, jacaranda, hibiscus and bougain-villaea. Colourful lizards ranged at ground level and fruit bats lodged in the taller trees. Beyond the garden fence flowed the majestic river Congo (now also called the Zaire), second only to the Amazon in volume of

water. By day we watched fishermen in their dugout canoes among the
water hyacinth. By night we saw the lights of Brazzaville and heard
gunfire, as armed police pursued smugglers. The centre of Kinshasa lay
upstream, with the ferry port and the embassy offices above Barclays
Bank. Downstream the rapids began, below Mount Ngaliema where
President Mobutu had his palace. From here a colossal bronze statue of
the explorer Stanley had once gazed up-river. Now it lay prone in a
junk-yard, broken off at the ankles.

The indoor staff in the residence had worked for the British for a long
time and knew exactly what was wanted of them. Sebastien the first boy,
Pierre the cook and Jean the second boy were like elderly gnomes, while
André the laundryman was younger and taller. Pedro and Simon, the
gardeners, were recent refugees from Angola who had been well trained
by our predecessors. The staff did not live in, following Belgian colonial
practice, but arrived early each day and left before dark, so that we had
the house to ourselves at night and on weekends. My chauffeur
Nkwenia, better educated and less deferential, was calm and resourceful
at the wheel and always well-informed. My team at the office was small
but well-chosen. Robin Crompton, my deputy, was on his third African
post. James Bevan at the political desk had a degree in social
anthropology. Joe McGoran was an experienced consul and his skills
were often tested. Joyce Milner, my secretary, was efficient and
motherly. Across the river the resourceful Clive Almond, with his wife
Auriol, maintained our presence in Brazzaville as chargé d'affaires.

Zairean protocol prevented me from doing any government business
till I had presented credentials to President Mobutu. So at first I
concentrated on the diplomatic and expatriate community. European
Community ambassadors met regularly and we all got on well together,
united in our dislike of the overbearing Commission representative. I
found a kindred spirit in Kees Lanjouw, the Dutch chargé d'affaires;
Kees, his wife Helga and their zoologist daughter Annette became close
friends. Commonwealth ambassadors also held periodic lunches and I
went to one on my first working day. Next day (Saturday) the phone
rang late at night and a faint voice reached us from Isiro, 1,500 miles
away in the far north-east of the country. It told us that a Canadian
travelling with a British overland expedition had been run over and
killed. I was glad I had already met my Canadian colleague before
contacting him with this sad news. His embassy had to retrieve the body

and repatriate it to Canada; inexplicably, the only reliable telephone link with Isiro was through the British residence. It was the first indication of why Zaire was a diplomatic experience like no other.

Every month the ambassador invited the heads of local British firms for an information-sharing session at the residence. I worried about how to handle this, as the businessmen all had much greater experience of Africa than I. But I was lucky in that Zaire had just rescheduled its debts with the Paris Club. On that subject I could hold forth with authority, so that I won their respect from the start. I got to know many of them well: Richard Wynne, the enterprising head of INZAL, that assembled Land Rovers; Tony I'Anson, the level-headed Yorkshireman in charge of CPA (Calico Printers Association), whose factory produced the brightly printed cloth worn by Zairean women; Muhammad Vayid, the gifted Mauritian running BAT (British American Tobacco), which had its own aircraft; and two reliable bankers, Geoff Thomas of Barclays and Peter Tomkins of Grindlays.

The development community consisted mainly of NGOs and missionaries. Paul Simon headed an Oxfam team operating in the Kinshasa area and we would invite them and their families to the residence. British Baptist missionaries, long established in the country, ran three hospitals along the river. We relied on the American Baptists in Kinshasa for their clinic, run by Dr Bill Macpherson, and their church, where an eloquent Welshman, Pastor Lewis, took the service. Once a month a Zairean Anglican priest, Fr Beni Bataaga, celebrated the eucharist there.

The Christmas holidays brought out Tom and his girl-friend Pamela from Oxford, followed by Charlie and Dick from Eton (Plate 13). We made cheerful family excursions to the botanical gardens at Kisantu and the spectacular Zongo Falls. We put our Avon inflatable dinghy on the river, where its outboard motor performed well. There were many other young people around, with whom our contingent sampled Kinshasa's nightlife and its vibrant musical scene. We hosted a large carol party on Christmas Eve and the boys played in a football match on New Year's Day 1984.

It was a light-hearted family interlude before more serious matters. Tom was into his last year at Oxford. He had enjoyed his engineering studies, but turned against it as a profession. Over the months ahead he tested his prospects in finance and finally settled for accountancy; he also parted with Pamela. Charlie, meanwhile, had chosen his university career in his own way. We had expected him to follow Tom to Oxford and read history there. But he was attracted by the course on Anglo-Saxon, Norse and Celtic offered by Cambridge and secured a place at Trinity College to study under Simon Keynes. His friend Uday Khemka was also bound for Cambridge. Having left Eton in December, Charlie planned to stay with us and experience life in Africa.

Early in January 1984 I was called to present my credentials to President Mobutu. Escorted by presidential guards, I descended a ceremonial stairway high above the rapids, poured a libation of palm wine to the ancestors, and inspected a cage of leopards, the national beast. I had a brief exchange with the burly Mobutu himself and perceived the determination and ruthlessness that sustained his despotic authority (Plate 12). Originally a journalist and then a soldier, he had seized power in 1965 at a time of chronic unrest. At first he served his country well, restoring order and creating a sense of national unity. But he became increasingly nationalistic and promoted the concept of 'authenticité' to remove all traces of the country's colonial past. He renamed the river, the country and its currency as Zaire and changed the names of all major cities. Zaireans had to adopt African instead of European names and were addressed as citoyen and citoyenne, as in the French Revolution. Suits and ties were outlawed and replaced by the abacost, a dark, formal bush-shirt worn with a cravat. Mobutu converted Zaire to a one-party state, founding the Mouvement Populaire de la République, so that his formal title was Citoyen Président Fondateur. The day after I met him he announced that he would run, unopposed, for another term of office.

Mobutu governed Zaire as if he were its paramount chief. He exerted power through patronage, providing his supporters both with direct financial rewards and with political office through which they could enrich themselves further. He constantly reshuffled his cabinet, so that no one else could build up a rival power base. He would share out ministries between different tribal leaders and they would give lesser government posts to their own people. By now all opposition to Mobutu had been driven into exile, but he was taking no chances. The rich mining province of Shaba had tried to secede in 1978. Mobutu ensured that all local office-holders came from outside the province and that it depended on electricity from the Inga Dam near Kinshasa, which could be cut off at will.

Governing by patronage was expensive and Mobutu enriched himself as well, with a personal fortune then estimated at $4 billion. Though Zaire was rich in resources, Mobutu's policies had bankrupted it. Public salaries went unpaid. The output of rich copper and cobalt mines shrank, as equipment was not replaced. Diamonds were smuggled out of the country in search of fairer prices. Major projects financed with aid money, such as a steel works, oil refinery and cement factory near Kinshasa, ceased to function. Initially Mobutu had expropriated all foreign-owned enterprises. Later foreign capital was allowed in again, but firms like INZAL and CPA were forbidden to repatriate their profits. They remained in business by over-pricing the inputs they were able to import. Over time Zaire had run up some $5 billion in international debt, which was now in arrears. The Paris Club had just agreed to reschedule that debt, but only if Zaire introduced corrective measures agreed with the IMF. These had begun to take effect before my arrival, with an 80 per cent devaluation of the currency. Mobutu had brought in a new prime minister, Kengo wa Dondo, and given him full authority. When I met him I found him determined to bring the public finances under control, and wished him well.

I could now do business with the government but found Zairean public figures very elusive. I called on ministers, but the exchanges seldom went beyond generalities. I had hopes of state dinners for visiting presidents, to which the diplomatic corps, the Cabinet and other leading Zaireans were invited. We would gather in the vast Palais du Peuple, said to be the largest building in sub-Saharan Africa, built and still maintained by China. We always sat down on arrival and the music began *fortissimo*. The singers, though loud, were good and were supported by undulating Zairoises clad in CPA fabrics which, in this election year, bore Mobutu's features spread across their ample busts and bottoms. But serious conversation was impossible. Starved of direct contact, and with press and television only serving to glorify Mobutu, we were reduced to relying on street rumour to learn what was going on. Here I found my East African Commonwealth colleagues very useful, as they picked up the gossip from the many Swahili-speakers in Kinshasa.

The Foreign Minister, Umba di Lutete, was friendly after he visited London in February, but weak as compared to his two deputies. One was Nyiwa Mobutu, son of the president. The other was Citoyen

Lengema, State Secretary for Development and the key figure on aid questions. The British aid programme totalled £1 million per year and London wanted it to reach the people and not be stolen by the government. After bad experiences with British experts, we preferred to donate equipment. We had had great success with supplying bailey bridges for river crossings, which could hardly be stolen, but the demand was now satisfied. After much debate with London and Citoyen Lengema, the year's allocation was split. Half went to supply new buses for Kinshasa's decrepit transport system, on which the local people depended. These would come in under the keen eye of Richard Wynne of INZAL. The remainder provided equipment for the Zaire river-boats operated by ONATRA, which was headed by a Belgian expatriate who had worked in Kenya. (Later in the year British viewers learnt all about these boats, as they followed Michael Wood up the Zaire on one of the BBC's 'Great River Journeys'. Nkwenia and my predecessor John Snodgrass featured in the opening sequence.) At the other end of the scale, I could make gifts of up to £1,000 from the Head of Mission Gift Scheme. For example, Dee and I gave a new washing machine to a maternity clinic run by the Salvation Army.

In my early months I spent a lot of time in Congo across the river, braving the unreliable ferry crossing. The regime here was just as despotic as in Zaire, but President Sassou-Nguessou was not as acquisitive as Mobutu. French colonial rule had left a stronger foundation and the country enjoyed good revenues from offshore oilfields. Brazzaville was in better shape than Kinshasa, apart from chronic power cuts. In January 1984 Colin Fletcher, a British trade minister, passed through. Clive Almond and I took him to see Congolese ministers, and we inspected a new railway tunnel and a eucalyptus plantation being financed by European Community aid. In February Brazzaville hosted an assembly of parliamentarians from the European Community and its African, Caribbean and Pacific associated countries. Dee and I looked after the dozen British MEPs who took part, including John de Courcy Ling, a former colleague from the embassy in Paris. Thanks to these events I became known in Brazzaville and in March was able to present my credentials to the president. But the main burden was borne by the Almonds, who were still living and working out of a hotel. Later in the year London authorised them to move into a new combined house and office (Plate 14). I visited them as often as I could and sent over other

Kinshasa staff to help them, including Simon from the residence to plant out their garden.

After Tom and Dick had gone back, Charlie needed some occupation and we approached Paul Simon of Oxfam. He arranged that Charlie and his friend Jamie Gow could work on the agricultural projects run by Mike Fitzgerald in Bas-Zaire, west of Kinshasa. They set off by bus and we lost touch with them. Without warning Charlie reappeared again a month later, tanned, self-reliant and full of his adventures. He and Jamie had spent their time digging fishponds in two villages deep in the bush, as part of a tilapia farming project. They had lived off beans and manioc, supplemented each evening with palm wine drunk with the village chief and his elders. They had gone hunting crocodile and monkey with the project leader, Lusumbisa, though without seeing either. They had travelled great distances clinging to the top of market lorries, one of which had brought them back to Kinshasa.

Encouraged by this experience, Charlie and Jamie planned a more ambitious trip, under the aegis of two British firms. Richard Wynne arranged for them to travel up the Zaire on the INZAL tankers taking fuel to Kisangani, 1,000 miles upstream, a voyage of three weeks or more. Then they would visit BAT's tobacco plantations in the north-east of Zaire, before returning to Kinshasa in the company plane. Dee saw them off from the docks and once more they passed out of contact. Dick appeared for the Easter holidays; Charlie's friend Uday Khemka turned up; my mother was also due for a visit. Late on Friday 30 March, a Lebanese working for INZAL brought us disturbing news received by radio. Charlie had had a bad diving accident upriver, near Kisangani; we had to get him out for urgent hospital treatment.

As the telephone was not working, Dee and I drove out to Richard Wynne's house, which was next door to Muhammad Vayid of BAT. We hoped that the INZAL agent in Kisangani, who was also the British honorary consul, could look after Charlie until Clive Wicks of BAT could fetch him back to Kinshasa in the company plane. But the BAT plane was away being serviced, so the five of us sat out the small hours together trying to reach Kisangani by phone and radio. We learnt that Charlie and his party had reached the airport and at length chartered a small plane from a German company. When morning came, we had to decide where Charlie should go next. Kinshasa to London took ten hours or more and there were no direct flights. South Africa was only five hours away, so I sent an urgent telegram to the embassy in Pretoria, who said at once they would receive him. I found Citoyen Kalonji, the friendly chief of protocol, at his desk on a Saturday and he authorised all the facilities I needed at the airport. Charlie's plane landed at mid-afternoon, with him on a stretcher, conscious but unable to move. The INZAL ambulance took him to Dr Macpherson, who gave us a diagnosis to pass to Pretoria. Charlie, he said, was 'quadriplegic'. 'Will that tell them enough?' I asked, not knowing what it meant. 'Oh yes,' he said, without explaining further.

That night the Johannesburg flight left with Charlie still on his stretcher, accompanied by Dee and Dr Macpherson. I gave lodging to Lisa Moon, a British nurse from the Baptist hospital at Yakusu, near Kisangani, who had flown in with Charlie. Before she left me on Sunday she tried to explain gently the consequences of diving accidents, but I was not taking it in. Monday morning brought a telegram from Dee. Charlie was now in hospital; his condition was very serious; she was staying with him and they were well looked after. Mercifully, the embassy phones were working and I was able to speak to her direct. She could hardly bring herself to tell me how bad the news was. Charlie had broken his neck and severed his spinal cord. He was paralysed from the neck downwards.

As soon as I could I flew down to Pretoria and found them in the spinal unit of the H. F. Verwoerd hospital. Charlie lay supine in traction, with a metal ring screwed to his skull and connected to weights, so as to straighten his neck. Dee was at his side and was able to stay there throughout the day. He told me what had happened. The tanker had moored for their last night before reaching Kisangani. They were restless after their long voyage and decided to dive off the ship's side into the river. Charlie dived twice safely, but the third time he hit his head, and when he surfaced, face downwards, he could not move. Jamie saw something was wrong, hauled him onto the bank and gave him artificial respiration. The ship's captain managed to establish contact with the Baptist hospital at Yakusu, which was close by. The hospital took care of him until they could transport him by motorised dugout canoe as far as Kisangani airport. Dee then told of their arrival at Johannesburg, after her second night without sleep, to be met by Gerry McCrudden, the embassy duty officer. He had been a tower of strength and secured

Charlie's entry to the spinal unit. This was headed by Dr Dommisse, now near retirement, who had made it the best in Africa. He explained that all the damage had been done on the first impact; Charlie had come through the rest of his long journey unscathed.

Charlie realised that he was only alive by a miracle. Having survived so far, he determined to make the most of his qualities of mind and spirit to compensate for his physical handicap. Dee dedicated herself to this cause too, however much effort and sacrifice it took. I went back to Zaire heartened by their courage and devotion, as Charlie began to dictate letters to his friends, coming to terms with his condition as he explained it. Everyone in Kinshasa was deeply distressed at the accident and wished Charlie well, none more than his friend Uday. At once he paid for Dick and then Tom to fly out to visit Charlie and support Dee; later he was able to go himself, overcoming all the obstacles created by apartheid.

After consulting London, I went back to Pretoria myself to confer with Dee and the doctors about Charlie's future. The embassy had installed her in a spare flat and helped her to buy a little car, while many of the staff had taken to visiting Charlie, from the faithful Gerry McCrudden to Ewen Fergusson the ambassador and his wife Sarah. It was decided that Charlie would come out of traction in late May and have an operation to fuse his broken vertebrae, as otherwise his head would flop forward. If this went well he would be flown back to England in early July, to enter the spinal unit at Stoke Mandeville, where the FCO had persuaded Dr Frankel to admit him.

Charlie was always in my thoughts, but I had to keep up my professional duties. These now took me to the two remaining capitals on my patch, four hours' flight away across unbroken forest. In April I presented my credentials to Rwanda's President Habyarimana in Kigali and in June to Burundi's President Bagaza in Bujumbura, visiting both countries on each occasion. Originally German colonies, they had passed to the Belgians after 1919, who administered them separately from the Congo until their independence in 1961. Their population was divided between cattle-breeding Tutsi, tall Nilotic people, and Hutu cultivators, of shorter Bantu stock. While racial differences had blurred over time, economic and social distinctions persisted, with the minority Tutsi being the traditional rulers. This was challenged after independence, leading to bloody civil wars in both countries. Bagaza had governed Burundi for eight years and still maintained the Tutsi supremacy. There was thus an unresolved tension in the country, which hampered good government. Habyarimana, in power since 1973, was a Hutu and many Rwandan Tutsis had gone into exile in Uganda. Rwanda therefore appeared much calmer, with a more efficient administration. Of the four countries in my charge, Rwanda seemed to me the best run, with the best prospects.

Britain's interests were looked after by two honorary consuls. Tony Wood in Kigali was a British coffee magnate, a bachelor and *bon viveur*. He looked after his visitors very well and gave me generous support. Charles Callot in Bujumbura was a serious-minded Belgian, who took his duties conscientiously. He and his wife Lily were well-liked and well-connected. In both countries the consuls set up calls for me on the foreign and education ministers and the local diplomatic corps. They enabled me to meet the teachers financed by the British aid programme. In Rwanda there was a strong Anglican presence and I enjoyed the packed Whit-Sunday service in Kigali cathedral, with hymns translated into Kinyarwanda sung to familiar tunes. I saw the impressive hospital at Gahini run by Anglican medical missionaries, which included a spinal unit (Plate 15). Missionaries were regarded with more suspicion in Burundi. But in general aid-workers felt they were making progress in both countries, in contrast to the chaos in Zaire. President Bagaza told me plainly that he would welcome more aid from Britain. I was pleased to tell his ambassador in Kinshasa, later in the year, that I had persuaded London to make Burundi and Rwanda eligible for loans from the Commonwealth Development Corporation.

Both countries were mountainous and scenically very beautiful. The land was fertile and villages were scattered thickly over the hillsides, each with its cluster of coffee trees, the main cash crop. Bujumbura had a fine site looking across Lake Tanganyika. Kigali was higher and its crisp climate was welcome after the steamy heat of Kinshasa. On my April visit to Rwanda, after my official programme, Tony Wood arranged for Dick and me to visit the mountain gorillas on Mount Visoke. We met two guides at the edge of the national park and plunged into the dense and dripping bamboo forest. After an hour's muddy climb up the extinct volcano we came upon a small gorilla group of a young adult male and an adolescent. We kept close to the ground, so as not to appear threatening, but they were very relaxed. The huge barrel-chested male basked in the sun, scratching himself with fingers as big as bananas. The younger ape was fascinated by the fair hair of a small girl in our party and she bravely let him stroke it. I had never been so close to dangerous animals in the wild (Plate 16).

British ambassadors regularly give a party to mark the Queen's Birthday in June, but are not tied to a special day. This allowed me to hold four Queen's Birthday Parties. I began in Kigali on 9 June, where Tony Wood laid on a lively event for over 150 people, with dancing in his garden. Charles Callot gave a more sober party for 90-odd in Bujumbura in 12 June, to which key Burundian ministers came. Pierre the cook spent a month preparing food for the Kinshasa reception held on 19 June. The Salvation Army band, in immaculate white uniforms with purple piping, played alternate British and Zairean tunes. There were three hundred guests in the garden, headed by Foreign Minister Umba and Nyiwa Mobutu, with whom I proposed toasts to Queen and President from the veranda. Finally, on 21 June, I crossed the ferry to Brazzaville, where the Almonds had gathered a varied group of about two hundred guests. So a grand total of 750 people came to honour the Queen in 1984.

The FCO granted me a month's special leave in July, to welcome Charlie and Dee back from Pretoria and install him in Stoke Mandeville. He could now sit up in a wheelchair, though he still had the metal ring round his head, connected to a sort of plastic cuirass, which supported his neck. But his early days in Stoke Mandeville were demoralising, as he was plagued by unexplained abdominal pain and nausea. Dr Frankel did wonders with his paraplegic patients, who could still use their arms. But he gave less priority to the immobile ones like Charlie and it was over a month before he got to grips with the problem. Meanwhile the family settled in with my mother at Long Compton, from where we could visit Charlie daily. Both the FCO and Cambridge gave us all the support we could wish. Personnel Department proposed that I should leave Kinshasa at the end of the year, spend six months in London at the Civil Service Selection Board and then become British Representative to the OECD in Paris. This was an ideal programme, which gave time for Charlie's rehabilitation before bringing me back into economic diplomacy. Trinity College made clear that they still wanted Charlie and would provide suitable rooms for him. His future tutor Kevin Gray and supervisor Simon Keynes visited him in Stoke Mandeville, which raised his spirits. I flew back to Zaire much reassured about the future. I faced several anxious months of separation, but then we would all be together again.

I settled to a solitary life in Kinshasa. Mobutu had received 99 per cent of the votes in the presidential elections and gone off on a triumphal tour of the provinces. Consular cases kept us busy. An Englishwoman in Kisangani was falsely accused of murder. Robin Crompton flew up and got her released from prison. (She was distantly related to the Royal Family and personally known to the Queen.) We helped to extract the British firm GKN from a disastrous mining venture with a Zairean partner, Citoyen Tambwe. A Zairean judge awarded all the assets to GKN, including a light aircraft. But when GKN sent a pilot and mechanic to collect the plane, Tambwe refused to release it and charged the mechanic, Nigel Tulloch, with criminal damage. Luckily the matter came before the same judge, who declared there was no case to answer. Tulloch, in his relief, went on a terrific bender in Kinshasa. As he drove home, he put his van into the ditch just outside the headquarters of the AND, Mobutu's dreaded security police. When two guards came out, he punched one on the nose and was sick over the other, so they promptly put him in a cell. Joe McGoran, by turns impressed and terrified by the AND, extracted him after a long argument.

The Anglican bishop came down from Kisangani and gathered a large congregation, including me, for an open-air service lasting four hours. We worked our way through confirmation, ordination and communion, with music from several choirs and a rousing sermon from Bishop Tibafa. The service shifted between French, English, Swahili and Lingala, the local language. For the offertory, the congregation went dancing down the aisle to put fat bundles of Zaire notes into a large laundry basket. The money was intended to buy land for a proper Anglican church in Kinshasa, and I visited the site with the bishop, Father Beni and the local treasurer, Denis Lejeune, an anglophile Belgian expatriate. He and his South African wife Mary Anne had helped me greatly when Dee and Charlie were in Pretoria. Another day I read the epistle at the nuptial mass in the Jesuit chapel for David Harvey, the embassy archivist, and his bride Bernadette. She had got dressed in the residence and Nkwenia had driven her to church in the official Jaguar. In due course the Jaguar brought bride and groom back to the residence and we had the wedding reception in the garden.

I took the opportunity to broaden my knowledge of other parts of Zaire. I flew south to the mining centre of Lubumbashi in Shaba, whose production of copper, cobalt and other metals, though well below capacity, still made up two-thirds of Zaire's exports. I gazed over the vast pit at Kolwezi, one of the world's largest open-cast mines, and went a kilometre down the deep mine at Kipushi, where it became uncomfortably hot. Once extracted, these metals followed a complicated journey by rail to a tributary of the Zaire, by boat to Kinshasa and again by rail to the seaport of Matadi.

Later Nkwenia drove me down to Matadi, 200 miles on Zaire's only good metalled road. The port had a dramatic setting in a gorge below the rapids that stretched all the way back to Kinshasa. There were ships being unloaded on the docks, but only a small pile of metal ingots waiting for export, showing the decline in Zaire's output. The Inga Dam nearby told the same story. The two great hydro-power stations, which only tapped ten per cent of the river's potential, could generate 1550 MW. But the whole of Zaire, including a new high-tension link to Shaba, consumed no more than 450 MW, so that most of the great turbines lay idle.

Down by the river at Matadi, under a great suspension bridge funded by Japan, I was moved to find a small graveyard of Baptist missionaries, dating back to the 1880s. Kimpese, the oldest and largest of the three British Baptist hospitals in Zaire, was not far away; there I was equally moved by the dedication of the staff, who stretched their resources to the limit to serve as many people as they could. Separately I visited the Baptist hospital at Bolobo, an hour's flight upstream from Kinshasa. This was a more remote operation, with only a few expatriates doing their utmost to provide maternity and child services and keep down tuberculosis. In 1972 the Baptists had been told to leave and let a Zairean enterprise take it over. A decade later they were asked to return and found the Zairean staff had not been paid for years. They had sold all the drugs and in consequence had no patients – a vivid example of the misgovernment rife under Mobutu. Seeing another Baptist team at work, I realised how much Charlie owed to their hospital at Yakusu after his accident. On the flight back, the pilot revealed he was a Tutsi refugee from Rwanda and spoke of the neglect suffered by his compatriots in Uganda under President Obote.

I had another vivid reminder of Charlie when I met Mike Fitzgerald of Oxfam on my way back from Matadi. I spent a day with him going round small projects to help the locals improve their agriculture and nutrition. We visited vegetable gardens, fields of new crops and fish-ponds like the ones Charlie and Jamie had dug. I also met their friend Lusumbisa and was able to tell him that Charlie was now making good progress. His nausea had been checked. He had built up just enough strength in his arms to use a powered wheelchair. He was learning to write on a computer with a 'mouth-stick' held in his teeth and I had already received letters he had typed in this way. It looked as if he would be released from Stoke Mandeville into our charge early next year. I therefore persuaded Dee to make a farewell visit to Africa in November, while Charlie was still being cared for in hospital.

Dee and I had a very happy reunion after three months' separation. She spent two weeks in Kinshasa renewing contact with the faithful residence staff and with all the friends she had made in our early months, who had showed such concern after Charlie's accident. She was able to say goodbye properly and to thank them all, not only for their earlier help and good wishes, but also for a very generous cheque subscribed for Charlie by the British community. Then we flew together to Burundi and Rwanda for me to make my final calls. These were soon accomplished and we had time to enjoy the scenery together. Charles Callot showed me hippos emerging from Lake Tanganyika at dusk. He led us both to a lakeside rock that marked the passage of Livingstone and Stanley and then up into the mountains to visit a tea plantation. In Rwanda I took Dee to see the mountain gorillas. We met a larger group this time, led by a majestic silverback male and including a female with an enchanting round-eyed toddler. At one moment the silverback rushed directly at me and I threw myself to the ground as he hurtled by. Then we drove through the Akagera game park, spotting elephant, hippo, buffalo, warthog and varied antelope. It was an elegiac joint farewell to Africa.

Dee flew home from Kigali. I had three weeks remaining in Kinshasa, with time to give a final carol party before I left on 20 December 1984. I had obtained a large wage increase for the residence staff, who fully deserved it, and Sebastien took me to see the house he was building for his family. Mobutu was then riding high. In a brief trip to the UN via Europe he had managed to see eight major heads of government, including Margaret Thatcher, Ronald Reagan and the Pope. He was inaugurated again as president with great pomp and made a speech lasting three-and-a-half hours. But the omens for Zaire's future were not good as I left. Prime Minister Kengo, as he thanked the ambassadors concerned for the President's good reception in Europe, said Mobutu considered economic restraint had lasted long enough. The people deserved some relaxation, so Zaire needed more foreign aid and debt relief. In mid-December a rebel group, led by Laurent Kabila, made a landing at Kalemie on the far eastern border. It was driven off easily, but on my final call Mobutu said he would have to divert funds from economic programmes to strengthen the army and security police.

In the twenty-five years since then, Rwanda has been torn apart by genocide and the Democratic Republic of the Congo (as Zaire now is) has suffered a chronic civil war in which four million people have died. I did not foresee the Rwandan tragedy, which was triggered by regime change in Uganda. The Tutsi refugees, maltreated under President Obote, gave valuable support to Museveni's successful bid to replace him. In return Museveni provided the backing they needed to invade Rwanda. Hutu extremists, fearing defeat, unleashed the horror of the genocide in 1994. Yet Rwanda survived as a country and has recovered strongly under President Kagame. The Hutu militia guilty of the massacre were driven across the border into eastern Zaire. This was the final straw that brought down Mobutu's tottering regime in 1997, to be replaced by his old enemy Laurent Kabila. The disintegration of the state had gone so far as to leave it only an empty shell, in which disorder continues unchecked and the UN's largest peacekeeping force can make little headway.

I was aware during my stay in Kinshasa that the seeds of this disaster were already being sown. I told the FCO that the longer Mobutu remained in power, the longer it would take to bring the country back to normal life. Yet his tyranny and corruption is not the strongest impression I retain from my time in Africa. Instead I remember the dedication of the aid-workers and the missionary doctors and nurses I met, as well as the capacity of ordinary Zaireans to survive against all odds. Most of all I recall the great kindness shown to me and my family following Charlie's accident.

# CHAPTER 14

# At the Organisation for Economic Cooperation and Development

I MADE AN ABRUPT TRANSITION from Africa to the routine of Whitehall. In mid-January 1985 I began my secondment to the Civil Service Selection Board (CSSB) as resident Diplomatic Service chairman. There I found the procedure little changed since I had been a candidate myself. Entrants to both Diplomatic Service and Home Civil Service went through the process together. Each applicant faced three stages: a set of written tests, as a first weeding-out process; a two-day interview board, run by CSSB; and a final interview, which brought in people from outside the civil service. I spent sixth months chairing interview boards, supported each time by a psychologist and a middle-level civil servant or diplomat. The board would test groups of five or six candidates in written and oral exercises and one-to-one interviews with each board member. Then we would grade them as Acceptable, Near-Miss, Not Acceptable and Far from Acceptable. The acceptable candidates and near-misses went on to their final interview, which almost always confirmed our choice.

In all, I assessed seventy-five candidates in my six months. The total field bidding for the Diplomatic Service was about 200 and I saw a quarter of these, with a smaller share of Home Civil Service candidates. I found it a demanding but generally encouraging experience. The FCO was looking for up to twenty-five new entrants and filled that quota easily. The candidates were not intellectually brilliant – few had first-class degrees – but they made up for this in sound judgement and resourcefulness. We were also making progress, if slowly, in attracting more women, more people from non-Oxbridge universities and more holders of science or economics degrees. I was especially pleased to recommend a woman microbiologist from Bristol, who has since had the most successful career of all those I was involved in selecting. The message for the Home Civil Service was less positive. They wanted eighty people, but attracted fewer candidates for each place offered and ended up with a shortfall. In part I attributed this to the wicked satire offered on television by *Yes Minister*, which undermined the public's good opinion of the civil service.

I enjoyed my spell at CSSB and worked conscientiously. But its great merit was its flexibility, so that I could devote time to Charlie's rehabilitation. I got back from Kinshasa just as he was being allowed out of hospital to spend Christmas with the family. We had a happy reunion at the Malt House, where my mother had been a tremendous support to Dee. Charlie went briefly back into Stoke Mandeville, but was discharged in late January 1985. It was now up to Dee and me to get him used to life at home and ready to start at Cambridge in October. We decided against moving back into Chetwynd House because it had too many stairs. Instead, we rented a small modern house in Thames Ditton, just across the river. Charlie in his wheelchair could enter from the garden on the level and operate freely all over the ground floor, sleeping in what was originally the dining-room. We were still close to our local friends, our very helpful family doctor and my brother Christopher and his wife Anne in Petersham, who gave us great support.

We moved with Charlie to Thames Ditton and established a routine. His condition was now stable, with movement and sensation in head and neck, plus a little in his arms; the rest of his body functioned automatically. He slept on a special adjustable bed with an inflatable mattress, to distribute his weight. Each morning Dee would dress him in bed. She would renew the condom he wore linked to a urine bag and strap this to his calf; every second day she would empty his bowels with a suppository. She would transfer him to his wheelchair, which had an inflatable cushion, though Charlie needed to be lifted regularly during the day to prevent pressure sores from forming. I would give a hand if I was around, as moving Charlie was easier with two, and I could do everything on my own if necessary.

Once in his wheelchair, Charlie sat up erect and could do some things for himself. He could drink from a straw, write with a pen in his teeth and draw vivid African pictures by the same method. His 'mouth-stick', fixed to a grip moulded to his teeth, enabled him to turn the pages of a book and operate a hands-free telephone or a cassette player. Best of all, he could use the personal computer that we bought with the money collected for him in Kinshasa. He was soon writing letters to his friends and dramatic stories with a Zairean setting. He was quick to perceive the potential of his computer and wrote presciently in his diary:

> It isn't until you've started to learn some of the things that even a little personal computer can do that you begin to understand the enormous power that computers as a whole represent. I do wonder what life is going to be like in twenty or thirty years' time. It really could be very different.

Charlie could travel further afield by being transferred from his wheelchair to the front seat of a car, but this was a laborious process. His mobility was greatly increased by the arrival of a second-hand Minivan specially adapted to accommodate his wheelchair. This was a generous gift from his friends and contemporaries at Eton, mobilised through the initiative of Raef Payne. In this vehicle we travelled down to Devon, to visit Tom Wilde, and up to Northamptonshire, where we spent a week on a canal boat converted for wheelchair users. In August the three of us, plus Dick, borrowed a house near the Sussex coast, where late one night we received a call for help from Tom. He had gone windsurfing at Hayling Island with Kristin Collyns, a fellow trainee accountant, but his car had broken down. I went out to rescue them and we found beds for them on sofas. Kristin took it all very calmly and we warmed to her at once. She and Tom soon became inseparable and two years later they were married.

As the year went on and Charlie grew in confidence, we began looking for suitable helpers to care for him at Cambridge. We identified a service called Community Service Volunteers (CSV) and our local council agreed to bear the cost. The volunteers had no special training but were prepared to do anything within reason. Most of them were fresh out of university and many were from abroad. Throughout his spell at Cambridge Charlie was supported by two CSVs at a time, who usually stayed through the academic year. At the outset we would train them in what they had to do for Charlie, which they all handled very responsibly. Once in Cambridge they would look after him physically and take him wherever he wanted to go, either in his chair or his van. Two strong young men could even get Charlie's wheelchair over stiles or up the spiral staircase to his supervisor's room. The bond between Charlie and his CSVs became very close. He inspired strong loyalty in them and, with rare exceptions, was able to trust them completely.

We installed Charlie in Cambridge with his first pair of volunteers as the academic year began. Trinity College had earmarked a suite of three rooms on the ground floor for him and his helpers. (These were the rooms earlier occupied by the Prince of Wales and his security team.) As Charlie would do all his academic work on his computer, the college carpenter constructed a suitable desk. Sadly, his original Minivan proved unable to stand up to the demands put upon it. So we replaced it with a new adapted Ford Escort van, bright scarlet, in which Charlie would cover many thousands of miles in the years ahead. Then Dee and I, hoping for the best, left for Paris, where I took up my post as UK Representative to the Organisation for Economic Cooperation and Development (OECD) in October 1985.

Economic diplomacy had been at a low ebb when I left it in 1982. Industrial countries were in recession, the debt crisis threatened the financial system and protectionist pressures were mounting. The Americans, in Reagan's first term, showed little interest in economic cooperation. Returning three years later I found things in much better shape. An economic recovery had set in from 1983 and would last the rest of the decade. James Baker became Treasury Secretary for Reagan's second term and was there throughout my time at OECD. He proved an enthusiast for collective international action. In September 1985 he invited the G5 finance ministers to meet at the Plaza Hotel in New York, where they issued a public statement for the first time. The Plaza accord brought about a controlled decline in the strong dollar, which had been making US exports uncompetitive. This eased protectionist pressures at once and opened the way to launch a new round of trade negotiations (the Uruguay Round) in the GATT in 1986. But now the G5 was out in the open, Italy and Canada forced their way in and it became the G7. When it met at the Louvre in Paris early in 1987, James Baker pressed for closer macroeconomic coordination, but this proved less durable. His 'Baker Plan' to end the debt crisis also had only limited success. Even so, this greater American engagement was widely welcomed.

The OECD was involved in every aspect of this international activity. It embraced the industrial democracies of Western Europe, North America, Australasia and Japan and covered a comprehensive range of economic issues. Unlike the economic summit, the OECD was a low-key body and did not court publicity. It could not provide finance like the IMF or impose treaty constraints like the European Community, but made its impact entirely by persuasion. It worked behind the scenes, by convincing its members to adapt their policies in their own interest and leaving them to take the credit. The main work was done in a series of specialist committees, which reached conclusions based on papers prepared by the expert secretariat. Officials would come from capitals to attend these committees and at times ministers would meet to give high-level direction. My main task was to brief British delegates to these meetings and suggest how the OECD could advance our objectives, rather than taking the front seat myself. British officials and ministers were always happy to travel to Paris, so that the delegation looked after a constant stream of visitors.

The OECD occupied a former Rothschild chateau near the Bois de Boulogne, with an anonymous annex for the secretariat, where our delegation offices also were. I was in charge of a compact team, composed at first of two counsellors and four desk officers. The counsellors – Emrys Davies and Timothy George – soon left to become ambassadors to Vietnam and Nepal and were replaced by only one, Hugh Davies. He and the desk officers – Kevin Passmore, John Dew, Charles Gray (later Chris Segar) and Richard Tauwhare divided up the economic issues between them. For all administrative matters we were looked after by our embassy to France, though I did have a chauffeur, Gerard Roselle, who drove my armoured Jaguar. He was a long-distance walker in his spare time and once walked from Paris to London in six days.

When the FCO first bought my residence, No 6 Villa Said off the Avenue Foch, it was criticised for extravagance. But we found it very well suited to our needs and made it work hard. There were four spare bedrooms, one very suitable for ministers; a large drawing-room for receptions; and a dining-room that could seat up to twenty. The large basement kitchen was the domain of Clare, the cook we brought with us, who turned out delicious meals for every occasion. She learnt to vary the quantities according to the guest-list: my OECD colleagues ate sparingly, but visitors from London would put away twice the amount. Her stepfather was president of the International Association of Airline Caterers. She got us invited to a grand dinner for six hundred guests in the Galerie des Batailles at Versailles, at which the airlines competed to serve the best food and drink.

Every year in May we welcomed three British ministers for the High-Level Council – the Chancellor of the Exchequer, Foreign Secretary and Minister for Trade. Nigel Lawson had no taste for the

OECD and would fly in, make a speech and fly out again. But Geoffrey Howe had become a strong supporter and took an active part, even when the meeting coincided with the American bombing of Libya in 1986 (Plate 18). One year his formidable wife Elspeth came as well. Alan Clark, as Trade Minister, was a courteous guest but unpredictable at the conference table; I was relieved to find we did not feature in his memoirs. Other ministers came for special events, including Kenneth Clarke (Employment), Chris Patten (Overseas Development), John Patten (Housing) and David Mitchell (Transport). They seemed to enjoy their stay and we often laid on lunches and dinners for them.

Among the officials who stayed with us, our favourites were the three Treasury knights – Peter Middleton (Permanent Secretary), Terry Burns (Chief Economist) and my former boss Geoffrey Littler. I successfully lobbied for Littler to become chairman of the OECD working-party on international monetary matters. Middleton and Burns came for the main Economic Committee and relished this rare opportunity to escape from London. To reinforce macroeconomic policies, the OECD was developing a technique for coordinating other economic measures under the slogan of 'structural adjustment'. This involved looking at a whole range of issues, like education, research, industrial policy, labour and financial markets and the size of the public sector, to see how they could be combined to improve economic performance. Peter Middleton was an able advocate of this approach: he and I encouraged David Henderson, the British head of the Economics Department in the secretariat, to follow it through. Meanwhile Dee and I learnt a lot of London gossip from the knights as, whisky in hand, they relaxed on our sofa at the end of the day.

We had frequent visitors from the Department of Trade and Industry (DTI), as the Uruguay Round got under way in the GATT: first Tony Lane and then my old friend Tony Hutton. For the first time, the negotiations would cover not only trade in manufactured goods, but also agriculture and services, two areas of great interest to Britain. As the GATT had no experience in handling either subject, it fell to the OECD Trade and Agriculture Committees to define the scope of the negotiations and to outline possible deals.

As the world's second supplier of services, after the US, Britain wanted to see the widest possible scope for removing trade barriers. Michael Palliser visited with members of the City-based Liberalisation of Trade in Services (LOTIS) committee, to feed in private sector experience. The OECD was able to classify the different varieties of services transactions and the obstacles to them. Services were not just traded across borders, like goods. They could also be consumed overseas, as in tourism; supplied by foreign firms established in the market, as in banking; or offered by foreign professionals on the spot, like lawyers and accountants. Barriers to services trade usually took the form of government regulations, rather than tariffs. The aim was to make them more transparent and avoid discrimination against foreign suppliers. The OECD's work laid the foundation for the General Agreement on Trade in Services negotiated in the Uruguay Round, which covered investment as well as trade.

Liberalising agricultural trade was even harder. OECD countries not only kept out food imports but subsidised farm production and prices in a bewildering variety of ways. The EC's Common Agricultural Policy was one of the worst offenders and British attempts at internal reform had made little headway. We therefore encouraged the OECD's work to develop a technique for measuring all varieties of support and protection for agriculture, in a way that allowed for comparison between different countries. The 'Production Subsidy Equivalents' worked out by the OECD were the first step on the road to the GATT Agriculture Agreement, whose conclusion, many years later, was essential to complete the Uruguay Round. The OECD was a useful place to pursue these aims, because the European Community did not have to speak with a single voice. The Commission delegate (often my old FCO colleague Leslie Fielding) would put across the agreed EC line, but member states could add further comments, provided we did not contradict it.

The OECD brought me new contacts from hitherto unknown parts of Whitehall. Grahame Reid came to the Employment Committee, which advocated labour market flexibility, a more congenial concept for Britain than the heavy regulation favoured in the EC. Sydney Fremantle was a regular visitor to the International Energy Agency, for debates on how to respond when oil prices fell sharply after 1986 – no easy decision for Britain, as we were now a net oil exporter from the North Sea. Fiona McConnell attended the Environment Committee, where the issues of climate change and biodiversity were attracting attention. I did not neglect my links with the FCO and did my best for Rodric Braithwaite, now the Economic Director, and Humphrey Maud, the under-secretary working with him. Rodric would come to discuss issues that spanned economics and politics in the obscurely named Executive Committee in Special Session (ECSS) and became the chair of it. I also kept up with summitry, as every year the sherpa of the host country gave a briefing to the OECD to explain the outcome. In May 1988, shortly before I left, the sherpas met on the margins of the ECSS and I entertained the British team at 6 Villa Said. Nigel Wicks, then Margaret Thatcher's private secretary, was our sherpa, supported by Rodric Braithwaite and Geoffrey Littler as sous-sherpas.

Our house in Paris proved highly attractive not only to official visitors but to friends and family too. Many people from earlier in this book made their way to 6 Villa Said to eat at our table and sleep in our beds. My mother and Aunt Diana visited regularly. My brothers Christopher and David came with their children. We welcomed our Hampton Court neighbours Colin and Kathy White, Bob and Rosemary Putnam from Harvard, and old Oxford friends, like Christopher Roberts, Richard and Kate Sorabji and Timothy Gee. FCO colleagues came on private visits, like Clive and Auriol Almond from Brazzaville and John Boyd, now back in London. We became expert guides to the local sights, including the Musée d'Orsay, Musée Picasso and Monet's house at Giverny, all of which had opened since our last stay.

Above all, 6 Villa Said offered admirable quarters for Charlie during his vacations. What had once been the coach-house was converted to provide generous ground-floor accommodation for him, with a bedroom above for helpers or friends and a terrace outside shaded by lilac trees. Embassy workmen took out a partition to create his bedroom, installed ramps leading to the main house and redecorated everything. All this was ready when Charlie arrived for Christmas 1985, driven across the Channel in his red van. Thereafter it served as a haven between Cambridge terms and his increasingly ambitious travels.

Charlie made the most of life at Trinity from the very start. At first this took such a toll that he had to recuperate in bed when he reached Paris. With time, however, he established a better rhythm, so that he would invite groups of friends and take them round the city, staying out far into the night. He even did some academic work, as he had to take exams in 1986 and 1987 to complete his Part I in Anglo-Saxon, Norse and Celtic. He wrote his exam papers on his computer and ended up with a very creditable 2:1, not far off a first. This earned him a round of applause from his examiners and promotion to be an honorary scholar of Trinity. He decided to take Social Anthropology for Part II, which gave him another two years at Cambridge.

Tom also invited lots of friends to stay, especially Kristin. He proposed to her in the house on New Year's Eve 1986 and the wedding was set for September 1987. Both of them finished their accountancy exams; Tom got a job with the investment banking arm of the NatWest Bank, while Kristin joined Lazards. We moved back briefly into Chetwynd House for the wedding, even though a leak in the water-pipes had brought down the drawing-room ceiling (Plate 17). Kristin's parents, Philip and Gisela Collyns, lived not far away in East Horsley and held the wedding party in their garden, under a tent designed by her engineer father. Back in Paris we learnt of the gale, a few weeks later, that blew down half the trees in Bushy Park. We invited Kristin's parents and grandmother to spend Christmas 1987 with us at 6 Villa Said. We all had a very cheerful time, helped by delicious food from Clare, and got on very well together.

Dick left Eton in the summer of 1986, having secured a place to read French and Italian also at Trinity. After a trip down the Niger with his friend Angus, son of the ambassador to Senegal, he moved in with us in Paris. He worked for a bank, passed his driving test in deep snow and became very attached to Helen, whose parents were in the embassy. To their dismay she was determined to become an actress. In due course Dick and Helen moved back to England and set up house together in Finsbury Park. After a grim period selling fire-extinguishers, Dick found an agreeable billet as a gardener. In due course he went up to Trinity, where he had rooms on Charlie's staircase, while Helen entered the Central School of Drama. But once their studies began, they gradually drifted apart. Helen McCrory, being dedicated to her profession, soon made a name for herself. Dick did well too in his own way, getting a First in French Part I, so that there were now two Bayne scholars at Trinity.

We only managed two long-distance trips in France: a summer holiday with Charlie on the Ile d'Oléron and an official OECD visit to Toulouse. But we had plenty of scope for weekend sorties. We went to the Loire Valley in midwinter, with ice on the moat at Azay-le-Rideau, and again in spring, when Angers and Saumur were full of lilac and wisteria. We toured Burgundy in pursuit of Romanesque churches, from Vézélay to Cluny via Fontenay Abbey, among cowslips and lady's-smock. We went north to Rouen and west to La Rochelle, returning each time with local ceramics. We sensed we would never have such a good opportunity again.

For longer journeys we re-discovered Italy. In spring 1987 I helped to launch the Italian edition of *Hanging Together* in Milan. Afterwards we went on to Lake Garda, where we found the delightful little town of Lazise, with painted houses and a Venetian customs-house reflected in its tiny harbour. Our friend Ivor Rawlinson, now British Consul in Florence, very kindly offered us his house for a holiday in August with Charlie. It began cheerfully, with visits from Dick, then studying in Perugia, and Tom on his last bachelor outing. But it ended in confusion when a local terrorist scare obliged us to flee back to Paris. Dee and I, however, were not discouraged from returning to Italy in May 1988. Gabriele Scimemi worked in the OECD Environment Directorate and his wife Zora was a friend of Dee. The Scimemi family owned a *palazzo* in Padua and Gabriele lent us the mezzanine reserved for his use. Padua had marvellous works of art – Giotto, Donatello, Mantegna and Titian – but few tourists. We were in easy reach of Venice, Vicenza and the Palladian villas of the Veneto. This made a splendid final excursion, as within a few weeks we were back in London.

Rodric Braithwaite was going as ambassador to Moscow and I would replace him as Economic Director. My three years at OECD had been an excellent preparation, but I still felt rather daunted by this promotion. In my last speech to my fellow ambassadors I said how much I appreciated the calm, reflective atmosphere of the OECD, so different from the frenetic demands for action that confronted most diplomats. I likened the OECD to a medieval monastery, which I now had to leave, reluctantly, to join the itinerant order of sherpas.

# CHAPTER 15

# Economic Director in the FCO

I RETURNED TO WORK IN THE FCO main building, after a long absence, and found it transformed from its earlier scruffy condition. The public areas, like the Locarno Rooms and the Durbar Court, were now restored to their original splendour. I thought the architecture pretentious and deplored the chauvinistic murals on the grand staircase, but it was vastly better than what went before. Work was still in progress on the Economic Director's office, so I moved into quarters just vacated by the Home Office. I would start my working day early, to read as much as I could before the telephone started ringing and the daily cycle of meetings began. I seldom stayed late, preferring to take papers home to read after dinner or over the weekend.

I went regularly to the gathering of senior staff at 10.30, chaired by Patrick Wright, the magisterial Permanent Under-Secretary (PUS), to review the issues requiring action that day. While the other under-secretaries were ranged round the wall, the eight most senior staff sat at an oval table. John Boyd as Chief Clerk (Director for Personnel) faced Patrick Wright across the middle; the Political Director (John Fretwell, later John Weston) took one end; I took the other, in the only chair with arms. The small group at the table would reconvene at other times, as the FCO Board of Management, the PUS's Planning Committee, the No 1 Board to select new ambassadors, or simply for a picnic lunch once a month.

Economic Director was a wide-ranging, open-ended job. I was responsible for all economic issues of concern to the FCO, both in Whitehall and in the world at large. As I could not do everything, I had to choose where to make my personal impact. This was not difficult. I was now sous-sherpa for the G7 summit. The FCO was responsible for commissioning and coordinating all briefing for the sherpa process and for the summit itself. I made summitry my main activity and was very well served by the team in Economic Relations Department (ERD). Tom Richardson and then Roger Bone headed it, in my old job; Nicola Brewer, followed by Richard Tauwhare from OECD, occupied the G7 desk. I took an active part in all issues that came to the summit: finance and debt, trade policy, the environment, and the economic future of Eastern Europe.

At times I intervened in other matters: aid policy, drug trafficking, energy, European issues, export credit, financial fraud, science, trade promotion and transport. But wherever possible I left these to my three under-secretaries. I gave John Kerr and later Michael Jay a free hand to deal with the European Community. They were star performers and both rose to become PUS. I only concerned myself with the EU's impact on the wider world, through trade and the single market. Roger Carrick, whose office was next to mine, was expert in trade promotion. Hitherto the FCO had handled export work overseas, while the DTI was responsible at home. Roger and I negotiated with David Dell of the DTI the formation of the FCO/DTI Joint Directorate, the foundation for today's UK Trade and Investment. (I had hoped that Roger would be its first head, but this went to his successor Oliver Miles.) Duncan Slater looked after energy, science and transport, but often had to give priority to terrorism, for which he was also responsible. In addition Simon Broadbent, the Chief Economic Adviser, was a valuable support at home and an ideal travelling companion.

My work took me all around Whitehall, but three departments were especially important. First came the Treasury, where Nigel Wicks had moved from No 10 to take Geoffrey Littler's post, while remaining UK sherpa. He was an excellent negotiator, being calm, patient and ingenious, and enjoyed the Prime Minister's total confidence. My finance sous-sherpa colleague was Tim Lankester, just returned from Washington. When he moved to be Permanent Secretary of the ODA, Huw Evans took his place. The sherpa team had to work very closely together and I found them all admirable colleagues. My office in the FCO was close to a concealed bridge giving access to the Treasury across King Charles Street (Plate 19). I acquired the key to this bridge and was back and forth almost every day. My links with the DTI on trade policy were almost as close. The GATT Uruguay Round was gathering momentum and became a key summit issue. Christopher Roberts, whom I had known since Oxford, was the UK chief trade negotiator and I regularly attended his GATT Round Group. Finally I got to know the Department of Environment team very well – Derek Osborn, David Fisk and Fiona McConnell – as this subject moved fast up the summit agenda.

Beyond the FCO and Whitehall, I pursued international contacts, giving priority to summit countries. With Treasury blessing, I would attend IMF sessions in Washington. I would stay on to meet the US sherpa, Dick McCormack, and his sous-sherpa, Tim Deal, as well as other influential figures. I would go to Paris for OECD meetings and then talk to my counterpart at the Quai d'Orsay, Pierre de Boissieu. He was a dominant figure on the French scene, eloquent and decisive, and though we got on well, I was always nervous he would talk me into something. With Germany we held an annual Anglo-German Economic Committee, which helpfully involved people from other departments to balance my mercurial foreign ministry partner, Alois Jelonek. I twice hosted this in the Foreign Secretary's elegant country mansion at Chevening.

Rodric Braithwaite had initiated regular consultations with Japan, so that I went there every autumn to confer with their sherpa and other officials. My first visit, in November 1988, was the most memorable. I developed a cold on the flight out and completely lost my voice. The formidable Michihiko Kunihiro and his team strained to hear my painful whispers in our talks, while at the traditional Japanese meals I had to keep silent. But an elderly geisha massaged my throat to such good effect that next day I was cured. After the formal talks Stephen Gomersall from the embassy took me off on a provincial tour. We went first to Kyoto, where I admired the Buddhist temples among the autumn maples. In Osaka we visited factories and learnt about the new airport. We returned to Tokyo via Ise, to observe Japanese agriculture and visit the ancient Shinto shrine (Plate 20). This was set in a forest of tall red cedars and built from their wood. Every twenty-five years a new temple was constructed, an exact replica of the previous one, and this had been going on continuously for twelve centuries. This organic link between past and present greatly appealed to me as an archaeologist.

I did not just talk summit business on these visits. I became an advocate of the European single market and linked it to the GATT negotiations. The European Community aimed to achieve free movement of goods, services, people and capital by 1992. A dangerous rumour was spreading that this would create 'Fortress Europe', which discriminated against countries outside the EC. I set out to demonstrate, from the measures already adopted, that the opposite was true. As the barriers came down, non-European firms could operate as freely as European ones. Once established in any one EC member state, they could do business in all the others. The EC therefore welcomed trade and investment from outside, and Britain offered especially attractive conditions. We hoped that our partners would follow this example of openness and make strong commitments to remove barriers in the GATT Uruguay Round negotiations. At first I carried this message to Washington and Tokyo. Later I took it to the capitals of fast-growing economies round East Asia and the Pacific, in recognition of their growing international impact.

As we came home from Paris, Charlie was ending his third year at Cambridge. He had already taken his red van, driven by friends or CSVs, all over the British Isles, from western Ireland to northern Scotland. He now set off on an ambitious trip through Scandinavia, escorted by Dick and Burckhardt, a German CSV. Dee and I decided we did not want to give up Chetwynd House, but hauling Charlie up six steps to the front door and another nineteen to his bedroom would not be tolerable for long. So we set about installing some lifts. We had a hard time persuading Richmond Council that we could put lifts into a listed building, but at last they relented and gave us a generous grant as well. When all was in place, an outdoor lift carried Charlie in his wheelchair down to basement level, where he entered the house by the kitchen door. An indoor lift took him from the kitchen up to the study on the ground floor and then to his own room above that. His CSV helpers, when in residence, had a room on the top floor just over his. This all worked very well and still left Dick with his cabin and a spare room for Dee's father or other visitors.

As his final Cambridge year began, Charlie, without much prompting from us, decided to apply for the Home Civil Service. Though he did not relish working in an office, he knew the civil service would provide the support and special facilities he needed. With the help of the CSVs and his computer, he got through the written tests in October and passed his interview board in spring 1989 with flying colours, making a powerful impression on everyone he met. He was accepted by the Department of the Environment to start work at the end of the year. He left Cambridge with a 2:1 in Social Anthropology and we went to the moving degree ceremony. Then he prepared for a final spell of adventurous travel to Eastern Europe and the United States. Meanwhile Dee and I contrived a nostalgic summer holiday round my official duties. We began at St Malo and the Mont St Michel and then broke off for the

OECD Ministerial Council and a sherpa meeting. We went on to spend another happy fortnight in the Scimemi *palazzo* in Padua, with a side trip to Lazise. Back in France for a short break in September, we learnt of the birth of Felix, our first grandson, and drank his health beside the Loire. We returned to wave off Dick, who was spending a year in Paris as part of his Cambridge course.

France chaired the G7 summit in 1989. The first preparatory meeting was held in the Perigord, near Lascaux, where the sherpas were taken to see the real painted cave. Sous-sherpas only got to see the replica, but I found this as evocative as the original. The second meeting was on the small Caribbean island of St Martin. I had a difficult journey, which included two hours before dawn at Cayenne airport in French Guiana, my only visit to South America. The sherpas met beside an intense blue sea, with pelicans dive-bombing for fish (Plate 21). The sun was baking hot, the land was parched, and it did not attract me. The third meeting, at Evian on Lake Geneva, was interrupted by the news of China's brutal suppression of demonstrators in Tiananmen Square.

Jacques Attali, the French sherpa, was decisive and full of ideas, but so arrogant that he put everyone's backs up. The US finance sous-sherpa, David Mulford, became apoplectic, but Jean-Claude Trichet (today President of the European Central Bank) was able to calm him down. Together they brokered a financial deal which finally put an end to the debt crisis that had broken out as I left ERD in 1982. Since then the creditor banks had allowed developing countries to postpone repayment of their loans, provided they followed reforms agreed with the IMF. But the banks still wanted full repayment eventually and refused to make the new loans envisaged in James Baker's earlier plan to end the crisis. In consequence the debtor countries could never escape from the austerity imposed by the IMF and the crisis dragged on. The new US Treasury Secretary, Nicholas Brady, decided the banks would not get all their money back, but must accept 'debt reduction'. The G7 backed the Brady Plan at the summit and it was then blessed by the whole IMF membership. The banks had seen it coming and acquiesced. This resolved the crisis for middle-income debtors to banks, though not for poor debtors to governments.

Attali wanted the summit to concentrate on the global environment, which had never been a lead subject before. We readily supported this, as Margaret Thatcher had been converted to the cause by the persuasive Crispin Tickell, now her environment adviser. The focus was on principles for domestic policy action, encouraged where necessary by the OECD. Environment policy should involve the whole range of government: it should be based on sound economics and work with markets, rather than relying on regulations. Subjects were also identified for international treatment, without prescribing specific measures: climate change, the ozone layer, biological diversity, forests, deserts and oceans. This approach proved uncontroversial and the sherpas prepared a long text that made up nearly half the economic declaration. The G7 decisions led to greater attention to environment policy in all industrial countries, so that it was integrated into overall government strategy.

In a gap in the sherpa programme Simon Broadbent and I made the first of our Asia-Pacific tours. We headed first to Australia for regular bilateral economic talks. I had never been there before and made sure we took in Sydney and Melbourne as well as Canberra, where I was happy to find Clare cooking for John Coles, the High Commissioner. The Australians were key players in the GATT negotiations, as founders of the Cairns Group of agricultural exporters. They complained vigorously about the EC's protection of its farmers, but I reminded them that Britain was one of the few member states that was pressing for reform. Australia was also launching a new regional economic initiative, called Asia-Pacific Economic Cooperation (APEC), and we got a full briefing on this.

On the way home we stopped off in Kuala Lumpur and Singapore, to see some dynamic Asian economies at first hand and show their governments that we took them seriously. I was amazed at the economic advances made by both countries, as compared with the Philippines I had known in the 1960s. I put over my message about the European single market and liberalising trade through the GATT Round. I found the Malaysians more open-minded than I expected. Singapore's economic regime was already very open, but they were reluctant to persuade others to follow their example. Throughout these visits I benefited greatly from Simon's economic curiosity, so that we would escape from official talks to visit factories, markets and shopping centres. He shared his wife Margaret's interest in plants and we found time to visit four magnificent botanical gardens.

The last sherpa meeting was at Rambouillet, site of the original summit back in 1975. With only two weeks left before the summit itself, the sherpas finally caught up with the extraordinary developments in Central and Eastern Europe. President Mikhail Gorbachev had already introduced *glasnost* (openness) and *perestroika* (restructuring) in the Soviet Union. Simon Broadbent and I had gone to Moscow in January to learn about its economic impact. We got an impression of turmoil and indecision. There were some signs of private enterprise, with new restaurants opening, but the GUM department store still had long queues for little stock. Many of the non-government people we met understood that radical economic reform was essential. In a side trip to Minsk in Byelorussia (now Belarus) we found Dr Kebich, the enlightened local leader, eager for more freedom of action. But our official contacts in Moscow either denied the need for change or, like Viktor Geraschenko at the Foreign Trade Bank, were determined to frustrate it and hold on to power.

Gorbachev's spokesman later said that no one would give him a Nobel Prize for economics. But by permitting opposition to communism in the Soviet Union he encouraged both political and economic change elsewhere in Central Europe. In Poland the Solidarity movement was gaining strength: in June it won elections and formed a government, without any objection from Moscow. The same was happening in Hungary. Britain had already created a 'Know-How Fund' to provide technical assistance to these countries emerging from communism, and other G7 countries were doing likewise. The sherpas realised that helping Central Europe must be on the summit agenda.

The summit followed directly after the 200th anniversary of the French Revolution. On Bastille Day, 14 July, the G7 delegations mingled with other visiting heads of government in spectacular celebrations under a cloudless sky. The junketing continued at night, when President Mitterrand hoped that G7 and non-G7 leaders would dine together. But the others were a motley bunch, including Mobutu from Zaire, and President Bush insisted that the G7 stay apart. Separately a letter arrived from Gorbachev, suggesting that he should join the G7. This was politely declined: it later emerged that Attali had stimulated the letter and even provided a draft.

Next day the summit leaders gathered in the newly opened 'Arch' building in the modern Défense quarter, a conscious homage to the Arc de Triomphe. The financial and environment issues were easily settled and the heads gave greatest attention to Central Europe. They agreed to set up a mechanism to coordinate their assistance to Poland, Hungary and other countries introducing open democracies and market economies. Bush proposed that the European Commission should chair the new body and Jacques Delors accepted with alacrity, to Margaret Thatcher's chagrin. As all twenty-four OECD countries joined in, it was called the G24 and soon began work in Brussels. Overall, the decisions reached on debt reduction, the environment and Central Europe made this the most productive summit for many years.

Throughout the summit, Margaret Thatcher was barely on speaking terms with Geoffrey Howe and Nigel Lawson, because they had just manoeuvred her into agreeing that Britain would join the European Exchange Rate Mechanism. She sacked Geoffrey Howe as Foreign Secretary before the month was out, while Lawson only lasted till November as Chancellor of the Exchequer. I was very sorry to see Geoffrey Howe go. He retained a strong interest in economic issues, after his years as Chancellor, and took an increasingly positive approach to the European Community. His successor Douglas Hurd involved himself less in economic matters. But he was a formidable negotiator when needed.

I had hoped to go to China on my next Pacific sortie, but the Tiananmen Square outrage made this impossible. Instead Simon and I went to Hong Kong, where the local inhabitants were in great need of reassurance. They wondered what would happen to them when they were absorbed into China, which was due in eight years' time. I did my best to calm any economic fears in my talks with the Trade Secretary, Anson Chan, and other officials. I argued that the authorities in Beijing would not want to undermine Hong Kong's economic success, which contributed so much to the development of China itself. But as they were preparing to take over, they would naturally seek to build up their own authority at the expense of Britain as the colonial power. Meanwhile, the nearest I got to China was a glimpse of Shenzhen from the edge of the New Territories.

On the same trip we visited New Zealand, to attend the Pacific Economic Cooperation Council in Auckland. This informal public-private gathering was a dress rehearsal for the new Asia-Pacific Economic Cooperation (APEC). All the potential members were there, from Canada clockwise round the Pacific to South Korea, including the US and Japan. An ingenious formula allowed China, Hong Kong and Taiwan all to take part. As an observer, I spoke last in the general debate and said how much, as a European, I welcomed the move to economic integration in the Pacific. I especially commended the concept of 'open regionalism', whereby any trade liberalisation among APEC members would be extended to non-members, as provided by GATT rules. APEC has since proved a durable institution, meeting at ministerial level and later adding an annual summit, though it has not fulfilled all its early promise. Auckland had another impressive botanical garden.

I was back in time to welcome Charlie home from an epic journey round Eastern Europe with Holger, another German CSV, and a friend Anthony Wilson. They had put the red van on a ferry to Helsinki and visited Leningrad, Estonia, Latvia, Lithuania, Minsk, Poland, Czechoslovakia and Hungary before heading home. They had slept in campsites and youth hostels and driven vast distances on dodgy communist petrol. The travellers brought first-hand evidence of continuing political ferment. In Tallinn they had seen the start of a human chain stretching four hundred miles through Riga to Vilnius, made up of two million people demanding independence for the Baltic States. They had finally left Hungary with a mass of East German cars heading for West Germany via Austria, as the border had just been opened.

The disintegration of the Soviet empire accelerated through the autumn. Mass demonstrations in Leipzig panicked the East German authorities into opening the Berlin wall and it was soon bodily torn down. Czechoslovakia abandoned communism with its 'velvet revolution'. Finally the Romanians rose up and removed their tyrannical leader Nicolae Ceaucescu. These historic events unleashed a tremendous surge of excitement throughout Europe.

I was now leading the British team to the G24 meetings in Brussels, chaired by my sous-sherpa colleague from the Commission, the painstaking Horst Krenzler. At every session we seemed to add new beneficiaries. Our aim was to coordinate western assistance, to avoid a glut of some sorts of aid and a dearth of others. We advised recipients on routes to a market economy, but did not impose a policy formula on them. I insisted that, having at last escaped from a command economy, these countries must be free to make their own choices. Poland was the star performer, where Finance Minister Leslek Balcerowitz put through 'shock therapy' that had the economy growing again within three years.

Others took longer to eradicate the poisoned legacy of Marxist economics.

Meanwhile Attali had one last initiative up his sleeve. He summoned the sherpas in December, just before handing over the chair, to propose a European Bank for Reconstruction and Development (EBRD) to finance the transition from communism. The British and American Treasuries overcame their initial doubts and agreed to back it, provided it was set up with minimum delay. It became the only development bank to be established with an explicitly political purpose, to support the move to democracy and open economies.

Amid all this excitement, Simon Broadbent and I fitted in one more Asian outing in November 1989. These tours gave me a welcome respite from the overwhelming pressures in London. We went back to Hong Kong, for some more morale building, visited Tokyo to meet the affable new sherpa, Koji Watanabe, and continued on to Seoul. I found the South Koreans receptive to my arguments about the European single market and the GATT, though I expected them to drive a hard bargain. They saw much merit in APEC, as they were not part of other groupings. After the talks, we travelled across no-mans-land to the North Korean frontier at Panmunjon. This had suddenly become the last communist barrier in the world. The divisions in Europe that had shaped my earlier career, when I worked in IRD and negotiated the Berlin agreement, were all vanishing. The Cold War, in force for most of my life, was coming to an end. Now, twenty years later, it is only a distant memory.

CHAPTER 16

# Summitry and the end of the Soviet Union

A S 1990 BEGAN, THE ECONOMIC future of Eastern Europe took all my attention. I made frequent trips to Brussels for the G24 and Paris for work on the EBRD. The new bank made rapid progress, with agreement on its founding statute by April. Donors embraced all OECD countries and some others, while the beneficiaries covered all Central and Eastern Europe, including East Germany and the Soviet Union. Debate moved on to practical arrangements, such as the site of the bank, and I left that to others. Paris and London were the main contenders. London emerged the winner, as President Mitterrand preferred to have Jacques Attali chosen as the first president. I privately thought Attali most unsuitable to head the bank and in fact his extravagant style soon led to his downfall.

The reunification of Germany dominated political debate early in the year. By the time I went to Frankfurt for the Anglo-German Economic Committee in April, it was already decided that West and East Germany would be formally united. Simon Broadbent and I, with Huw Evans of the Treasury, travelled on to visit East Berlin and Leipzig, to see at first hand how economic reunification might work. It was my first trip into East Germany since 1968 and I had the same impression of going back in time. The whole place was shabby and rundown, with smog from brown coal hanging everywhere. The university professors we met in East Berlin were keen to join the open economy, while the factories in Leipzig were proud of their workmanship. Even so, it would be hard to make the East German economy competitive, and we doubted whether the new West German measures to promote privatisation and determine property rights would help the process. At the official rate, one East German Ostmark equalled one West German Deutschmark (DM), but in fact the Ostmark was worth much less and black market exchanges were busy. When Chancellor Kohl decided that most East German savings could be converted to DM at the official rate, he gained political advantage but aggravated the economic problems.

Kohl had not consulted the Bundesbank over this move. When German fiscal policy was loosened to allow for massive grants to the East, the Bundesbank tightened monetary policy to compensate, thus asserting its independence. In Whitehall debates, Simon Broadbent pointed out that this would put pressure on other currencies in the European Exchange Rate Mechanism (ERM), unless the Bundesbank agreed to revalue the DM. This would soon become a problem for Britain too. John Major, as Chancellor of the Exchequer, was gradually persuading Margaret Thatcher to honour her pledge to join the ERM. He finally put the pound into the ERM in October 1990 and cut interest rates at the same time. I should have rejoiced at this, as I had always supported such a move, but in fact I had deep forebodings. At first my fears seemed groundless, as the pound was buoyant and the inflation rate dropped steadily. But this false dawn only made our final exit from the ERM, in September 1992, all the more catastrophic.

Charlie had finished off his period of freedom with a long trip to the United States. He based himself in Atlanta, home to Chad, an earlier CSV, and made a wide circuit through New Orleans and Texas, Florida and Tennessee. In January 1990 Charlie began working in the Department of the Environment. His division was concerned with local issues, like noise and waste, and was supervised by Derek Osborn and Fiona McConnell. The department's workshops built him two special desks, one for his computer and the other for reading. A colleague in his division, Joanne Sallek, doubled as his carer while he was in the office. He soon became a valued member of the team, as his word-processing skills were at a premium in the days before there was a computer on every desk. Charlie was based at home and his CSV, the Franco-Algerian Kader, drove him to work every day. I was sometimes glad to hitch a lift, especially when another great gale closed Waterloo because of falling glass.

I too made trips to the United States, as the Americans chaired the 1990 summit. They held the early sherpa meetings in the scenic surroundings of San Francisco and Newport, Rhode Island, but the preparations were more frustrating than the year before. Dick McCormack, the US sherpa, did not offend people, as Attali had, but he could not resolve the inter-agency battles in his own administration. President Bush himself seemed undecided. As a result, the Houston summit in July approached without a clear sense of what it would achieve. There would, however, be three main themes: the GATT trade negotiations; the environment, as in Paris last year; and future attitudes to Eastern Europe. On the flight out in the Prime Minister's plane I briefed John Major on trade issues. I found him much more confident as Chancellor than during his short spell as Foreign Secretary. Margaret Thatcher kept to herself. Houston was hot and steamy and the meetings were held on a university campus.

The summit started with international trade. The Uruguay Round of GATT negotiations were meant to be completed at a ministerial conference in Brussels in December. Many issues in the long agenda had made good progress. But agriculture was holding everything up and the European Community was a major obstacle. In the EC agricultural trade policy was decided by Agriculture Ministers and the same applied in London too. In the GATT Round Group, chaired by Christopher Roberts, I often argued with the dogmatic Richard Parker from Agriculture (his deputy, Richard Carden, was more reasonable). The key issue was which barriers should be lowered. Exporters of food, like the US and the Cairns Group led by Australia, were insisting on separate commitments to reduce import restrictions, export subsidies and levels of domestic support. The EC offered to reduce domestic support only, arguing that this in itself would lead to higher imports and make export subsidies unnecessary. This division had led to open disagreement at the OECD ministerial. The summit offered another chance to close the gap.

Margaret Thatcher had studied her brief and worked out a formula which she thought would get negotiations started again. To our surprise, she introduced it at the summit session, as normally the leaders did not engage in drafting. Bush, taken aback, accepted that her language should be reflected in the declaration which sherpas would prepare later. This process took the whole night and I had to negotiate the trade text. We made good progress on non-agricultural topics. All agreed to resolve future trade disputes multilaterally and strengthen the GATT's dispute settlement mechanism. This meant the US would no longer impose unilaterally the provisions of its Trade Acts. We agreed to make the GATT, which was institutionally weak, into a stronger multilateral trade organisation once the Uruguay Round was over. I fought hard to protect the Prime Minister's ideas on agriculture. I had strong support from the European Commission, which was lucky, as trade was really their responsibility. We ended up with an agreed text that, on the face of it, reconciled the American approach with the EC position.

The next topic was the environment. While the Paris summit had addressed domestic policy, Houston turned to action on global issues like climate change and biodiversity. The break-up of the Soviet empire had made it easier to negotiate on subjects which required worldwide participation. However, differences now appeared between the United States and the others. Policy in Europe was driven by consumer groups, who were worried by threats to the planet and were pressing for measures to avert them. But powerful producer interests in the energy and food industries made the Americans reluctant either to admit the problems or to take corrective action. President Bush, however, strongly supported a plan to protect forests in Brazil advanced by Chancellor Kohl. Overnight Nigel Wicks sat at the table dealing with the environment text. This could only paper over the cracks between the US and the rest, while it watered down the forest proposal, as the Brazilians had not been consulted.

On the second day the leaders welcomed the great strides made in Central Europe, which President Bush described as a 'new world order'. But discord soon broke out over the Soviet Union, where the economy was deteriorating from month to month. Kohl, Mitterrand and Thatcher all wanted to help Gorbachev. The European Council in June had charged the Commission to draw up a plan for collective economic aid to the Soviet Union. The Europeans expected the other G7 countries to join in. But American preparations for Houston had only covered Central Europe, not the USSR. Bush would not commit American funds, as he believed Congress would not approve them. Prime Minister Kaifu of Japan also opposed helping the Soviet Union, as long as a territorial dispute was unresolved. The most that could be agreed was that a group of international institutions should prepare a report on reforms to the Soviet economy and criteria for western assistance, in parallel to the work done by the Commission. Houston was a more fractious and less productive summit than the year before and set a daunting task for the British sherpa team, who would take over the chair in 1991.

Senior officers in the FCO usually gave parties at Christmas for their staff and outside contacts. Roger Carrick and I preferred to give our party in the summer instead, once the summit was safely over. On the morning before our post-Houston party I had to go home with a severe pain in my stomach and put myself to bed. As I lay there, my brother David rang with news that my mother, now eighty-five, had been in a collision while driving to visit him in Cheltenham. She was badly shaken, but not hurt, and David had collected her and brought her home. We both hoped that her usual resilience would carry her through.

Next morning I was no better and went to my doctor. Dr Parry laid me down and pressed firmly on my navel. I let out a yelp of pain. 'You have an acute abdomen,' he said, and reached for the telephone. In no time, it seemed, I was admitted to the New Victoria Hospital in Kingston, so that the surgeon, Mr Jarrett, could operate at once. When I came round, he told me that acute diverticulitis had perforated my colon; if he had not operated it would have been fatal. He had checked the infection, so that I was out of danger, but I would need two more operations over the weeks ahead. He never explained what had caused this outbreak, but I concluded it was stress and exhaustion from the summit, plus unsuitable Texan food. Once I was feeling better, Dee broke to me sad news about my mother. While at David's she had gradually weakened. She was admitted to hospital where she died of kidney failure. I grieved for her, alone in my hospital bed. But worse was to follow.

When the weekend arrived, Charlie came in to visit me. He had now served over six months in the Department of the Environment. He had made his mark as secretary of the Noise Review Working Party, a group of experts advising on how to reduce the disturbance from noise in the community. He had earned an excellent initial report and was due to move to the climate change division, who had asked for him. He had snatched some weekend outings to Ireland and Guernsey and was preparing a trip to the Balkans on his summer leave, with Dick in support. At a recent meeting with my brother Christopher's family, Charlie and his cousin Caroline discussed how they might set up a flat together in London. His prospects looked good.

Two days after Charlie's visit Mr Jarrett told me I could soon go home. I rang Dee to pass on the good news, but she was clearly in great distress. 'What's wrong?' I asked. 'It's Charlie,' she said, 'he's gone.' Charlie had come home from work around lunchtime feeling ill and short of breath. She put him to bed and was soon worried enough to ring Dr Parry, who came at once and called an ambulance. But before it arrived Charlie died in Dee's arms. It was viral pneumonia that killed him, against which his paralysed body had no defences. Most likely he had picked it up when visiting me.

Mercifully, I was soon released from hospital, so that Dee and I could comfort one another at home and prepare for two funerals. We first drove to Long Compton for my mother's service in the parish church, attended by many old family friends. Later my brothers and I scattered her ashes in the churchyard, as we had done for my father, and found a way to commemorate them both. The most striking landmark in Long Compton is the thatched lych-gate, with a garden beside it that my father had tended in his lifetime. We put up a tablet on the lych-gate wall that recorded our parents' long residence in the village and their support for the church.

My brother Christopher and his wife Anne, to our eternal gratitude, enabled us to give Charlie a worthy funeral in their church at Petersham. They found a priest to take the service and an organist to play; they also laid on flowers. The little church was packed with Charlie's loyal friends from Eton, Cambridge and elsewhere. I was touched to see FCO colleagues there too, as it was the day that Iraq invaded Kuwait. Dick read from one of Charlie's favourite Anglo-Saxon poems, 'The Seafarer', which vividly evoked his yearning to travel and see new places. After the funeral we invited his friends back to Chetwynd House, where they spilled out over the green and the park in the sunshine and drank to his memory.

Over the next three months I went twice back into hospital, where Mr Jarrett removed a foot of my colon. I had spells of convalescence and brief periods back in the office. William and Helen Wallace very generously lent us their house in Saltaire near Bradford for a week and we also spent time at the Malt House in Long Compton. We scattered Charlie's ashes under his favourite trees in Bushy Park and on a cliff-top in North Devon. The Noise Review was published and submitted to Parliament; the chairman explicitly commended Charlie for his tenacity and hard work. Thanks to our MP Toby Jessel, we were in the gallery of the House of Commons to hear Charlie's achievement recognised by David Trippier, the responsible minister, by Toby himself and by Geoffrey Howe.

Over this time Dee and I were able to come to terms with his death. We remembered Charlie with sorrow, but also with pride at what he had achieved. Though physically helpless, he had lived a full life at

Cambridge, with a good degree and quantities of friends. He had held down a demanding job in the civil service. He had found great satisfaction in travelling on ever more ambitious expeditions, so that his red van had covered 74,000 miles in less than five years. He was completely dependent on his CSV helpers, which put great demands on them, but they became so dedicated to him that they never let him down. Indeed, Charlie brought out the best in everyone with whom he was in contact, so that we had unstinting help and support from the FCO, Trinity College, the Department of the Environment and so many others besides, to whom we owed a great debt of gratitude. Throughout these years he remained the Charlie we had always known: humorous, imaginative and with a mind of his own.

After much debate in the family, we decided to honour his memory in two ways. First, we extracted everything he had written from his computer, to form the basis for a book. We hesitated about revealing what he had kept secret, but we found nothing that he would be ashamed of. Dick set to work to select and edit passages from his diaries, letters, poems and other writings. He put these together in a privately printed volume called *A Travelling Man*, with a minimum of linking passages, so that Charlie could speak for himself. Second, we set up a charity called the Charlie Bayne Travel Trust, getting valuable guidance from Margaret Spufford, who had founded a hostel for disabled students in Cambridge, called Bridget's in memory of her daughter. As Charlie had died as a serving civil servant, his ministry paid a death grant of £25,000, which became the trust's endowment. The trust would make grants to disabled students in Cambridge to enable them to travel either within Britain or abroad. Tom and Dick became trustees, with others from Cambridge, while my brother Christopher was treasurer. Every year from 1992 the trust has helped half-a-dozen beneficiaries with travel grants from £100 to £500. The travels have ranged from sampling roller-coasters round Britain to research in Ethiopia and charitable work in Belarus. Charlie, we think, would approve of all of them.

Early in November I returned to my desk in the FCO. Michael Jay, who had succeeded John Kerr as European under-secretary, gave a drinks party to welcome me back. There he told me he thought Margaret Thatcher would not survive much longer. I was astounded, but soon saw why he thought so. The introduction of the poll tax had made her widely unpopular, while her attacks on the European Community were increasingly strident. Michael Heseltine headed a group of Conservatives who believed she had become an electoral liability. With his resignation speech attacking her leadership, Geoffrey Howe became Brutus to Heseltine's Cassius and obliged him to challenge her openly. I went to hear a lecture by Chris Patten, the Environment Secretary, just as the results were expected from the first round of the contest. No one paid much attention to the talk, not even the speaker himself. Then a buzz went round the hall: she was ahead on votes, but not by enough. Two days later she was gone. I did not regret her departure. In her earlier years she had transformed the British economy, but now she had turned against the FCO. 'Everyone knows I am no diplomat,' she once said, 'we have more than enough of them!' She always needed enemies to overcome, and by now the only adversaries available were her fellow European leaders. I welcomed her successor, John Major, with his more conciliatory approach. But in the end her combative legacy destroyed him and his government.

The GATT trade negotiations came to a climax in December with the ministerial conference intended to conclude the Uruguay Round. I joined Christopher Roberts in supporting Peter Lilley, the Trade and Industry Secretary, at this meeting. It was held in the Heysel exhibition centre in Brussels, next to the ill-omened football stadium, and was the worst international conference I had ever attended. The preparations were fraught, as the formula on agriculture worked out at Houston had soon crumbled. The European Community was still only offering to reduce domestic support, which did not satisfy the Americans and other food exporters. Without a deal on agriculture, all the rest of the agenda, including services and dispute settlement, was in abeyance. At the Heysel site the European delegations were housed together, isolated from the rest, and spent the time in acrimonious consultations. To reach any others, like the Australians or Americans, we had to cross a gallery teeming with media folk, who would surround and immobilise anyone they recognised.

After an unproductive first day, Peter Lilley, Christopher and I went out to unwind over dinner. Lilley's private secretary, who made up the fourth, had her handbag snatched as we walked back to our hotel. The minister set off in hot pursuit, but to no avail. Next day the EC, with great difficulty, was brought to offer some moves on imports and export subsidies in agriculture, but this was too little, too late. The Latin Americans walked out in disgust and the conference came to an abrupt end. The whole round faced collapse, as the Americans' negotiating authority from Congress ran out in March 1991. Fortunately the EC saw the light at last. It undertook to negotiate reductions in import barriers and export subsidies on an equal footing with domestic support. It also launched a programme for the fundamental reform of the Common Agricultural Policy. The US administration persuaded Congress to extend its authority for two more years, so that the round was back on track again.

The United Kingdom took over the chair of the G7 summit in January 1991. Nigel Wicks, Huw Evans and I began the preparatory process and I drafted the first outline of what we hoped to see in the economic declaration. Our greatest problem was to keep the agenda under control. The crisis in the Gulf raised issues of energy supply, but mercifully these were settled before the summit met. Many industrial countries had gone into economic recession, but the response was delegated to the finance ministers. Trade was an essential topic, after the failure at the Heysel. So was the environment, with the approach of the UN Conference on Environment and Development in Rio in June 1992. John Major added debt to the list, to advance an initiative he had launched when Chancellor of the Exchequer. After initial euphoria, the Central European countries were struggling economically and needed more help. In August 1990 Margaret Thatcher had publicly proposed that the Soviet Union should be associated with the summit and Major had endorsed this approach. Officials felt obliged to pursue it, though I had private doubts. John Major longed to simplify the process and escape this heavy agenda. But since this was his first summit as head of government, he felt inhibited about proposing radical reform.

Since the arrogant Attali had left for the EBRD, Nigel Wicks had an easier time in chairing the sherpas. Many of them would go on to greater things: Robert Zoellick, the forceful new US sherpa, is today President of the World Bank; Pascal Lamy, the Commission sherpa, is head of the World Trade Organization; Horst Köhler became head of the IMF and then President of Germany. I too had a congenial group of sous-sherpas to chair and knew them all well. Tim Deal, Alois Jelonek, Pierre de Boissieu and Horst Krenzler were complemented by Francesco Aloisi (Italy) and Louise Frechette (Canada), both very helpful colleagues. We held the first sherpa session in Brocket Hall, a small stately home near London. For the second we took our sherpa colleagues to Hong Kong, to make them aware of the great progress being made there. Simon Broadbent then joined me and we went on to Indonesia, Australia and New Zealand. Roger Carrick was now our ambassador in Jakarta and made us very welcome. Despite their problems in managing such a populous country, I found the Indonesians were keen to be active internationally. In Canberra and Wellington I argued that the EC was at last moving on agriculture in the GATT. The Australians remained combative, seeking to shame the Europeans into action; the New Zealanders were more conciliatory.

The London summit took place in Lancaster House in mid-July. We had wanted to hold it outside the capital, but no provincial centre met our standards for meeting-place, accommodation and transport links. The evening before the summit opened, disaster threatened. A water-main burst just outside Lancaster House, flooding the forecourt shin-deep. The emergency services worked all night, pouring in rapidly setting concrete, and by morning all signs of the flood had disappeared. Thereafter all ran smoothly. The leaders dined on the first night in the Tower of London, ending up at the Ceremony of the Keys at 10 p.m. (Sadly the meal had to be hurried, as President Mitterrand arrived forty-five minutes late.) On the second night they were guests of the Queen at Buckingham Palace and were treated to spectacular fireworks.

As at Houston, the first day was devoted to the economic agenda. On trade, we decided against drafting detailed provisions on the Uruguay Round, as this had proved fruitless the year before. Instead, we concentrated on getting personal commitments from the leaders present to conclude the round by the end of the year. This came out well in the published summit declaration. But it was a bad omen that, in the actual trade debate, neither Mitterrand nor Kohl spoke; only their ministers intervened. Our forebodings were borne out. As the end of the year approached, John Major, Jacques Delors and Ruud Lubbers for the Dutch Presidency all worked strenuously to get enough flexibility into the European position to achieve agreement. But France and Germany prevented this. The round staggered on for two more years before it was finally concluded late in 1993.

On the environment the Americans were still unforthcoming. However, we brought them to agree that the forthcoming UN conference should conclude a framework convention on climate change and mobilise financial resources through an environment facility set up in the World Bank. This duly happened at Rio in 1992. There was also consensus at the summit that framework conventions should be negotiated on protecting forests and preserving biodiversity. But in the event developing countries opposed the first and the US did not adhere to the second.

Other economic items went better. Many poor countries were still burdened with debts incurred in the 1970s and 1980s. The Toronto summit of 1988 had agreed to relieve up to one-third of their debts if they followed IMF programmes. These 'Toronto terms' covered aid loans and government-guaranteed export credits. But it was soon clear that Toronto terms were insufficient, as not all G7 countries offered debt reduction. In 1990 John Major had proposed at the Commonwealth Finance Ministers' meeting in Trinidad that relief for poor countries should apply to half or even two-thirds of their debts. 'Trinidad terms' were resisted by the US and Japan, who disliked the idea of forgiving government loans. But Major secured agreement in London to 50 per cent relief, which marked the first of many times that the summit would return to this issue. Eventually the 2005 Gleneagles summit endorsed 100 per cent relief on debts to governments and to institutions like the IMF and World Bank.

The record on help to Central Europe over the last two years had been impressive. The G24 process had mobilised $31 billion in bilateral aid and financial support, while the new EBRD had already started lending. But the development of open economies in these countries had been set back by the troubles of the Soviet Union, which had hitherto taken most of their exports. The summit focused on improving their access to western markets, which in turn would help them to attract investment. In consequence, the EC concluded association agreements with Poland, Hungary and Czechoslovakia later in the year and the US launched a comparable programme.

On the second day the G7 leaders debated conditions in the Soviet Union and then invited President Gorbachev to join them. The invitation followed much agonised debate among the sherpas. Up till the Hong Kong meeting in April it looked unlikely, as Gorbachev was getting nowhere with economic reform in the USSR. Then he launched a diplomatic offensive, promoting a set of measures recommended by a team of Harvard advisers. The G7 leaders faced a dilemma: they wanted to encourage Gorbachev and to see him persist in reform; but they could see that he was steadily losing power to Boris Yeltsin and other leaders of Soviet republics. In the end they decided to invite him and offer economic cooperation, but not to provide financial assistance without clearer evidence of measures to transform the economy. I defended this decision at the time, but now I think it was the wrong one. It did nothing to help Gorbachev. It established an unwelcome precedent of inviting the Russian leader, which weakened the summit as an economic instrument.

I managed to attend the post-summit party in the FCO this year, to which we invited the many people who had helped us in staging the event. I also went to a reception at No. 10 (Plate 22). Soon Dee and I went off on holiday to a house in the hills behind Menton, on the Côte d'Azur. Tom, Kristin and Felix, now nearly two, joined us there and Dick soon arrived as well. He had hiked round Mont Blanc with some friends and then walked over two hundred miles to reach us. After a few days we went into Menton to buy newspapers and were amazed to learn of the coup against Gorbachev. In September, not long after my return to the office, the three Baltic republics achieved their independence, two years after Charlie had joined their human chain. It looked as if the Soviet Union was disintegrating before our eyes. I planned a trip to Moscow to learn what might happen next. But before that I achieved my long-deferred aim of visiting China.

Simon Broadbent and I travelled via Tokyo and Hong Kong. The Japanese were worried at what might happen in neighbouring Russia, while Hong Kong was feeling more confident about China. As we drove through Guangdong province to Guangzhou, we could see how Hong Kong investment was generating local prosperity. We learnt that, because it was growing so fast, the province enjoyed considerable autonomy, but was careful not to get across Beijing. Guangzhou was a curious mixture of old and new: skyscrapers and swanky hotels among exotic markets, ancient pagodas and the surviving houses of British merchants. We ate snake, the local delicacy, though only in soup.

We flew on to Beijing, where I found the officials unforthcoming, until I met a senior figure from MOFTEC (Ministry of Foreign Trade and Economic Cooperation) at my final dinner. He explained how

China planned to open up its economy by stages. The streets of Beijing were teeming with cyclists, interspersed with lorries laden with cabbage; this was stored as the only vegetable available in winter. On Sunday, after a morning in the Forbidden City, Robin MacLaren, the ambassador, took us out to the Ming Tombs. We picnicked by the overgrown tomb of the last Ming emperor, where the crowds of the capital seemed far away. Before leaving Beijing I bought a fur hat, as my next post would be Canada.

In contrast to the sense of purpose palpable in China, Simon and I found the Soviet Union wavering on the brink of collapse. My foreign ministry counterparts in Moscow assured me the USSR would survive, but I did not believe it and nor I think did they. We got more sense from those close to Boris Yeltsin and from people in the nascent private sector, with all of whom Rodric Braithwaite, as ambassador, had excellent contacts. We took time off to see *The Queen of Spades* at the Bolshoi before going on to Leningrad. There we found the consul-general, Barbara Hay, established in two rooms in a hotel. One room was her office and living quarters; the other was full of her communications equipment. Leningrad was a centre of heavy industry, mainly supplying armaments, and would find it hard to adapt to the new Russia. Price controls produced strange distortions: a trader had flown from Dushanbe in Tajikistan to sell a bag of lemons in the market, as his airfare cost next to nothing.

We were impressed in Moscow by the economic strategy for Russia being prepared by Yegor Gaidar, Yeltsin's economics minister. This made more sense than anything Gorbachev had produced. Gaidar proposed to free all controlled prices first, to allow them to rise to market levels. After this first surge, inflation would be controlled by tight monetary policy, while most of Russia's industry would be privatised. This was the strategy followed by Balcerowitz in Poland and had a fair chance of success. Gaidar introduced it in January 1992, but it was sabotaged by Viktor Geraschenko, whom we had met back in 1989 and who was now governor of the central bank. He loosened monetary policy instead of tightening it, so that inflation went on rising. Economic reform in Russia never really recovered from this setback.

The twilight of the Soviet Union was causing a more immediate crisis. As the government lost its authority, the economic machinery ground to a halt. The Soviet Union ceased to service its debts, hospitals ran out of medicines and agricultural production shrank so far that famine threatened. The western powers could not allow the end of communism in Europe to be associated with starvation and disease. The UK still held the summit chair and we revived the sherpa machinery to address these problems. Nigel Wicks and Huw Evans initiated the negotiation of a debt deferral. I called together my sous-sherpa group to coordinate emergency food assistance, combining what was being offered by the United States, the European Community and Canada. By the end of the year $15 billion had been mobilised for Russia and the other Soviet republics.

January 1992 was the most hectic month in all my time as Economic Director, and my official diary survives to prove it. The United States called a meeting, at minister level, of all potential donors of humanitarian aid for what was now the *former* Soviet Union. This meant two trips to Washington, one for a preparatory session of officials and the second for the ministerial conference. I co-chaired the official group on food aid and made the presentation to ministers. Our findings were that enough food was pledged and ready for shipment to meet all the republics' needs. The task now was for the Russians and others to get it distributed. The meeting ended with a ministerial press conference, at which Douglas Hurd, who had arrived late, asked me to take his place. This earned me a rare appearance on the television news.

The G7 summit chair had passed to the Germans, who organised a group to fly from Frankfurt to Minsk in Belarus, where we could explain to the recipients the outcome of the Washington conference. This was the first opportunity to meet people from the new ex-Soviet republics, especially in Asia, and Kevin Tebbit, just arrived as head of ERD, made good use of his Turkish. Many of the newcomers were baffled by our message that the food aid was ready and it was their responsibility to distribute it. Happily, this did not matter very much. As soon as Gaidar's price reforms took effect, agricultural production revived and the crisis disappeared.

The Germans held their first sherpa meeting, and my last, at the Petersburg Hotel, where Hitler once met Neville Chamberlain. I attended farewell sessions of the OECD in Paris and the G24 in Brussels. I even fitted in a reconnaissance trip to Ottawa. Finally the pace slackened and in February I handed over to my successor, Brian Crowe. He had experience from Washington and the EC mission in Brussels, so that I was leaving the post in good hands. I had served as Economic

Director during a time of historic change and seen the communist system in Europe crumble away. This had a powerful impact not only on Europe, but on the economic system as a whole. From now on economic diplomacy would encompass the entire globe, with no one left out. As a result, it would involve new subjects and many new players, and penetrate deeper into domestic policy than ever before.

CHAPTER 17

# High Commissioner in Ottawa

IN MY THIRD YEAR AS Economic Director, I began to think of where I wanted to go for my next diplomatic post, which would probably be my last. The system had recently changed, so that officers had to bid for their new posts, rather than just going where they were sent. I decided to bid for an embassy in a G7 country and went through the list. Washington was above my class and had already gone to Robin Renwick. Paris, Berlin or Tokyo would be possible, but Christopher Mallaby, Nigel Broomfield and John Boyd were strong favourites and I preferred not to compete against them. Ottawa, however, had many attractions: I really liked my Canadian sherpa colleagues; I had never served in the Western Hemisphere; I could use my French in Quebec; I should have a fairly free hand, without getting too many instructions. The field was open and I was duly chosen to be High Commissioner to Canada, arriving in Ottawa two days before the British elections in April 1992. As the Queen was also Canada's head of state, I did not have credentials signed by her but a letter from John Major commending me to his Canadian colleague, Brian Mulroney, also a Conservative. When I met Mulroney, he said that, unlike others, he had been sure Major would win a new mandate. He was less prescient about the fate of his own party. This chapter deals mainly with Canadian politics, while the next covers economics.

Canada proved a happy posting for Dee and me and we made many friends. The Canadians were people after my own heart: calm, tolerant, considerate, public-spirited and self-effacing. They would 'do good by stealth and blush to find it fame'. The country was vast, second only to Russia in area (see Map 4). From Ottawa the province of Ontario spread out to the south and Quebec to the north. Eastwards were the four Atlantic provinces: bilingual New Brunswick, Nova Scotia with its Scottish links, tiny Prince Edward Island and remote Newfoundland. Westwards the country was split by the barren rocks of the Canadian Shield, bearing only woods and lakes. Beyond this came the three prairie provinces of Manitoba, Saskatchewan and Alberta, and then British Columbia on the Pacific Coast. The main settlements kept close to the

US border, but Canadian territory stretched far beyond the Arctic Circle. The opportunities for travel were limitless and I made the most of them, with Dee usually coming too.

Ottawa was the world's coldest capital, after Ulan Bator. We enjoyed the crisp icy weather, deep snow and frozen rivers, and learnt cross-country skiing. But the winter lasted too long, so that we would arrange to be in Vancouver in April, to find some green grass and spring flowers. Then the touring season would begin. I made a point of visiting each province at least once a year, with more frequent trips to Toronto and Montreal and occasional sorties to the United States. In addition, many friends and relations came to visit us. Tom twice brought his family, including new grandchildren Claudia and Roland, for seaside holidays on the Atlantic coast. Dick took his current girl-friend Natasha in our inflatable dinghy down the Rideau Canal to Lake Ontario, a week's voyage. My most memorable journey was the 'Northern Tour' laid on for diplomatic heads of mission by the Canadian government in the North-West Territories and the Yukon. This lasted a week in midsummer, when it never got dark and for three days we were beyond the tree line. We flew over the North Magnetic Pole, first located by my remote uncle James Clark Ross, and from the frozen landscape I got a sense of what my explorer ancestors had endured. I also learnt about today's northern issues: high-latitude mining, fur-trapping and the problems facing the Inuit and the Dene Indians.

It was said that 'Canada has too much geography but not enough history', but we did not find it so. We would come upon restored historic sites in the most distant parts of the country. At the remote northern tip of Newfoundland we visited the turf huts from the Viking settlement at Anse aux Meadows. In Nova Scotia we wandered through the great French fortress at Louisbourg, lovingly recreated. After its capture in 1758, James Wolfe made it his base for attacking Quebec. In Manitoba we pursued the Hudson Bay Company. We inspected the Company's earliest archives in Winnipeg, where a replica of its first ship, the *Nonsuch* of 1670, was displayed in the city museum. Then we flew north to Churchill on the frozen shores of Hudson's Bay itself. There the Company's great stone fort still survived, complete with its cannon and full of snow (Plate 25). It took twenty years to complete Fort Prince of Wales, which then fell to a French squadron in 1783 without firing a shot.

There was evidence everywhere of Canada's historical links with

Britain and we ourselves became part of it. Our Ottawa residence, Earnscliffe, had been the house of Sir John A. Macdonald, the architect of modern Canada. On 1 July 1867, still commemorated as Canada Day, he brought about the Confederation of the eastern provinces. Twenty years later he had joined them to British Columbia by the Canadian Pacific Railway and opened up the lands in mid-continent claimed by the Hudson Bay Company. We still used Sir John A.'s library, the dining-room he had built and the bedroom where he died.

Upper Canada Village was a collection of nineteenth century houses on the banks of the St Lawrence River, rescued from being flooded when the seaway was created. There was a working farm, a sawmill, a bakery and a cheese factory, while a hotel served food of the period. On Queen Victoria's birthday (still a public holiday in Canada) Dee and I took the parts of the visiting governor-general and his lady in a historical recreation (Plate 24). Canada had made an exceptional contribution to the defence of Britain in both world wars. In 1994 I was in London to see the Queen and Prime Minister Jean Chrétien inaugurate the Canada Memorial in Green Park. A year later Nicholas Soames, Defence Minister and Winston Churchill's grandson, laid a stone at the war memorial in Ottawa (Plate 27). This recorded the abiding gratitude of the British people to the Canadians, fifty years after World War II had ended.

This historical legacy laid the foundation for a rich and varied relationship between Canada and Britain. Many people had dual Canadian-British nationality, so that Ottawa issued more British passports than any post except Canberra. Scots were strong on the Atlantic coast, Irish in Toronto and English in British Columbia. Links to the Crown were embodied in the Governor-General in Ottawa and lieutenant governors in the provinces. I was careful not to come between the Canadians and their Queen and kept a low profile during visits by the Royal Family. But I once joined the Lieutenant Governor of Nova Scotia on Canada Day and took the salute at the Halifax Tattoo. Canada's parliamentary system, both at federal level and in the provinces, was closely modelled on Britain's and there were frequent exchanges with Westminster. Like Ottawa itself, many provincial capitals were built round monumental legislative buildings, where I would call on the premier, the speaker and the leader of the opposition whenever I visited.

The ties between our armed forces and intelligence agencies were extremely close, as I saw during some exciting visits. At Suffield in

Alberta armoured units of the British army conducted exercises using live ammunition – Tom had been there years before. I got up before dawn, under a spectacular display of the aurora borealis, to see squadrons of tanks capture their final objective. Pronghorn antelopes moved over the virgin prairie unperturbed by falling shells. I visited Goose Bay in Labrador, where RAF Tornadoes conducted low-flying exercises over vast expanses of moor and forest inhabited only by caribou. I flew in a C30 Hercules, via Thule airbase among the glaciers of Greenland, to the Canadian army base at Alert. At 82 degrees of latitude, this was the most northerly settlement on the planet, set on bare frozen ground looking over the icebound Arctic Ocean (Plate 26). I saw a wolf there – they were regular visitors – but no signs yet of global warming.

In culture and the arts, Canada's impressive achievements often drew on British inspiration. We regularly went to the two finest drama festivals in North America: at Stratford, Ontario, mainly of Shakespeare; and at Niagara-on-the-Lake (downstream from the falls) of works written during the lifetime of George Bernard Shaw. Canadian orchestras often played music by British composers. Canadian novelists sold more books in Britain than in Canada itself. After the British Council exhibited sculptures by Anish Kapoor in Ottawa, the National Gallery of Canada bought one. Later the gallery held an exhibition of the Queen's Pictures, the first time works from the Royal Collection had been shown abroad.

This was my first Commonwealth post and I came to understand the breadth of this relationship. I visited the Commonwealth of Learning in Vancouver and attended a session of the Commonwealth Parliamentary Association in Banff, Alberta. The most spectacular event was the Commonwealth Games at Victoria, British Columbia, in 1994. For two weeks Dee and I, based in the old-style Empress Hotel, spent our days cheering on the separate teams of athletes from England, Scotland, Wales, Northern Ireland, Jersey, Guernsey and the Isle of Man. In the evenings we went to cultural shows, once with the Queen present, or watched firework displays. It was a most agreeable diplomatic experience, crowned by securing a commitment that Manchester would host the games in 2002.

To pursue such a kaleidoscopic relationship, I had an effective staff spread across the country. In Ottawa I relied greatly on my deputy, Bruce Dinwiddy, as I travelled so much, and on my economic counsellor, first Richard Fell and then Boyd McCleary. The political officer, Doug

Scrafton and later Patrick Holdich, usually came with me on provincial visits. Trade and investment promotion was run from Toronto by the experienced consul-general there, Peter Davies. Our old friend Ivor Rawlinson followed Alan Clark as consul-general in Montreal and developed an excellent feel for Quebec politics. The consul-general in Vancouver was isolated from the other posts and had to be self-motivating; Tony Joy and later Brian Austin achieved this very well. The team was completed by three honorary consuls – Frank Smith in St John's, Les Straughan in Halifax and Jack Hignell in Winnipeg, who served us loyally and became good friends. I was able to propose the latter two for the MBE.

At Earnscliffe, Vanessa Hynes, the wife of a Canadian diplomat, was our social secretary, until she became information officer at the High Commission and Pat Robson took her place. The cosmopolitan domestic staff comprised George the butler, originally from Scotland; Henrick the chef, from Denmark, assisted by Devaraj from Madras; and two maids, Maria from Madeira and Hilmiye from Turkey. The house itself, which looked like an outsize Scottish manse, was well adapted for its purpose and we made full use of it (Plate 23). It had plenty of room downstairs for entertaining, including chamber concerts, and upstairs for lodging guests, while still retaining a family atmosphere. It looked out over the Ottawa River, which froze hard in winter, and its spacious garden, cared for by Pat Dunn, was very good for summer parties.

The High Commission served a very wide variety of government departments back in the UK. Officials and ministers in Britain and Canada took very similar approaches to public affairs, so they were always looking to learn from each other's experience. We therefore received a great many visitors on a bewildering range of subjects, from the Lord Chancellor to the Governor of the Bank of England, from Douglas Hurd as Foreign Secretary to David Hunt at Employment, from a Home Office team interested in prisons to Christopher Roberts seeking common ground on trade negotiations. Hong Kong personalities also came through: Chris Patten the Governor and my old contact Anson Chan, now Chief Secretary.

There were frequent visitors concerned with Northern Ireland, including Patrick Mayhew, the Secretary of State. Both Protestants and Catholics from Northern Ireland were well represented in Canada. The communities got on well together and both were keen to help the peace process, which was just then getting under way. I was able to recommend General John de Chastelain, the outgoing Canadian Chief of Defence Staff, as head of the Decommissioning Body. Once the Lord Mayors of Dublin and Belfast came to Ottawa, at the end of a joint tour of North America. After a formal dinner with speeches, they stayed up late drinking with a local mayor of Irish origin. The Belfast mayor was staying at Earnscliffe and crept in during the small hours. At breakfast he announced that he had lost his passport – and he was flying home that day. 'You are staying in the right house, Lord Mayor,' I said, and had the office opened (it was Saturday) to issue him a new one.

In 1992 Canada was going through an identity crisis. Throughout the twentieth century there had been recurrent friction between the French-speaking Canadians in Quebec and the English-speakers in the rest of the country. Pierre Trudeau, as Liberal Prime Minister in the 1970s, had tried to resolve matters by reforming the Canadian constitution. But the Quebeckers had rejected this and a political movement gained ground there in favour of separation from the rest of Canada. When Brian Mulroney came to power in 1984, thanks to support in Quebec, he had tried to promote reconciliation. His first attempt produced the Meech Lake accord of 1990, which had recognised Quebec's distinctive qualities. Quebec accepted the deal, but it collapsed when two other provinces refused to ratify it. Undeterred, Mulroney tried again, but the process now became much more complicated. To balance provisions that gave Quebec a special status, the western provinces were demanding reform of the Canadian Senate and the aboriginal peoples were seeking better definition of their rights. As I arrived in April, I found intricate negotiations under way at ministerial level between Ottawa and nine of the ten provinces, with Quebec not at the table but active behind the scenes. As soon as I had got my head round the subject, I fired off an assessment to London, prepared with the help of Doug Scrafton.

The 125th anniversary of Confederation fell in 1992 and the Queen came out for the Canada Day ceremonies on 1 July. In her speech she urged all the parties to come to agreement and this seemed to have a salutary effect. The negotiations were raised to the provincial premiers' level, including Robert Bourassa of Quebec, while Brian Mulroney himself joined in. Agreement was finally reached on a complex package at Charlottetown, Prince Edward Island, in August. Quebec was recognised as a 'distinct society'; more powers were moved from the centre to the provinces; the Senate would be elected and provide more equal representation; the native peoples would get self-government. This won support from the federal government, all the provinces including Quebec, the main political parties, the key aboriginal leaders and most of the media. I told London I thought the reforms could work, if they were adopted country-wide. Mulroney declared a national plebiscite on 26 October to confirm the constitutional changes.

Despite such wide endorsement, the Canadian people rejected the Charlottetown Agreement by a large majority. Some opposed it because Quebec got too much or too little, or from concern about the aboriginal provisions. But for most people it was a vote against Mulroney and his government. During the year of constitutional debate, the economy had gone into recession. Its effects were aggravated by tax increases brought in to correct the gaping budget deficit. The population blamed Mulroney for wasting time on the constitution when he should have focused on their economic troubles. Canadians at large did not reject the reforms because they wanted to divide the country. But in Quebec this second failure of reconciliation encouraged the separatists.

Opinion polls now showed Brian Mulroney to be the most unpopular prime minister since they had started fifty years before. His Irish charm told against him, as it made him seem insincere. The Conservative government had to call an election within a year, but Mulroney dithered. He waited till February 1993 before saying he would step down and did not leave office till June. That gave little time for his successor, Kim Campbell, to make her mark before the elections in October. I had met her as Justice Minister and she had impressed me as intelligent and ready to listen. But she proved a hopeless campaigner, coming across as wordy and arrogant, with no clear policies to propose. In contrast the Liberals ran a well-prepared campaign, under their leader Jean Chrétien, and commanded trust, if not enthusiasm, with their 'red book' of election promises. Like everyone else, I tipped the Liberals to win, but I was amazed at the annihilation of the Conservatives, who won just two seats. The Liberals had a large majority over an opposition split three ways, between separatist Bloc Québecois, right-wing Reform and centre-left New Democrats. Jean Chrétien became Prime Minister and remained in office for the next ten years.

★   ★   ★

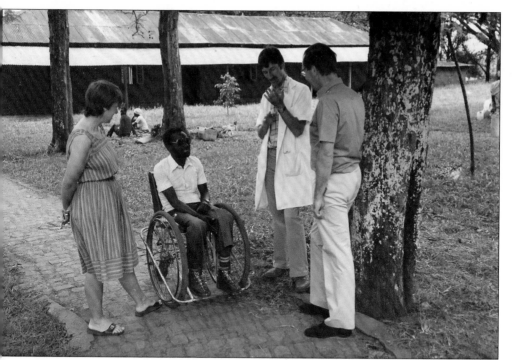

15. *Spinal unit at Gahini hospital, Rwanda (page 127)*

16. *Young male gorilla on Mount Visoke (page 128); Dick's head in foreground*

17. *At Chetwynd House before Tom's wedding (page 141); Charlie (in wheelchair) and Tom on left, Tom Wilde on right*

18. *With Sir Geoffrey Howe at the OECD (page 138)*

19. *Bridge from FCO (left) to Treasury, carrying secret passage lit by round window (page 144)*

20. *At the Ise shrine, Japan, with Stephen Gomersall (page 145)*

*21. Relaxing after a sherpa meeting, St Martin (page 147), with two Canadians, Si Taylor and John Paynter*

*22. John Major's reception after the London G7 summit (page 164)*

23. *Outside Earnscliffe, the residence at Ottawa (page 172)*

24. *As a Victorian governor-general and his lady, Upper Canada Village (page 170)*

*25. In Fort Prince of Wales, Hudson's Bay (page 169)*

*26. At Alert, the world's northernmost settlement (page 171)*

27. *Defence Minister Nicholas Soames, at lectern, with Canadian colleague David Collenette, in dark raincoat, at ceremony in Ottawa (page 170)*

28. *Prime ministers at Earnscliffe; John and Norma Major and Brian Mulroney (page 179)*

29. *At a financial services meeting at the WTO, Geneva (page 190)*

30. *Our grandchildren: Felix, Claudia, Max and Roland (page 211)*

Throughout my time in Ottawa, my main foreign policy preoccupation was Canada's defence policy and its presence in Bosnia. Canada was a founder member of NATO and a strong supporter of UN peacekeeping operations, which owed much to the original ideas of Lester Pearson. The Conservative government had launched several equipment programmes, especially a fleet of ten new patrol frigates, which I saw being built at Saint John, New Brunswick. It ordered a new helicopter, the EH101 made by Westland Agusta, to put on the frigates and to use for search and rescue.

By the time I arrived, however, budgetary pressures were obliging Mulroney to cut back on defence spending. He had withdrawn all Canadian NATO forces stationed in Germany, followed by the long-serving UN peacekeepers in Cyprus. But elsewhere Canada's commitment to peacekeeping remained strong. There were two Canadian battalions in former Yugoslavia, one in Croatia and a second earmarked for the new UN Protection Force (UNPROFOR) in Bosnia. UN-PROFOR was commanded by a Canadian general, Lewis Mackenzie. On Canada Day 1992 the Queen announced in her speech that he had successfully led his troops into Sarajevo. This earned tremendous applause, as the Canadians were proud of their peacekeeping achievements.

The Liberals were instinctively less favourable to defence. During the election campaign they promised to cancel the EH101 helicopter contract and Jean Chrétien announced this on his first day in office. This was a setback for British defence sales; but later an economy version of the helicopter was ordered for search and rescue, while Canada also purchased four Upholder submarines no longer needed by the Royal Navy. For a time there were doubts about Canada's commitments in former Yugoslavia. Chrétien's first overseas trip, in January 1994, took him via London to a NATO summit in Brussels. There Bill Clinton, backed by John Major, wanted to bomb the Serbs who were blocking a Dutch contingent from replacing the Canadian troops then stationed at Srebrenica. Chrétien opposed this vigorously and the Canadians secured a negotiated handover, but London worried about the new government's resolve. However, Chrétien took a robust line when he came to London for the D-Day commemoration in June, after visiting the two Canadian battalions. He told John Major that he was ready to keep the troops in place and duly renewed their mandate in August 1994.

By then the Contact Group on Bosnia had been set up, composed of the US, Russia, Britain, France and Germany. The Canadians were displeased to be left out, when they were providing two thousand troops. I tried to explain to my helpful contacts in the foreign ministry, Gaetan Lavertu and Michael Kergin, that the Contact Group was intended to plan for Bosnia's political future, in which its European neighbours had the closest interest. But their omission rankled and Chrétien complained to Douglas Hurd when he visited Ottawa on his way home from the UN General Assembly in September. I therefore took pains to brief both the foreign and defence ministries regularly on what was going on. Despite tense debates in Cabinet, the Canadian battalions stayed until the conclusion of the Dawson Field agreements late in 1995, thanks to the efforts of the sympathetic Defence Minister, David Collenette. Once the Implementation Force (IFOR) took over from UNPROFOR, the battalions were replaced by a smaller mixed contingent of mainly non-combat troops.

In 1995 another Canadian identity crisis broke out, with an explicit threat from Quebec to break away. Quebec separatism had a long history, but a great symbolic boost came in 1967, when French President Charles de Gaulle cried out '*Vive le Québec libre!*' during an official visit to the province. In 1970 violent separatists kidnapped James Cross, the British Trade Commissioner in Montreal, from the house later occupied by our consul-general. He was released unharmed, but a provincial minister was murdered, so that Prime Minister Pierre Trudeau brought in a strict anti-terrorist regime. The violence ended, but the political movement grew stronger, so that the separatist Parti Québecois, headed by René Lévesque, governed Quebec from 1976 to 1985. A referendum held in 1980, however, showed only 40 per cent support for Quebec leaving Canada.

After Mulroney's constitutional reforms failed, the separatists were quick to take advantage. The Bloc Québecois, led by Lucien Bouchard, won nearly all the Quebec seats in the 1993 federal elections. In 1994 the Parti Québecois regained power in the province. Their leader Jacques Parizeau, a plump and wily politician with a doctorate from the LSE, undertook to hold a referendum on Quebec 'sovereignty' (i.e. independence) within a year. Jean Chrétien took a very relaxed attitude. He could not believe that his fellow-Quebeckers could really want to leave Canada.

For a long time Chrétien's laid-back approach seemed justified. The Quebec government passed legislation providing for a referendum, but was divided over the timing and the wording of the question. Eventually the date was fixed for 30 October 1995, with a question that began clearly enough but then became obscure: 'Do you agree that Quebec should become sovereign, after having made a formal offer to Canada for a new economic and political partnership?' Parizeau, however, told the European ambassadors over a private lunch that a 'Yes' vote would certainly mean independence. The Quebeckers, he said in English, would be in a 'lobster-pot', i.e. they could not escape. This leaked to the francophone press, which thought the Quebeckers were being tipped into boiling water. It provided a rare diversion in a boring campaign, as Parizeau failed to arouse the Quebeckers. Opinion polls right through to early October never showed more than 45 per cent support for separation. But Ivor Rawlinson in Montreal warned that the campaign could suddenly catch fire, especially as Lucien Bouchard, a gifted orator, was taking over the lead role from Parizeau.

In mid-October Dee and I went back to London to help inaugurate the Barking Reach power station, an Anglo-Canadian joint venture. On my return, with the referendum a week away, I found the position transformed. Bouchard's inspirational rhetoric had electrified the Quebeckers and the polls were all showing the separatists in the lead. Rapidly I advised London on what might happen if they should win. The Canadian government could try to erect legal and economic obstacles to separation, but these might only make the Quebeckers more determined to leave. The economic conditions for Quebec would be very unfavourable. There would be a haemorrhage of capital. An independent Quebec could not count on using the Canadian dollar and could not automatically join NAFTA – the US ambassador had made that clear in public. There would be tough negotiations on debt and public property. But Canada would suffer damage too. Higher interest rates would be needed to defend the currency, making it harder to maintain growth and reduce the fiscal deficit.

Meanwhile the federal government was close to panic, as it had made no contingency plans. Jean Chrétien gave a sombre television address. Federalist opinion mobilised at last and mounted a huge rally in Montreal, to show that the rest of Canada wanted Quebec to stay. While I would have liked to speak out myself, I thought it wisest to keep quiet and London agreed. But John Major sent Chrétien a message of support, which I transmitted to him by telephone, and he was grateful. My admirable French colleague also said nothing, though Jacques Chirac wanted the separatists to win and was all set to recognise an independent Quebec.

On referendum day John Coles, now the PUS, was in Ottawa for talks with his counterpart Gordon Smith, arranged long before. He was devoted to the Flemish painter Hans Memling and we found time to look at his *Virgin with St Anthony Abbot*, complete with pig, in the National Gallery of Canada. After supper we settled down before the television to watch the results come in. There were reports of an exceptionally high turnout, later confirmed at 93 per cent. The results from the francophone rural areas came in first and showed the separatist vote mounting rapidly. But as the night wore on, more votes were counted from Montreal districts, where English-speakers and other federalists prevailed. The balance slowly crept back again. The final count was 49.4 per cent Yes to separation against 50.6 per cent No. Quebec would stay in Canada, by the narrowest possible margin. I sent John Coles to bed and set off for the High Commission to concoct a telegram with Patrick Holdich. London would need this first thing next morning, which meant sending it soon after midnight Ottawa time.

My first reaction was that this result settled nothing. The detailed breakdown showed a 60 per cent majority of francophone Quebeckers favouring independence. English-speakers had been leaving the province steadily for years and this was bound to accelerate. Recent immigrants were instinctively federalist; Jacques Parizeau had angrily attributed his defeat to 'money and the ethnic vote'. But they soon tended to move on. This suggested that the separatists only had to wait a few years before getting the right answer. By the time I left Canada early in 1996, however, I was a bit more hopeful. Chrétien was at last introducing measures to make secession more difficult. Parizeau had resigned as premier after his racist remark. Lucien Bouchard had taken his place and adopted a more cautious strategy, aiming to build up the Quebec economy first. Although the conventional wisdom was still that Quebec was bound to leave, I reflected that it had always been wrong in the past. My prudence has since been justified. Canada held together, the Parti Québecois lost ground and separation is off the agenda. The country has survived the identity crises of the 1990s.

CHAPTER 18

# Economic diplomacy in Canada

O N I JULY 1992, CANADA DAY, Britain assumed the Presidency of the
European Union (EU) for six months. In consequence, Dee and I
were offered a ride in the EU's hot air balloon that took part in the
Ottawa balloon festival in September. We flew for an hour over the river
and the town and found it an admirably calm and steady form of
transport, offering splendid views. But EU–Canada relations were far
from calm and steady. They were often fractious and dominated by
tiresome trade disputes, so that Canadian public opinion regarded the EU
as a source of trouble. Throughout my time I worked hard to improve
them. I had more chance to intervene in this economic diplomacy than
in the politics of the last chapter, where I was often only an observer.

In December we received John Major and his wife Norma, plus
Jacques Delors, for a regular EU–Canada summit. The visit got off to a
bad start. On the point of setting off to meet their plane, we learnt that
Ottawa airport was closed by fog and they had been diverted to
Montreal. The Canadian motorcade drove off for Montreal airport, a
hundred miles away through the snow, but we prudently stayed behind
at Earnscliffe. The party eventually reached us four hours late, after a
hair-raising drive over the icy roads. Norma Major was prostrated by the
journey and retired to bed, not to appear again till next morning. The
formal EU–Canada summit lasted barely an hour, before the party
adjourned to a grand dinner. Next morning Brian Mulroney called at
Earnscliffe to say goodbye to John and Norma Major before they left to
spend the weekend with George Bush, who was in his last few days as
president (Plate 28). During the visit we had put up seven visitors in the
house, nearly all of the Prime Minister's party. Despite its brevity, the
summit did useful business on Yugoslavia and the GATT Uruguay
Round. It concluded a British Presidency that had managed to make
some progress in EU–Canada issues.

The state of the Canadian economy now attracted my attention. I
found it had been sadly mismanaged by Mulroney's government. By
1993 the budget deficit had risen to 6 per cent of GDP. Net public debt

was over 70 per cent of GDP, with foreign loans a large share of this. Debt service was the largest single item of government expenditure, absorbing one-third of all tax revenue. There were rumours that Canada might have to seek help from the IMF. This was the principal reason for the Conservatives' shattering electoral defeat. Rescuing the economy became the new Liberal government's most urgent problem.

When Jean Chrétien drew up his new Cabinet, I already knew his key economic ministers from their time in opposition. Roy MacLaren, the Trade Minister, who was proud of his links with Scotland and Cambridge, was a good friend. His office was in the foreign ministry, just across the street from Earnscliffe, and he sometimes dropped in for lunch. John Manley at Industry was an Ottawa MP, while David Anderson at Environment was a fellow parishioner at St Bartholomew's church. I knew the Finance Minister, Paul Martin, less well. But I had worked with David Dodge, his Permanent Secretary, as Canadian finance sous-sherpa, and I kept close to him.

In their pre-election 'red book' the Liberals had promised to halve the budget deficit to 3 per cent of GDP in three years. Though this was an ambitious target, action was essential. Paul Martin told parliament: 'We are in hock up to our eyeballs.' In fact, Martin met his initial target and went on to bring the budget into balance and then surplus. But the process required deep cuts in spending at every level of government. Public expenditure overall was eventually reduced by 22 per cent. The federal public service lost 45,000 posts, 19 per cent of the total. This was a painful process for all, but the electorate accepted it as necessary. The cuts were widely spread, with nothing spared, and their impact was eased by a steady economic recovery. By the time I left in 1996, the programme was bearing fruit and a new deficit target of 2 per cent of GDP was set for the following year, when debt levels were expected to start falling. Martin eventually achieved budget surpluses in eleven successive years and reduced public debt to 30 per cent of GDP. This remarkable performance has lessons for western governments today, faced with the huge debts generated by recovery programmes following the financial crisis.

The Canada-EU relationship, however, got no better. The EU threatened to ban imports of fur from animals caught in leg-hold traps. In reply, the Canadians argued that fur-trapping was a vital livelihood for the native peoples, as I saw on the Northern Tour. Canada's timber trade with Britain shrank by 70 per cent when the EU insisted all softwood be treated against the pinewood nematode, a destructive parasite. On my first call on Anne McClellan, the Liberal Resources Minister, she complained about the tough line taken by the British Forestry Commission official who chaired the EU expert committee imposing these restrictions. The nematode would be harmless in Britain, as it was in Canada, because of our relatively cold climate. The EU action looked like trade discrimination in favour of Scandinavia. I pointed out that forests had to be protected throughout Europe, including the warmer Mediterranean regions. It was widely believed that Dutch elm disease had entered Europe from Canada and we could not risk another disaster.

These disputes were irritating, but they affected only a fraction of trade and investment exchanges between Canada and the EU. In particular, business ties with Britain were as strong and diverse as the political links described in the last chapter. The Rolls-Royce plant in Montreal was the world leader in making land-based gas turbines, used in pipelines. The Hongkong Bank of Canada, part of HSBC, was the most successful foreign bank in the country. Rio Tinto was preparing to exploit newly found diamond deposits that I had learnt about on the Northern Tour. In the other direction, the versatile firm Bombardier, based in Montreal, had acquired Shorts Aerospace in Belfast and was supplying the car-carrying coaches for the Channel Tunnel. Olympia and York of Toronto pioneered the new financial district at Canary Wharf, though it bankrupted itself in the process. Canadian Utilities of Calgary helped to build the Barking Reach power station. The head of this firm, Ron Southern, with his wife, organised an international show-jumping event at Spruce Meadows that Dee and I visited every September. British competitors often won and the event attracted a crowd of Canadian politicians and other leading figures.

I therefore worked hard to get the EU-Canada relationship seen in broader perspective, building on the arguments I had developed as Economic Director. With the completion of the European single market, there were now fewer barriers, in some respects, between EU member states than there were between Canadian provinces. There were greatly increased opportunities for Canadian firms trading or investing in Europe. Britain could serve as the gateway of Europe, as it already received 60 per cent of Canadian investment in the EU. Conversely, Canada was now linked to the US and Mexico through the North-

American Free Trade Agreement (NAFTA), which meant that British firms could use Canada as a base to penetrate the whole North American market. This was the rationale for the 'North America Now' campaign to increase Britain's trade and investment with the US and Canada, in both directions.

I deployed my arguments in frequent public speeches and lectures across Canada. They found a satisfying echo in an initiative by Roy MacLaren, an eloquent advocate of open markets, for a Trans-Atlantic Free Trade Area embracing the EU, the US, Canada and possibly Mexico too. This attracted favourable comment from Douglas Hurd and his successor Malcolm Rifkind, as well from other European foreign ministers, though the United States showed no interest. Trade officials, in contrast to ministers, were more sceptical and pointed out the technical obstacles. I shared many of their views, but I still saw merit in a wider political debate. This became all the more necessary after the fisheries crisis erupted.

The rich fishing grounds of the Grand Banks off Newfoundland had been famous for centuries. But the use of new technology had led to over-fishing and depletion of the stocks, for which the Canadians were as much to blame as outsiders. Canada extended its fishing rights to its 200-mile limit, but the stocks did not recover. The Mulroney government had to impose a moratorium on fishing for cod in 1992 and for redfish and flounder in 1993, which caused great hardship in fishing communities in Newfoundland and elsewhere. The Grand Banks, however, extended into international waters in places and European fishing-boats were active there. Canada got the moratoria accepted by the North-East Atlantic Fisheries Organisation, to which the EU belonged. Discipline was reinforced by an EU-Canada fisheries agreement concluded in December 1992, during the British Presidency. But there were persistent breaches of the rules, especially by Spanish trawlers.

Jean Chrétien chose Brian Tobin, an aggressive and outspoken Newfoundlander, as his Fisheries Minister, which showed from the start that he would support tough measures to protect the fish. At his first meeting with John Major, in January 1994, Chrétien insisted the problem must be solved. Major responded by saying it should be done by agreement, but Chrétien told me outside the meeting that he would act unilaterally if necessary. There were more danger signs throughout the year. Canada declined to ratify the EU–Canada fisheries agreement. It suspended its acceptance of the jurisdiction of the International Court of Justice, a sign that illegal acts could follow. Parliament passed a law authorising unilateral enforcement action. Even so, Tobin tried to work with the Commission to get the rules observed for the main fish stock not under moratorium, called turbot in Canada and halibut in Europe. But Spain and sometimes Portugal still resisted any controls. Tobin's patience ran out.

On 3 March 1995 Canada declared a moratorium on turbot fishing inside and outside the 200 mile limit, but the EU refused to accept it. Brian Tobin therefore had the Spanish trawler *Estai* arrested in international waters, strictly speaking an act of piracy. The *Estai* was escorted into St John's harbour in Newfoundland. Her net, when salvaged, proved to have too small a mesh. The European Commissioner, Emma Bonino, denounced the illegality of the seizure without recognising the abuse of the fishing rules. This infuriated the Canadians, who inflamed the row by cutting the nets of two more Spanish boats. Spain expected the rest of the EU to rally to its defence. In fact several member states, including Britain, were already exasperated by the predatory Spanish fishermen. I advised London not to come out for Canada against Spain, but to work within the EU to get greater discipline on their trawlers. I knew that Jim Bartleman, Chrétien's diplomatic adviser, was deeply worried about the wider damage to Canada's position in Europe if the row persisted.

This provided the opening for new negotiations between the EU and Canada on both fish quotas and conservation measures. The Canadians wisely gave ground on quotas in return for really tough discipline. The talks dragged on into Holy Week, with the Spanish at first digging their toes in. John Kerr in Brussels believed they would have to give way and I kept Jim Bartleman in close touch with his tactical advice. But Tobin was growing restive. Bartleman called me out of church on Good Friday to warn me that another high seas arrest was planned for Saturday. If this happened, it could lead to an exchange of fire between Spanish and Canadian warships. (Chrétien was aware of this, as he told his wife Aline he was starting a war with Spain.) Mercifully a European decision was imminent. I urged Bartleman to have the action at sea held back for another day and he got Chretien's authority for this. During Saturday EU member governments, including Spain, gave their consent to the deal worked out in Brussels. After a sleepless night, I rang John Kerr for news at 5 a.m. on Easter Sunday morning (10 a.m. his time). He said that an exceptional meeting that morning had confirmed agreement on terms acceptable to Canada. The crisis was over and I went to St Bartholomew's much relieved that a war had been averted.

British fishermen and public opinion generally had supported the Canadian position vigorously, which enhanced our reputation locally. But I took little pleasure in this, since I thought the crisis had damaged the reputation of both Canada and the EU. Inevitably Canada's position suffered during the six-month Spanish Presidency, which began in July. Canada was excluded from the EU-US Action Plan agreed in Madrid and had to wait till late in 1996 for a parallel EU-Canada Action Plan. Meanwhile my Spanish colleague, hitherto very friendly, would barely speak to me.

The fish dispute provided my first excitement in 1995; the second was the G7 summit held in Halifax in June. The 1994 Naples summit had launched a review of international institutions, to see if they were fitted for the post-Cold War world. Jean Chrétien had first attended the summit back in 1978, as finance minister. He decided that Halifax should focus on financial institutions, notably the IMF and World Bank, and aim to stabilise exchange rates.

The other G7 members resisted this at first, but the Mexican financial crisis at the end of 1994 changed the position fundamentally. The Americans constructed a rescue plan, but it was rejected by Congress. So they got Michel Camdessus, the IMF Managing Director, to endorse an outsize loan of $18 billion from the Fund, as part of a total package of $40 billion. This was presented to the other IMF members at very short notice as a *fait accompli*. Just after this, Kenneth Clarke, the Chancellor of the Exchequer, Eddie George, Governor of the Bank of England, and Nigel Wicks came to Toronto for a G7 Finance Ministers meeting early in February. I went with them on a coach trip to the icebound Niagara Falls and found them fuming at the way they had been bounced over Mexico. Paul Martin therefore found ready agreement that the summit should look at reforms to the IMF, which would help to prevent such crises and deal with them more effectively when they broke out.

I was happy to be back in the G7 preparatory process again, for my last summit as a diplomat. I knew all the key players very well, both in London and in Ottawa, and they allowed me privileged access on the strength of my earlier involvement. Alex Allan, the current UK sherpa, briefed me after the first preparatory meeting in Ottawa. Michael Jay, now FCO Economic Director, kept me well up to date. I had earned the trust of Gordon Smith, the Canadian sherpa, over Bosnia and fish, and he came to breakfast when Bob Putnam was visiting. Louise Frechette, who had been my counterpart as foreign affairs sous-sherpa, now wore the finance sous-sherpa hat. I also revived my quasi-academic role, with London's blessing, writing the introduction to a volume of pre-summit essays published by Dalhousie University in Halifax. After the summit, I published an article commenting on the progress made in the journal *Government and Opposition*. This updated an earlier article on economic relations after the Cold War, based on a public lecture I had given at the LSE.

Throughout the preparations, British and Canadian ideas were very close. We both knew what we wanted to achieve, while the others seemed confused or undecided. London was content now with what Chrétien proposed on the IMF and World Bank. In return Chrétien promised to promote John Major's ideas for reform of the United Nations, as part of the review of institutions. The two leaders agreed that the summit should be informal and unpretentious, with no distractions from serious work. Halifax proved an admirable setting for this. The meetings were held in modest lawyers' offices on the waterfront. The hotels for the delegations were all within walking distance and the leaders mingled with cheerful crowds of residents and holiday-makers. I brought Boyd McCleary and his deputy Jackie Barson from Ottawa to support me. Jackie miraculously silenced a rowdy pub outside John Major's hotel which was keeping him awake. The only entertainment was an evening performance by the Cirque du Soleil in a large tent, with the leaders sitting in the front row. Boris Yeltsin had arrived by then and had clearly drunk deep over dinner. When the troupe came forward for their final bow, Yeltsin lumbered to his feet and enveloped the youngest member, aged about nine, in a great bear hug. We could see her terrified face over his shoulder as he swayed on his feet, but he put her down safely.

The opening dinner of G7 leaders was meant to start on the economic issues. But French President Jacques Chirac, recently elected, arrived greatly excited by a visit to Bosnia. He hijacked the proceedings and made the foreign ministers interrupt their separate dinner to construct a Bosnia declaration for instant issue. Next morning, however, Chrétien regained control of proceedings and worked through the economic agenda during the day. Finance and foreign ministers met in parallel. Yeltsin arrived for dinner. As agreed at Naples the year before, Russia was a full participant in political discussions but not economic ones. Yeltsin accepted this with good grace, but refused to have any reference to Chechnya in the summit texts. Even so, Chrétien told the press that the other leaders had reproved Yeltsin for Russia's brutal tactics.

Overnight the sherpas agreed the economic declaration with unusual speed. (Gordon Smith later revealed that decaffeinated coffee was the secret.) In next morning's debate, John Major made a powerful presentation on reforming the economic and social activities of the UN. This gained unanimous support and the leaders endorsed a programme of work leading up to the 1996 summit in Lyon. The final press conferences were held in part of the hockey stadium, where I had earlier attended the tattoo, but Kenneth Clarke was missing. As finance ministers had finished their work early, the Chancellor had gone off bird-watching with Boyd McCleary. He got back in time, but found his tidy clothes had been packed up and sent to the aircraft. Douglas Hurd told me he had enjoyed Halifax more than any other summit he had attended and drew on it in his novel *The Shape of Ice*.

The most important outcome from the Halifax summit was the plan for reforming international financial institutions, which was endorsed by the entire IMF and World Bank membership. The plan contained four main measures. The IMF should strengthen its surveillance of members' economies, on the basis of better data, to give early warning of financial crises. A new emergency mechanism would provide faster help to countries in trouble and the Fund's main creditors would put up $18 billion to finance it. Finance ministers would explore the scope for an insolvency procedure for countries, comparable to the system used for firms. Financial regulators, together with ministers, should cooperate in the supervision of institutions and markets and reach concrete under-standings for the reduction of risks.

Unfortunately only the first measure, on improved surveillance, was put into effect fully and promptly. Congress delayed for over three years before voting the US contribution to the emergency mechanism. Ministers decided that a solvency regime for countries was unworkable. Cooperation between regulators made limited progress, mainly because of American and British reluctance to see international rules applied to their financial markets. In consequence the decisions were overtaken by the Asian financial crisis that broke out two years later, and the response to that sowed the seeds of the worldwide disaster which began in 2007. If the Halifax measures had been properly implemented, both these catastrophes could have been avoided.

The tense referendum campaign in Quebec followed the summit and completed an eventful and rewarding year. I could hardly expect 1996 to match it. Though I could stay in Ottawa till February 1997, I decided to leave early. I enjoyed working in Canada very much, but after thirty-five years I had had enough of being a British diplomat. The Conservative government had clearly run out of steam. Visitors to Ottawa confirmed the media reports of deep divisions in the Cabinet, particularly over European policy. There was no prospect of an election till after my retirement date. I knew that my old Paris colleague Anthony Goodenough was keen to succeed me and would do it very well. I therefore arranged that Dee and I should leave Canada in March 1996.

A memorable farewell dinner hosted by my French colleague Alfred Siefer-Gaillardin gave me the chance to quote Talleyrand's account of the ideal diplomat from his last great speech:

> There is one thing that I must say, in order to destroy a widely spread prejudice: no, diplomacy is not a science of deceit and duplicity. If good faith is necessary anywhere, it is above all in political transactions, for it is that which makes them firm and lasting.

This reflected the pattern I had tried to follow throughout my diplomatic career. Then Dee and I said goodbye to Earnscliffe and our loyal staff and left for a holiday in Mexico. We returned to spend a snowy day with the hospitable Rawlinsons in Montreal before our flight out. One last surprise awaited us. Retiring ambassadors, like newly appointed ones, are allowed to fly first-class. We were leaving on the very first day when British Airways offered beds to first-class passengers on their Montreal-London flight. We stretched out and slept soundly on our way to a new life.

CHAPTER 19

# Private sector experience: British Invisibles

M Y OBJECTIVE IN RETIREMENT WAS SIMPLE. I wanted to continue doing the things I had enjoyed most as a diplomat, like writing and making speeches, but avoid the things I had liked less, such as organising people and managing budgets. I hoped to find an academic niche where I could continue the research on international economic issues that I had started nearly fifteen years earlier. Before leaving Ottawa I made an approach to Chatham House, where I had been so well received before, and followed this up on my return. But this time the institute had no place for me.

While I digested this unexpected setback, my old friend and colleague Derek Thomas invited me to lunch. Derek was now with N. M. Rothschild, the merchant bank, and also worked for British Invisibles (BI), a grouping of firms and associations that promoted the international interests of the City of London. He had become chairman of BI's Liberalisation of Trade in Services (LOTIS) committee, following Michael Palliser, who had visited me at the OECD. Derek was looking for a successor and since my academic plans were in abeyance I agreed to take it on. Thanks to LOTIS, I got four more years of active involvement in economic diplomacy, which tested skills unused during my time in the FCO.

The Uruguay Round of trade negotiations in the GATT, which had occupied me at the OECD and in London, was finally concluded in 1993. It was three years overdue, but went much further than originally expected. Hitherto the GATT had mainly covered trade in manufactures. Now agreements were added on agriculture and services, so that the multilateral system embraced all civilian trade. The GATT, which had been institutionally weak, was replaced by the robust World Trade Organization (WTO). This began its work on 1 January 1995, including its wholly new regime on services.

In most countries services took a larger share of the economy than manufacturing or agriculture. But international exchanges were heavily restricted, often by government regulations. For the first time, the General Agreement on Trade in Services (GATS) laid down a multi-lateral regime covering all types of tradable services, drawing on the ideas developed while I was at the OECD. The GATS captured the full variety of international transactions in services, whether they were supplied across borders, as with transport; consumed abroad, as by tourists; or provided by firms or persons established in foreign markets, like banks or lawyers. The great drawback was that the GATS only obliged WTO members to offer access to their services markets where they made specific commitments to do so. Industrial countries with open services regimes undertook to preserve their existing practices, but most developing countries were less forthcoming. The commitments made before the round ended were not sufficient in some key sectors, especially in financial services like banking and insurance, the main concern of British Invisibles and its LOTIS committee.

Negotiations on financial services had continued till 1995, but were then suspended because the United States rejected the agreement on offer. Prompted by its private sector, the US administration declared that other WTO members, especially developing countries, had not put enough on the table. The US would have to allow foreign banks and insurance firms into its valuable market without getting satisfactory access to other countries' markets. In contrast, the European Union was ready to sign the draft agreement, even though many services firms in Europe would have liked it to press harder.

Andrew Buxton, the soft-spoken but decisive chairman of Barclays Bank, was keen to get an agreement concluded. He saw that the key to success lay in the American and European private sectors getting together and putting an agreed set of demands to their governments, which would shape their negotiating position. In July 1996 I joined a meeting between Buxton and Bob Vastine, head of the US Coalition of Service Industries (CSI), at which they agreed to create a transatlantic Financial Leaders Group, composed of heads of services firms dedicated to promoting a successful WTO agreement. This would be backed by a lower-level Financial Leaders' Working Group. Andrew Buxton and Ken Whipple, chief executive of Ford Financial Services, would jointly chair the leaders; Bob Vastine and I would co-chair the working group.

The Financial Leaders Group gathered in Washington in October, where many bankers and insurers were present for the IMF annual meeting. The twenty-five founder members came not only from the US and EU, but included financiers from Japan, Canada, Switzerland and Hong Kong. The London contingent included Douglas Hurd, now deputy chairman of NatWest Markets (where Tom worked) and shortly to become chairman of British Invisibles. Bob Vastine and I then mobilised the working group, communicating by fax, e-mail and monthly conference calls. On the British side, many of my LOTIS Committee colleagues took part. Josh Bolten from Goldman Sachs International (later a close aide to President George W. Bush) and John Cooke, an ex-DTI colleague now at the Association of British Insurers, were influential players. From the EU, Jacques Leglu of the European Insurance Committee and Pascal Kerneis of the European Banking Federation were both active.

Our first task was to construct an agreed position on what our governments should seek in the negotiations. It emerged that the American CSI and various European bodies had been compiling lists of obstacles to services business in major markets, mainly in developing countries. For example, banks and insurance companies often needed to be established in their target markets and could face a range of government restrictions. Some countries kept foreign suppliers out altogether; some would only allow foreign firms to take minority shareholdings; some would allow majority holdings, but not wholly-owned foreign firms. I took on the task of comparing and reconciling the different lists and got agreement on a *Common List of Barriers to Financial Services Trade*, known as the Barriers List. This set out in standard format the barriers in force in twenty key markets, all developing economies apart from three Central Europeans and Turkey. We wanted our negotiators to focus on getting these barriers removed.

When financial services negotiations resumed at the WTO in April 1997, Bob Vastine and I, supported by other members of the working group, made the first of many visits to Geneva (Plate 29). We held a joint meeting with the negotiators from the United States, European Union, Canada and Switzerland, where I handed over copies of the Barriers List and explained its rationale. We also visited the WTO delegations of countries targeted on the list, to argue with them the case for opening up their financial services markets. I had thought they might resent our lobbying, but in fact they were pleased that the private sector was taking such an interest in them.

WTO negotiations on manufactured goods or agriculture were based on bargaining. Members would open their own markets in return for getting better access for their exports to other countries. But in financial services we had to rely on persuasion, as most developing countries were not interested in international operations. We had to convince them that it was in their own domestic interests to open their markets to foreign banks and insurers. We argued that all countries needed a strong financial sector to underpin their development. Foreign firms would help to raise the standards of the domestic finance industry. Their presence would also help countries to attract the foreign direct investment they needed. Fortunately, we were not deploying these arguments in a vacuum. Many countries had already worked out for themselves the advantages of stronger and more competitive financial sectors. Making commitments in the WTO would reinforce what they were doing already.

In our Geneva lobbying, we did not just concentrate on the twenty countries on the Barriers List. We worked on some developed countries too, notably Canada, and persuaded the European Commission to negotiate more toughly with Japan. Luckily for me, two key players in the Commission were British: John Mogg, the Director General for the Internal Market, and Robert Madelin of the Trade Directorate, whom I had known when he was in the DTI. I kept close to them and to David Hartridge, the British head of services in the WTO Secretariat. In London Jeremy Seddon and Neil Jaggers at British Invisibles and the whole LOTIS committee gave me solid backing. I maintained regular contact with the services negotiators at the Treasury and at the DTI, where Christopher Roberts was just handing over as chief trade negotiator to Tony Hutton. But in Geneva the negotiations moved very slowly and I took time off to visit Schaffhausen, home of my im Thurn ancestors.

Finally, just before the negotiations were due to end in December 1997, commitments from our target countries began to appear. The Financial Leaders Working Group gathered in Geneva and set up panels to evaluate the offers as they came in. On Thursday of the final week the group met to take a view on the agreement as a whole. Douglas Hurd chaired this critical meeting, as Ken Whipple's plane was delayed, and I briefed him carefully. The Europeans all considered there was enough on the table for an agreement, while the Americans were divided. Large US firms, backed by Bob Vastine, wanted to hold out for more, but the associations representing smaller firms were keen to take the opportunity for a deal. Hurd summed up that that the private sector thought a good agreement was in prospect, but a final effort was needed. He gave this message to our chief negotiators – Leon Brittan, the European Commissioner, and Jeff Lang and Tim Geithner for the US – who were encouraged by it. By Friday morning, when Andrew Buxton arrived, all the US private sector people in Geneva had come round to supporting the agreement, but needed the blessing of their principals back home. Buxton spent the day working his top-level contacts and by 1 a.m. on Saturday morning all the American financial leaders were on board. Meanwhile the WTO negotiators had been working through the night, and the agreement was concluded at 4 a.m. I had lost track of events and gone to bed, but was woken with the good news.

The WTO financial services agreement was an excellent first step. A hundred countries made commitments, covering all the WTO members with markets of any size and 95 per cent of international financial exchanges. Many states improved on commitments they had made earlier in the negotiations. In most cases, countries undertook to preserve their regime in force, not to improve it; but this was still worth having, since it locked in domestic reforms and prevented backsliding. There were wide differences between countries, and some major areas, like the Indian insurance market, remained impenetrable. But it was an achievement to conclude the agreement at all, since a major financial crisis was now raging in Asia. There was widespread satisfaction in the private sector and government alike, in which I shared. I was especially pleased to get a letter from Gordon Brown, the Chancellor of the Exchequer, thanking me for the contribution made by the LOTIS committee.

Once home from Canada, Dee and I settled back into life at Hampton Court. We were happy to have more time to appreciate the parks and the palace, and returned to worshipping at the Chapel Royal, where I sometimes read the lesson. Dee did not go back to the Citizens' Advice Bureau, where she had worked before, but began volunteering for the local Samaritans. No 2 Chetwynd House was looking rather shabby and we embarked on a building campaign: repointing, rewiring, new central heating and thorough redecoration. After a tussle with the Royal Parks authorities, we enlarged our drawing-room windows looking over Bushy Park. We extended the dining-room, opening up a new fireplace, and rebuilt the staircase, which proved only to be held up by faith and friction. These works occupied the whole of our first year home. It was Christmas before we could have the house fully habitable again.

Tom Wilde, Dee's father, now in his late eighties, was still living alone in Bideford. During our time in Canada Dee had phoned him regularly and come back for visits every three months or so. But now we could go down more often and sometimes bring him back to stay with us. Tom and Kristin produced our fourth grandchild, Max, soon after our return. They were living in a house in Hammersmith, an easy drive away, and skilfully adapted their attic and basement to make room for their growing family. Tom's work on corporate finance for NatWest Markets produced a generous income, so that he could afford a holiday home in the south of France. At Montauroux, inland from Cannes, he bought a house with swimming-pool in an olive grove, which became their base for regular summer holidays and occasional Christmases too. It was on the edge of a spectacular gorge, with traces of a Roman aqueduct, and the sea was not far away.

When we were in Canada, Dick had begun working for the Alternative Travel Group (ATG), based in Oxford. ATG organised walking holidays, mainly in Italy, in which groups of clients, over a week, would walk from, say, Volterra to Siena in Tuscany or Norcia to Spoleto in Umbria. An ATG leader would guide them, while a manager would transport their baggage between hotels and provide a succulent picnic each day. Dick began as a leader on Sicily, worked through ATG's Italian mainland routes and finally became a specialist in the longest journey, 'Paths to Rome', leading groups over three weeks from Siena to St Peter's Square on foot. As he was so devoted to walking, he was assigned to update the handbooks issued to ATG's 'Footloose' clients, who followed the routes without a guide. We first walked with him when he was tracing ATG's only English route, from Oxford to Stratford-on-Avon. It appealed to us so much that we became regular Footloose travellers, eventually walking ten routes in Italy and one in France, in the Quercy. We especially enjoyed walking in sight of the sea, on the coast between Amalfi and Positano or on a route created by Dick himself along the Ligurian Riviera to Portofino and Camogli.

ATG had been founded by Christopher Whinney, who still ran it. Dick became very attached to his eldest daughter Laura, when they were both based in Tuscany. They spent one winter together in Colle Di Val d'Elsa, south of Siena, and then returned to England soon after we came home from Canada. Laura began working for the travel firm Abercrombie and Kent at their offices in Burford. She and Dick moved into a cottage beside the river Windrush in the village of Little Barrington. As well as leading walks and tracing routes for ATG, Dick tried his hand at writing fiction. He had an early success with a prize-winning short story, but found no one would publish his thrillers and turned to translation as a more reliable source of income. On a cloudless day in July 1999 Dick and Laura were married at Longleat House. The ceremony was held in the orangery, followed by a reception in the rose garden and dinner in a tent by the lake, across from the safari park. During dinner several hippos swam up the lake to inspect us, attracted by the merrymaking.

During 1998 the WTO financial services agreement entered into force. But I could not rest on my laurels, since more services negotiations, called GATS 2000, were due to start in January 2000. With Neil Jaggers' help, I produced a booklet called *The BI Guide to the WTO Financial Services Agreement*, explaining the advantages of the agreement and suggesting what more remained to be done. Since GATS 2000 would cover all services, I widened the scope of the LOTIS committee to go beyond banking and insurance and do more on shipping, telecommunications, accountancy and legal services. I drafted a comprehensive paper called *Objectives for GATS 2000 and the WTO*, which was agreed in LOTIS in February 1999 and sent to the DTI and the European Commission. The paper endorsed the European Union's view that services should form part of a new comprehensive round of trade negotiations, to be launched at the WTO ministerial meeting at Seattle in November 1999. It advocated 'pro-competitive regulation', which would be strict in ensuring solvency and financial stability, but avoid discrimination against foreign suppliers.

Andrew Buxton also kept me busy, as he set about mobilising the private sector in services across the European Union. Using his wide network of contacts, he persuaded a group of business leaders to come together as the European Services Forum (ESF). The heads of firms themselves would meet rarely, but could each nominate a member of the ESF's policy committee, which European associations representing service sectors, like airlines or accountants, could also join. The Forum was strongly backed by Leon Brittan, the EU Trade Commissioner, and was formally launched in Brussels early in 1999. A year later it had forty-six member companies from twenty different service sectors and all fifteen member states except Portugal, together with twenty-five sectoral associations.

Throughout 1999 I attended the ESF policy committee in Brussels as Andrew Buxton's nominee. We produced papers giving European private sector views on issues relevant to GATS 2000, which were discussed with the Commission and transmitted through them to the member governments. Pascal Kerneis volunteered to leave the European Banking Federation and to provide the ESF secretariat, which he did very efficiently. Not all the member associations were in favour of opening up their sectors: but if the film industry, for example, pleaded for protection, it would be countered by the music industry, which benefited from competition. Thus as the WTO negotiations approached, the European governments were comprehensively briefed on the hopes and objectives of the private services sector. Meanwhile the Financial Leaders' Working Group kept up transatlantic contacts and I took Dee to Ditchley Park for a conference laid on by Bob Vastine.

Yet the progress made on services was not matched elsewhere. There was growing tension in the WTO as it prepared for the Seattle ministerial meeting. The European Union had ambitious aims for a new 'Millennium Round', to include investment and competition policy as well as more familiar subjects. The United States, where the Clinton administration was nearing its end, wanted a more limited agenda, though this should include strict rules on labour standards. The developing countries were unhappy at the burdens imposed on them by the Uruguay Round and argued for more attention to their concerns. Work in Geneva made little progress in reconciling these views and many issues remained to be settled by ministers. Outside government, civil society NGOs began to target the WTO, which they saw as threatening the environment and penalising development. They promised vigorous protests in Seattle. Even so, I expected new negotiations to be launched. I was already in my fourth year at LOTIS and decided I could not cover another complete round. So I agreed with Christopher Roberts, who was now with the trade lawyers Covington and Burling, that he would replace me during 2000.

The WTO ministerial was to cover five days from Monday 29

November 1999. I arrived in Seattle over the weekend and fled from what I thought was an anti-WTO protest, but it was only the Seattle Marathon. On Monday, as one of over two thousand representatives from 776 registered NGOs, I attended a conference at which we could put our views to a WTO panel. Of the NGOs present, 80 per cent were hostile, accusing the WTO of being undemocratic and in the pocket of multinational companies. Few of the government spokesmen were prepared to stand up to them. Tuesday was to be the formal opening of the conference, but it never took place. An obstructive human chain surrounded the Seattle convention centre where the meeting was meant to happen. Going there early, I was firmly blocked by a burly demonstrator. I recoiled, circled the building till I spotted a weak link and broke my way in. But I found myself almost alone, as all the ministers were turned back. The Seattle police just looked on as the protestors occupied the streets.

Orders from Washington brought an abrupt change in tactics, as President Clinton was due to appear on Wednesday. Protests were broken up by tear gas and rubber bullets and five hundred demonstrators were arrested. A curfew was imposed and only those with official badges were allowed on the streets during the day. Instead of a war zone, central Seattle became a ghost town. Clinton duly spoke to the conference, which had now started work, and later to the press. He called for more NGO involvement in the WTO's work and advocated labour standards, to be enforced by sanctions. Both points were badly received by developing countries. They believed the WTO was for governments and labour standards were barriers to their exports.

A series of open-ended working groups now tried to resolve outstanding differences. But the US Trade Representative Charlene Barshefsky, in the chair, organised the proceedings clumsily and alienated smaller countries from Africa, Latin America and the Caribbean. By the end of Thursday they felt so excluded that they promised to reject any consensus reached in this way. In the early hours of Friday a small group of ministers began a final effort to reach agreement, but after a long debate on agriculture it was clear they would run out of time. Barshefsky thus suspended the meeting with nothing agreed. Although the NGOs had provided most of the excitement, in fact they had not caused this failure. The problem lay in the attitudes of the participating governments. The United States was inflexible, the European Union was complacent, and neither realised the determination of the developing countries to have a trade round that suited them.

Christopher Roberts duly took my place at LOTIS and from now on I devoted myself to my academic activities. But I had enjoyed my time there and learnt a lot. I had not negotiated directly with the Americans before and found this demanding and instructive. I had seen the private sector at work, though I noticed that those who took an interest in liberalising services were usually prompted by earlier experiences in government. This applied to Douglas Hurd and to Peter Sutherland, who had come to Goldman Sachs International after being European Commissioner and Director-General of the GATT. At my level, the LOTIS committee contained many refugees from government, and the same applied to my American counterparts. Andrew Buxton, who had made his life in Barclays but had a genuine concern for the international economic system, was a very rare figure.

LOTIS gave me a freedom of action I had not experienced before, with a personal sense of achievement. I could take pride in the success of the financial services negotiations and was also pleased that services was the only sector that did not cause controversy at Seattle. In fact, I chose a good moment to sign off, as the WTO was entering a troubled period. It was not able to launch a new round of trade negotiations, called the Doha Development Agenda, until November 2001. That round is still dragging on nine years later. Services negotiations began as forecast, but could make little progress while wider disagreement prevailed on other issues. The financial services agreement has proved to be the last substantive negotiation to be concluded at the WTO for more than a decade.

CHAPTER 20

# More summit books

THOUGH THE LOTIS COMMITTEE kept me busy, I was still looking for a permanent academic base. Meanwhile I took up activities related to Canada that kept me in touch with the FCO and the Canadian High Commission, where Roy MacLaren arrived as High Commissioner. I spoke at the service in Petersham church commemorating George Vancouver, who is buried there. I wrote a booklet for the FCO called *Britain and Canada – 500 Years*, to mark the anniversary of John Cabot's voyage to Newfoundland in 1497. I became Honorary President of the British side of the Canada-UK Colloquium, which organised an annual conference on public policy issues of interest to both countries. I joined the board of the Foundation for Canadian Studies, which supported British universities where Canadian literature, geography or politics formed part of the courses offered. All this took me regularly back to Canada and introduced me to unfamiliar parts of Britain. After a working life divided between London and abroad, I welcomed the chance to see more of my own country.

Peter Lyon, a colleague on the Colloquium, was editor of *The Round Table*, a long established journal of Commonwealth affairs. At his suggestion I joined its Editorial Board and wrote articles on the Commonwealth in the world economy. I had also been writing for the political science quarterly *Government and Opposition* since I was Economic Director, having got to know its founder, Ghiţa Ionescu, whose intellectual curiosity was inexhaustible. I joined its Editorial Board when I got home from Canada, though sadly Ghiţa died very soon afterwards. But I was still on the fringes of academic life.

My breakthrough came thanks to William Wallace, my former patron at Chatham House, who was now established in the International Relations Department at the LSE. Once again he changed my life, this time by introducing me to his colleague Mike Hodges. Mike was an engaging, outgoing character, well respected by his peers though far from a conventional academic. He rode a motor-bike and was devoted to horseracing. Mike Hodges opened the door for me to teach economic diplomacy at the LSE, the subject of the next chapter. More immediately, he encouraged me back into the study of economic summitry, the subject of this one.

I was already in touch with the G7 Research Group at the University of Toronto, created by another entrepreneurial academic, John Kirton. His courses based on G7 summitry were supported by an extensive database on the internet, while his academic conferences linked to each summit had attracted Mike Hodges' interest. John Kirton took groups of his students, and other like-minded academics, to the summit each year with media accreditation. He invited Mike Hodges and me to join him at the Denver summit in June 1997 and we went as the accredited correspondents of *LSE Magazine*, a publication intended for LSE alumni. It was my first experience of tracking the summit from the outside, disguised as a journalist, instead of from the inside as an official. I enjoyed it and wrote up my 'Impressions of the Denver Summit' for the G7 Research Group's website. Denver was in fact not a very productive summit, but I had greater hopes for the next one, to be chaired by Tony Blair in Birmingham.

Mike Hodges, John Kirton and I busied ourselves with conferences in the run-up to the 1998 summit, which was to focus on jobs, crime and finance. Mike persuaded his LSE colleague Richard Layard to sponsor a high-level meeting on employment. David Blunkett, the responsible Cabinet minister, spoke at it and so did Jacques Delors, while I took the chair. I organised a public conference on the summit agenda in the City, with the help of the law firm Clifford Chance, with whom I had set up similar events for British Invisibles. John put together a scholarly seminar, to which I contributed a paper. This appeared in the conference volume, which launched a series of books on summitry issued by the academic publishers Ashgate.

For the summit itself, Birmingham basked in Mediterranean weather. Journalists abandoned the media centre to stroll along by the canals, where the decaying warehouses I remembered from my youth had been tastefully smartened up. We were rewarded by the sight of Bill Clinton sharing a table with two unsuspecting pensioners on a pub balcony, as he too took a break. Demonstrators calling for debt relief for poor countries formed a human chain round the summit site on the second day, but it was all very peaceful, unlike what I later met in Seattle.

Blair had hoped for major progress on debt relief and on reforming the international financial system after the Asian crisis, but in fact neither issue could be fully resolved. The Cologne summit a year later had to complete the work on reshaping the IMF and World Bank, called the 'new international financial architecture', and on getting more generous relief for poor countries in debt to these institutions. In 1998 the great advances were in the summit process, as I explained in my 'Impressions of the Birmingham Summit'. Russia became a full summit member, making G7 into G8, and the leaders met without supporting ministers. With only nine or ten people at the table, the leaders could drop formality and talk seriously among themselves.

A month after the summit, Mike Hodges collapsed on Holborn Underground station and died of a heart attack. He was a great loss to me. Without his guidance, I failed to get to the 1999 Cologne summit. But I did attend the pre-summit conference held in Bonn, where John Kirton urged me to write a new summit book. Ashgate wanted more volumes for their new series on summitry. I had already published enough material to fill a sequel to *Hanging Together*. I agreed and settled down to prepare the first book I would write as sole author. With Bob Putnam's endorsement, I called it *Hanging In There: the G7 and G8 Summit in Maturity and Renewal* and dedicated it to the memory of Charlie, Mike Hodges and Ghiţa Ionescu.

The raw ingredients for *Hanging In There* consisted of ten articles, spread over a dozen years, including those written for *Government and Opposition* and *The Round Table*. These, I found, told a coherent story. While Bob Putnam and I had ended *Hanging Together* at a low point in G7 summitry, the end of the Cold War had stimulated a revival. The summits had then turned their attention to the impact of 'globalisation', the name given to the worldwide spread of open economic policies. But bringing new subjects to the summit had overloaded the agenda. Pressure from the leaders to simplify the process had led to the reforms introduced at Birmingham.

The book was based round chapters telling the story of the twelve summits held since *Hanging Together* appeared. These were drawn from my direct experience, as I had been at four of them as a serving diplomat and two more since I retired. Between the narratives I inserted chapters explaining how the summits had interacted with international economic organisations: the OECD for macroeconomic and energy policies; the GATT during the Uruguay Round of trade negotiations; the IMF and World Bank for financial reform and debt relief. I examined the consequences of the end of the Cold War for the international economy. With the collapse of communism in Europe, the open economic system prevailed worldwide and international institutions could achieve universal membership. But without the constraint of a security threat, the major powers were more inclined to let economic disputes drag on unresolved. Though the institutions became more representative, governments did not give them greater powers, but used them to resolve their own domestic problems.

The three objectives of exerting political leadership, reconciling domestic and external pressures, and providing collective management, identified in *Hanging Together*, remained as valid as ever. But the summit had moved a long way from its original austere conception. It now sat above a growing apparatus of ministerial and official groups, while the admission of Russia had opened the question of adding other countries. The founders had hoped that when leaders addressed an issue, they would resolve it definitively. In fact summits often needed several attempts before reaching a satisfactory conclusion. This process of iteration, though essential to summitry, tended to clutter the agenda with unfinished business. I was not sure if making the leaders meet on their own would check this trend. Even so, summit performance had slowly improved since the nadir of Reagan's time, with the two latest being among the most productive.

The book came out early in 2000, as I was detaching myself from LOTIS. My time as an active player in economic diplomacy was now over. Henceforth, for the next decade, I would be an observer and interpreter of economic diplomacy instead. The G8 summit gave me my best observation post. Accordingly, I became a faithful member of John Kirton's team at all the summits from 2000 to 2005, chaired in turn by Japan, Italy, Canada, France, the US and the UK. Each year's campaign developed on two levels. The academic level focused on a scholarly conference held just before the summit and close to its site. The speakers would be drawn from John Kirton's regular academic backers and contributors from the host country. The papers would form chapters in one or more conference volumes, published by Ashgate. This process was moved forward by the cheerful and efficient Madeline Koch, with whom I exchanged countless e-mails over these years as I produced a total of twelve chapters for this succession of books.

The second level was centred on the summit itself. I would go each year as the correspondent of *LSE Magazine*. In the media centre I would join John Kirton, Madeline Koch, other academic experts and an eager team of students. We would track all the summit documents and cover all the media briefings, especially the leaders' press conferences at the close of the summit. I followed the British position closely and went to hear Tony Blair whenever he spoke. I kept in touch with my former FCO colleagues, who were very open with me. I also attended Jacques Chirac's briefings regularly, as he was a lively performer and splendidly indiscreet. From these materials I would compile my 'Impressions' of each summit.

John Kirton's G8 Research Group, to which I now belonged, was not just a consumer in the summit process. We made our own contribution by briefing the media ourselves. We would appear on television, speak on the radio and talk to print journalists, drawing on our accumulated knowledge of summitry. We also kept in touch with the more responsible NGOs, like Oxfam, that now followed the summit with increasing attention. In fact the G8 Research Group provided a service which the summit governments could not offer themselves. Each year responsibility for the summit passed to a new country, which would put its national slant on any public material issued. Thus the G8 summit had no collective memory or joint information service. Those who wanted unbiased data and assessments on the summit, whether journalists, academics, non-G8 governments or the general public, would turn to the G8 Research Group. The G8 governments themselves were happy to see this happen.

The Birmingham and Cologne summits in 1998 and 1999 had mainly focused on international finance and debt relief, but had also addressed domestic issues like employment, crime, education and social policy. But the next three summits, held in Japan, Italy and Canada, abandoned domestic themes and concentrated on issues of international development. There were some valuable initiatives on promoting IT for development, fighting infectious diseases and starting a new trade round in the WTO. But the summits were gradually losing momentum until Jean Chrétien focused the 2002 summit on the revival of Africa. The G8 agreed a detailed 'Action Plan for Africa', covering peace and security, better political standards and economic development. This was designed to dovetail with the New Programme for Africa's Development

(NEPAD) launched by a group of African leaders, who were invited to meet the G8 heads on equal terms. I was very struck by the way the G8 and the Africans worked together. In my 'Impressions' I compared their joint actions with the Marshall Plan to revive Europe after World War II.

Meanwhile, the hostile demonstrators I had met at Seattle caught up with the G8 at Genoa in 2001. The summit site was in the port area, isolated by a double ring of barriers under heavy police guard. As John, Madeline and I arrived late at night, driving through a cataclysmic thunderstorm, the road was full of cars escaping from Genoa. Next morning revealed a city under siege, so that I could only reach the media centre in a special bus with an armed escort. Inside TV screens showed the brutal battles between police and rioting protesters, in which one luckless demonstrator was killed. The lingering smell of tear-gas drifted across the harbour. To avoid such scenes, the Canadians held the 2002 summit at Kananaskis, a remote ski resort, which also gave protection against terrorist threats after 9/11. The media grumbled at being kept in Calgary, sixty miles away from the action, but I took the opportunity of a Canadian holiday with Dee. Next year the French hosts kept demonstrators well away from the summit site at Evian. There were riots in Lausanne and Geneva instead, a nasty surprise for the Swiss, though the French later paid for the damage.

The Iraq War split the G8 down the middle and for several months George Bush and Jacques Chirac were not on speaking terms. It looked as if Bush would attend the 2003 summit, but not stay on French soil. Fortunately the tension eased and the Evian summit began a process of reconciliation, which continued at Sea Island, Georgia, the following year. But the G8 took few decisions of substance at either summit, though the volume of documents continued to grow. The key innovations were in outreach to non-G8 countries. In 2003 Chirac invited emerging powers like Brazil, China, and India to the summit, as well as the Africans. Bush tried to associate Middle Eastern leaders in 2004 with a programme of political and economic reform in the region, but key figures stayed away. The media were stuck in Savannah, eighty miles away from the summit, and the only consolation was that Bush himself gave a press conference. The security round him was very tight – in contrast to Chirac, who insisted on shaking my hand as he worked the room. Yet I was impressed by the visceral force with which Bush advanced his arguments, if not by the arguments themselves. On the way to Savannah I had joined a dinner-party given by Bob and Rosemary Putnam. The other guests, all Democrats, were sure John Kerry would defeat Bush later that year. Bob was less convinced and put more hope in a rising star called Barack Obama.

Each country had now hosted a G8 summit (except for Russia, which would first do so in 2006) and Tony Blair's turn came round again. With the encouragement of John Kirton and Kirstin Howgate at Ashgate, I sat down to write my third and last summit book. I called this *Staying Together: the G8 Summit Confronts the 21st Century* and timed it to appear shortly before the Gleneagles summit of July 2005. By now all our grandchildren were at school. Felix was at St Paul's and Claudia at St Paul's for Girls. Roly was at Colet Court, aiming for St Paul's too, and Max, the youngest, was about to start there as well. Tom and Kristin decided to give Roly and Max a summer term at the local primary school at Montauroux, where they had their holiday home. Dee and I undertook to stay with the boys in France *in loco parentis*. There I began the book, among the orchids and the olive trees.

*Staying Together* had the same structure as the two earlier books. There was a narrative chapter for each summit, based on my 'Impressions' written at the time. Between these I inserted chapters assessing their performance in the subjects getting the greatest attention: finance and debt relief at first; then trade and development issues; finally the revival of Africa, together with non-economic subjects like terrorism that became active after 9/11. I considered whether the summits were still meeting their original objectives of political leadership, reconciling domestic and external pressures, and collective management of the international system. I also examined whether summit decisions had been durable, acceptable to others and consistent between one policy area and another.

I concluded that the reformed G8 process had produced five years of improved performance up to 2002. But the last two summits had seen a marked falling-off, as the initial reforms lost their force and summit documents became too long and diffuse. The G8 summit had broadly given good results in political leadership, as shown by its capacity to innovate and to strike deals, sometimes across different issues. A new departure was the conscious integration of economic and political measures, which was particularly relevant to Africa. Collective management had also worked well and flexibly, with growing outreach by the

G8 to other countries. African leaders were regular participants, while key emerging powers had been invited to Evian and Middle Eastern states to Sea Island. The underlying concept was that the G8 would not add new members, but would invite other countries to join them each year, depending on the topics on the agenda.

The G8 summit proved much less successful, however, in reconciling domestic and external pressures on policy-making. The leaders increasingly avoided putting economic issues on the agenda that were sensitive at home. They gave way too easily to domestic resistance and sometimes even aggravated it. Their record in keeping promises made at the summits was unsatisfactory, which alienated the media. I was still convinced that the G8 summit was valuable, but it needed a new sense of purpose. As the book went to press, it was clear that Blair intended the Gleneagles summit to provide this.

Tony Blair was now meeting widespread opposition to his alliance with Bush over Iraq, which I shared. Even so, he set very ambitious goals for Gleneagles. He chose an agenda with two items only: Africa and climate change. He looked for major advances in debt relief, aid volume and trade access, to revitalise the G8's Africa programme. These would be complemented by a new approach to development, drawn up by his Commission for Africa, which had members from the G8, Africa and even China, and involved business and NGOs as well as governments. Climate change had been avoided by earlier summits, because of the gulf dividing the Americans from the rest. But Blair was convinced that the time had come to bridge this gap and bring the Americans back to the table. Both subjects involved domestic policy decisions of a kind that recent summits had avoided.

I was able to follow the preparations closely. Michael Jay was now the UK sherpa. I had good contacts with Martin Donnelly, who had my old job in the FCO; Charles Hay, the head of his G8 summit team; and Myles Wickstead, who ran the secretariat for the Commission for Africa. The British sherpa team went further in outreach than ever before. They conducted preparatory exchanges with the Africans on their development topics and with Brazil, China, India, Mexico and South Africa on climate change, so that both groups could be associated with the summit results. They successfully enlisted the backing of development NGOs like Oxfam, which generated a mass movement to 'Make Poverty History'.

Meanwhile, John Kirton and I helped the University of Glasgow to organise a pre-summit conference, at which Donnelly and Wickstead spoke, as well as Jack McConnell, the First Minister of Scotland.

The summit media centre was within walking distance of the Gleneagles Hotel, where the leaders were housed and held their meetings. I went to the frequent briefings from Blair, Chirac and other leaders, as well as celebrities like George Clooney and Bob Geldof. Access was difficult coming from Edinburgh or Glasgow as obstructive demonstrators would block the roads, but luckily I was lodged further north and had no trouble. The event began well for Tony Blair, as he learnt that London was chosen to host the 2012 Olympics. But early on the first full day news came through of terrorist attacks in London, with many killed and injured. The other leaders urged Blair to fly down there, leaving Michael Jay to take the chair. When Blair returned, he issued an eloquent condemnation of the terrorists, flanked by all the leaders present. Despite his absence, the summit completed its work on climate change and disposed of Africa ahead of schedule on the following day. Each G8 leader solemnly signed the main documents on Africa and climate change, to underline their commitment to keep their promises.

The results from Gleneagles were substantial. The leaders confirmed an earlier agreement by finance ministers to grant 100 per cent relief for African and other poor countries' debt. The summit pledged that aid to Africa should double by 2010, an extra $25 billion per year, while total aid should increase by $50 billion. Not all G8 members have met this target, but aid for Africa has risen strongly even so. The proposals of the Commission for Africa were reflected in the summit decisions, though with some dilution. Trade, however, was a disappointment, as the G8 leaders failed to invigorate the WTO negotiations, as they had promised. The cumulative effect of the Gleneagles measures, on top of the Africans' own efforts, was a steady improvement in growth for most countries in Africa. In climate change, Bush accepted for the first time that global warming was caused by human activity. The summit agreed to develop new technology to reduce greenhouse gas emissions and launched a dialogue embracing all the big emitters, including the United States and emerging powers like China. This enabled progress to restart in UN contexts, even before Bush left office.

After 2005 I gave up going to the summit. I thought Gleneagles would prove the zenith of G8 achievement and this turned out to be true.

Russia's first summit in 2006 was good for Vladimir Putin's prestige, but not much else. Germany's summit in 2007 had some useful results, but the meetings in Japan in 2008 and Italy in 2009 were disappointing. The G8 continued to avoid difficult domestic issues and failed to develop a consistent approach to the emerging powers, which would recognise their growing weight in the world system. As a result, when the international financial crisis struck in 2008, the response was orchestrated by summit meetings of the G20, rather than the G8. Hitherto the G20 had been a finance ministers' grouping, but it included Brazil, China, India and other key players, which the G8 did not. The G20 summit soon declared itself 'the premier forum for economic cooperation'. Thus the G8 summit's days may be numbered as an instrument of economic diplomacy. If so, I shall be sorry, as I have become very attached to it. But after three summit books I have said all I wanted to say.

CHAPTER 21

# Economic diplomacy at the LSE

T HROUGHOUT THIS BOOK I HAVE spoken freely of 'economic diplomacy', but the term was never current during my professional life. I
first heard it used by Mike Hodges, as the title of the course that he
proposed we should teach together at the LSE. He saw it as describing
the process by which states took domestic decisions and conducted
international negotiations in economic issues. He thought this process
deserved closer intellectual examination, which could best be done by
bringing scholars and policy practitioners together. I was happy to join
him in this, as it gave me the academic base I was seeking.

On our return from the Denver summit of June 1997, Mike got me
made a visiting fellow at the LSE's International Relations Department.
Most of the staff in the department, like William Wallace, focused on
political aspects of international relations. Mike Hodges was part of a
smaller group that offered a master's degree in the politics of the world
economy. Students took a core course of lectures and seminars and two
optional courses, each leading to exams. They also wrote a dissertation,
all within one year. Mike taught an option on international business;
other options covered trade, finance and energy. The initial plan was for
Mike and me to offer a new option on economic diplomacy, starting in
October 1998. But in January he told me he could not introduce a course
so soon. We would offer instead a series of ten special seminars, each one
with an academic and a practitioner speaker. The full course would only
begin in 1999 and meanwhile we would jointly write a book to go with
it.

Mike got departmental blessing for these seminars. We worked out a
list of topics before breaking off to organise the conferences linked to the
Birmingham summit. When Mike died suddenly in June I thought that
all our work would go for nothing. But his colleagues did not want his
projects to die with him and Hilary Parker, the departmental manager,
asked me if I could run the seminars on my own. I said that I needed a
partner from the LSE staff and suggested Stephen Woolcock, who had
recently joined as a lecturer. He was a trade expert whom I knew from

his time at Chatham House and the Confederation of British Industry, whose latest work was a study of financial services liberalisation. Steve Woolcock agreed to take it on and this was the start of a very fruitful partnership, which continues to this day. He struck me as very serious at first and rather diffident in manner, but we found it easy to work together. Steve's confidence grew as the seminars proved successful and led on to the full economic diplomacy option, now in its twelfth year.

Steve and I started work at once to approach academic and practitioner speakers for the seminars, which ran from November 1998 to February 1999. Leading experts from the LSE were ready to take part, while I got excellent support from my former government colleagues. Senior figures from the FCO, Treasury, Trade and Industry and Environment all seemed happy to talk at the LSE about the arms trade, debt relief, inward investment and climate change. Steve himself spoke on transatlantic economic relations, while I covered trade in services. The seminars were only voluntary for the students, as they did not lead to exams, but they were well attended. I circulated the details widely around Whitehall and the City, so that we had a good outside following too, with Christopher Roberts and John Cooke being faithful participants.

The Mike Hodges seminars went so well that we began to prepare for a full option course to run from October 1999, with Steve as the 'course proprietor'. We had a daunting meeting with the departmental professors, as some were loath to regard economic diplomacy as an academic subject. But we promised to include more theoretical content, where my earlier association with Bob Putnam made a good impression, and thus gained their approval. Steve and I worked out a programme of lectures and seminars and drew up a reading list. Only twenty students signed up for the full course in our first year, but the practitioner lectures attracted a wider audience. Economic diplomacy became accepted as an established option in the MSc in the Politics of the World Economy. The LSE gave me a contract as a guest teacher and paid me accordingly.

The twenty lectures and associated seminars soon settled into a standard pattern. Steve and I shared the early lectures between us. After a joint introduction, he would lecture on theories of economic diplomacy, while I spoke on how it worked in practice and had adjusted to the end of the Cold War and the advance of globalisation. We offered historical case studies on the creation of the GATT and the early G7 summits. The Michaelmas term ended with three practitioner lecturers, representing government, business and NGOs. My successors as FCO Economic Director would give the first of these, starting with Colin Budd.

In the Lent term Steve and I introduced different approaches to economic diplomacy – bilateral, regional and through wider institutions – which were illustrated by a range of practitioner speakers. Matthew Goodman of Goldman Sachs, a colleague from LOTIS, lectured on US economic diplomacy towards Japan, based on his experience as financial attaché in Tokyo. A senior Treasury figure would speak on the IMF and World Bank, starting with my sherpa colleagues Huw Evans and Nigel Wicks. The chief British trade negotiator (Tony Hutton, then Richard Carden) covered the WTO. A Commission expert showed how the EU conducted environment negotiations; a member of the Commonwealth Secretariat explained what economic diplomacy meant for poor countries; and an NGO speaker talked on debt relief. A final joint performance by Steve and me pulled it all together.

In the smaller seminar groups the students had to do the work themselves. They took it in turns to present short papers to the class, making imaginative use of the LSE's audio-visual resources, and wrote essays each term that I had to mark. Though I was nervous at the outset, it was most rewarding to teach them. I found them industrious and well-motivated, despite the constant distractions at the LSE. They were a highly cosmopolitan group, but had no problem in communicating with me or with one another. My first class of ten came from India, Italy, Korea, Mexico, Thailand, the US and Vietnam, plus three from Canada. Over the years Europe, North and South America and Asia (including China) were well represented on the course. African and Middle Eastern students were rare, while only about 5 per cent came from Britain. There was no teaching in the summer term, only revision classes and marking the exam paper that Steve and I had set earlier. This was my least agreeable task. Steve and I agreed readily on other things, but often differed on exam marks. Much depended on our decision, as the students were only graded on their exam performance. Marking always had to be done against the clock. It often clashed with G8 summits, so that in 2002 I sat up till the early hours marking scripts in Calgary and conferring with Steve in Brussels by unreliable fax. But I could hardly complain, when the summer was otherwise free.

★  ★  ★

For the first time in my life, I spent a whole decade doing the same job and living in the same place. This enabled Dee and me to follow the fortunes of our family. Tom was still working in corporate finance. His team split off from the NatWest, just before the takeover by Royal Bank of Scotland, and became Hawkpoint Partners, in which Douglas Hurd was still involved. After a time, Tom left to join the board of a construction firm, to get direct experience of running a business. He found this instructive at first but less satisfying in the long run. He therefore returned to corporate finance, joining with a few close colleagues to form Noventus Partners, which offered services to small firms that were neglected by the big banks.

Tom took to running marathons, first in London and then other European cities. Kristin worked for a charity active in Notting Hill. Our grandchildren developed their own personalities (Plate 30). Felix, to my great pleasure, became a keen classical scholar and aimed for Oxford. I went with him to an open day at Christ Church, but he preferred Corpus Christi, the strongest college for classics in the whole university. Before starting there he taught English in a Buddhist monastery in India. The warm-hearted Claudia was the most athletic, excelling at lacrosse, netball and throwing the discus. Roly was versatile, being keen on debating and rugby. Max preferred natural history and gardening.

We did not forget Charlie. On the tenth anniversary of his death I was moved to write one last poem.

### To My Dear Wife: Remembering Charlie

Often I think of Charlie, as I sit
　　Like him, at my computer. Close to me
I see him at the keyboard he would hit,
　　Making his mouth-stick dance from key to key.

And he is not just here: on roads in Spain,
　　Sweden or Poland, still the locals see
His scarlet van go by, to show again
　　How love of travel set his spirit free.

Yet from his travels he'd return to you,
　　My dear. You gave his life its stable base.
You gave him confidence to see things through
　　And hope, whatever setbacks he might face.
He could rely on your whole-hearted giving
Of all your love, to make his life worth living.

Over the next decade, Dick and Tom kept the Travel Trust going, with the support of the Cambridge Disability Centre. My brother Christopher, its treasurer, calculated that by 2009 the Trust had made grants totalling £30,000, well in excess of the original endowment, enabling about a hundred disabled students to go travelling. Dee and I replenished the funds and, on the twentieth anniversary of Charlie's death this year (2010), sent round a memento of him to all his friends with whom we were in contact. We were deeply touched to find how many of those who had known him, at Eton, Cambridge and elswhere, still remembered him vividly.

Dick and Laura bought a house in Eastleach, described by Simon Jenkins as 'the Cotswolds of which exiles dream'. In 2002 Dick fulfilled a long-cherished ambition, when he and Laura walked the whole length of Italy, starting in April from the tip of Calabria. They mainly kept to the mountains, but broke off to spend a week with us at Paestum, south of Naples, and we met them again at Laura's father's house near Siena. They came down to the sea to follow the Ligurian Riviera and finally crossed the French border in October. During their walk they were much attracted by the Majella massif, east of Rome, and went back to look for a holiday house there. They found one in Decontra, a small pastoral village deep in the mountains and overlooking the Orfento gorge. Dee and I went out to help them put the house in order, taking time off to walk through remote valleys to medieval hermitages.

Decontra provided the inspiration for an ambitious business venture that they launched with Ed Granville, who worked with Laura at Abercrombie and Kent. Their front room in Eastleach became the head office of Upland Escapes, which offered walking holidays based in European mountain villages similar to Decontra. Dick mainly researched the walks, wrote the handbooks and selected the Upland Managers in charge in each place, while Laura and Ed ran the business. Dee and I became enthusiastic Upland Escapers. We went first to the French Alps behind Nice, with Dick acting as our manager, which added to the pleasure. Next year we were at Decontra itself, where Christopher Roberts joined us. Later Escapes took us to the well-watered valleys of the French Pyrenees, the volcanic landscape of Grand Canary and the Welsh hills behind Harlech, covered with sheep and megalithic tombs.

Aunt Diana, my mother's sister, died in 1999, aged ninety-two. From her my brothers Christopher and David and I inherited what remained of Great-grandfather Fleischmann's fortune. We passed most of it directly to our children, the fifth generation to benefit. Sorting out her possessions brought us three brothers together and from then on we arranged six-monthly meetings to keep in touch. Aunt Diana was the last survivor of the previous generation of my family, but Dee's father Tom Wilde was still going strong. He lived alone in Bideford well into his nineties. When this became too much for him, he joined us at Hampton Court. Though less mobile than he was, he remained mentally alert and excellent company. He celebrated his 100th birthday on 2 August 2009, surrounded by his descendants.

I had not forgotten Mike Hodges' intention that there should be a book on economic diplomacy, based on the course. I persuaded Steve that this would be easy to produce, as each lecture would provide a chapter. Ashgate agreed to publish *The New Economic Diplomacy: Decision-Making and Negotiation in International Economic Relations*, and all our practitioner speakers undertook to write up their lectures. In fact it all took much longer than I expected and *The New Economic Diplomacy* was not on the shelves till early in 2003. But it sold well – much better than my two summit books – and soon Ashgate brought out a paperback version, which students could afford for themselves.

My chapters of the book enabled me to expound my interpretation of economic diplomacy to a wider audience than just my LSE students. I aimed to rationalise my professional experience and my later observation in a form suitable for an academic textbook. My thesis was that states tried to reconcile three tensions which would otherwise conflict: between politics and economics; between domestic and external pressures; and between government and other forces. In the first tension, for example, economics argued for removing trade barriers unilaterally, but politically this was much easier as part of a reciprocal bargain with others. The second tension was a consequence of the economic interdependence, long prevailing in OECD countries, which now applied world-wide as globalisation. The third reflected the growing pressure from private business and NGOs on governments and institutions.

I argued that the advance of globalisation increased the demands on states. Economic diplomacy did not stop at the border, but penetrated domestic policy. More subjects were covered and more countries were taking part. As governments saw their power to shape events was shrinking, they had developed four new strategies. They involved ministers alongside bureaucrats, thus raising the political stakes. They got non-state actors – business and NGOs – to bear more of the burden. They promoted transparency, i.e. better information and public explanation. They used international institutions to reinforce their domestic policy aims.

I outlined the domestic sequence of government decision-making. First a lead department was chosen, which would consult both outside parties – firms, NGOs, academic experts – and other departments, so as to produce an agreed national position. This would get political authority from ministers, who might take their own initiatives, and democratic legitimacy from parliament, which increased transparency. The process gave a mandate to national negotiators, sitting at the international table with partners who had gone through a similar sequence. Where negotiators could not agree by exchanges among themselves, they would seek to influence the domestic process in the other countries. Once agreement was reached at the international level, it returned to the domestic level for ratification, where it could always come unstuck.

In comparing different approaches to economic diplomacy, I showed how bilateralism favoured the stronger party and therefore appealed to the United States. Regionalism attracted medium-sized countries, as in the EU, since they could combine against more powerful rivals. International institutions had more political content than first appeared and were going deeper into domestic policies. The multilateral WTO could make formal rules with binding effect, but exclusive bodies like the OECD and G8 could not go beyond voluntary cooperation and peer pressure.

In our last chapter Steve and I found that the end of the Cold War had had a positive effect on the first and second tensions. There had been a striking advance in creating new, rule-based institutions, such as the WTO and the UN conventions on climate change and biodiversity. The Asian financial crisis had led to reforms at the IMF and World Bank; the G8 was paying more attention to poor countries, especially in Africa. But everywhere the early promise was running into obstacles: the new commitments provoked domestic resistance; developing countries felt rich states were still trying to dominate the system. We believed rule-based economic diplomacy would make progress, but it would be much harder than expected. As for the third tension, when governments wanted firms or NGOs to do more, they struggled to keep the initiative. They were often using independent agencies or even the private sector to regulate economic activity. But this had not always worked well, as the private sector made mistakes just as government did. In conclusion, we compared economic diplomacy to cookery, which produced very different dishes from the same ingredients.

While working on the book I got the chance to teach in Canada. The Canadian side of the Canada-UK Colloquium was run by Bob Wolfe, a former diplomat, and Keith Banting, who were based at Queen's University at Kingston, Ontario. From 2001 to 2003 they invited me to teach in a graduate summer school, where I compressed economic diplomacy (there called 'global governance') into an intensive three weeks. Many of my class were professionals studying in their spare time, who enjoyed bringing their own practitioner perspective to the course. I got them to simulate the G8 summit, which everyone enjoyed. Between classes I caught up with Canadian friends, as Ottawa and Toronto were within easy reach. In one year my three original Canadian students at the LSE gave me dinner in Kingston. One was now with the IMF, one had joined a bank and the third worked for a Quaker NGO.

From now on Steve and I had more flexibility with the course. Our original lectures were available in the book and did not need repeating. A helpful colleague, Mathias Koenig-Archibugi, joined us to lecture on theory. We brought in more practitioners from the emerging powers, starting with Celso Amorim, the Brazilian Ambassador in London who became President Lula's foreign minister. We found an excellent Indian lecturer in Kishan Rana, an ex-ambassador and writer on comparative diplomacy. We never found an equivalent Chinese speaker: but Matthew Goodman now lectured on US economic relations with East Asia, including China, which he had covered in the White House during Bush's first term. Two former students came back as lecturers: a Swedish diplomat at the EU and a Brazilian negotiator at the WTO.

The numbers choosing our course rose steadily. Its empirical focus and involvement of practitioners appealed to the students, some of whom cited our course as their reason for choosing the LSE. Instead of one seminar class apiece, Steve and I first had to take two and then bring in additional teachers. There were nearly a hundred students in 2005–6, requiring six seminar groups, which tested Steve's organising ability to the limit. Thereafter he had the numbers capped at seventy-five, so that only five groups were needed. Steve was now doing more, while I did less, after a bout of heart disease early in 2004. I retired from taking seminars and also escaped from marking, to my great relief. Instead I organised a simulation of each year's G8 summit, starting with Gleneagles. The students showed great aptitude for this role-playing exercise. I often thought they achieved better results than the actual summit.

Early in 2006 Ashgate suggested that we should produce a revised second edition of *The New Economic Diplomacy*, to appear in both hardback and paperback. No peer review would be needed, so that if we submitted the text by the end of April 2007, the book would be out in time for the new academic year. Steve and I agreed with some foreboding, but the process was much smoother this time. We simplified the analysis in our academic chapters and added some new practitioner authors. Martin Donnelly from the FCO focused on the Gleneagles summit and its aftermath; Roderick Abbott, a veteran of the Commission and WTO Secretariat, covered the world trading system; a chapter on the International Energy Agency (IEA) was contributed by Joan McNaughton, who had chaired its governing board. Our text reached Ashgate in time and they had the book out in September 2007 as promised.

The content of my analytical chapters in the new edition required little change, though I reflected the rise of emerging powers like Brazil, China and India and the distinctive policies of the Bush administration. But our conclusions struck a more sombre note. The prospects for economic diplomacy had not improved over the last four years, with the WTO negotiations marking time and the US dragging its feet over climate change. The financial system was calm, but the new regime had not been tested in the current period of strong economic growth. In reconciling politics and economics, there were moves to engage the emerging powers more fully in the system, but these were informal and unsystematic. In reconciling domestic and external pressures, rule-making was giving way to voluntary cooperation, especially at summit level, but the commitments made were not being met. Economic diplomacy was fragmenting, with bilateral agreements or even unilateral national actions being preferred to the use of institutions. In reconciling government and other forces, NGOs were becoming more influential, combining internal lobbying with public campaigns. But though this was accepted in industrial economies, developing countries were more resistant. Business preferred to act behind the scenes and to persuade governments to leave more to the operation of the markets. In short, economic diplomacy needed to become more inclusive internationally and more effective at overcoming resistance domestically. In our cookery metaphor, new exotic types of cuisine were gaining ground, but standards were not improving.

I delivered the corrected proofs of the book to Ashgate early in August 2007. Within days the European Central Bank advanced 128 billion euros to keep the banking system afloat, while next month Northern Rock collapsed. The credit crunch had begun, which, needless to say, we had not predicted. I became fascinated by the economic diplomacy of the crisis. For a whole year central banks were left on their own to fight it, while governments intervened only with great reluctance and did not mobilise the IMF. Even before Lehman Brothers failed, I sensed that historic changes were afoot, with greater impact than any of the crises I had known over thirty-five years' experience of economic diplomacy. The financial collapse generated a severe economic recession, which afflicted mature industrial states far worse than emerging powers. It became clear that a fresh edition of *The New Economic Diplomacy* was needed. That will be my next task, once these memoirs are finished.

CHAPTER 22

# Reflections of an Economic Diplomat

THERE ARE TWO WAYS OF THINKING about diplomacy. The first sees it as an instrument for exercising power. Countries seek to advance or defend their national interests against foreign encroachment. In international dealings, the objective is to gain advantage at the expense of the other participants and to get more out of the transaction than they do. Sporting metaphors are frequent, like 'game, set and match' used to describe Britain's performance in the Maastricht negotiations in the European Union. I call this approach 'competitive diplomacy', though the academic term is 'value claiming'.

The second approach sees diplomacy as a means of reaching agreements from which all parties benefit. The participants gain more by acting together than they could achieve on their own. The ideal is for all parties to make equal gains in all parts of the agreement, but this is seldom attainable. Some losses may have to be accepted, to secure greater gains elsewhere. Provided all benefit, it is acceptable that some gain more than others. I call this 'cooperative diplomacy': for academics it is 'value creating'.

Both types of diplomacy are necessary. Where political diplomacy focuses on assuring security against our adversaries, whether hostile states or terrorists, it has to be competitive. During the Cold War, which lasted for most of my time at the FCO, the aim of the West was to gain advantage over the communist bloc. Yet even then cooperative agreements could be achieved, as I learnt from the four-power negotiations on Berlin. The Russians wanted to restrain Federal German activity in Berlin more than the allies needed to increase it; they could grant at little cost the access improvements we wanted so much. Everyone gained more than they gave.

Some aspects of economic diplomacy are competitive too. Trade promotion involves competing against other bidders to secure export orders, though I did very little of this. The economic diplomacy that I practised always had the potential to be cooperative, as it aimed to expand the fruits of peace for the benefit of all. I found this the most satisfying professional activity, which suited my talents best. Though it was harder work, it gave everyone an incentive to meet their commitments. One successful exercise in cooperation could lay the foundation for the next. While competitive diplomacy favoured powerful countries, cooperative diplomacy gave a chance to the small and weak. If a cooperative agreement turned out to be ill-judged, of course everyone involved in it would suffer. But competitive diplomacy could be just as damaging, when a strong state involved weaker ones in its own mistakes. Cooperative diplomacy at its best led to durable, rule-based regimes. But if competitive attitudes prevailed, these regimes came under threat.

Throughout my career, economic diplomacy steadily penetrated deeper into domestic policy-making, as a consequence of opening markets. This brought economic benefits, but made cooperative diplomacy more difficult. While government operates collectively, especially in coalitions, domestic politics is adversarial, above all in Britain and the United States. The media prefers competitive diplomacy, as rivalry produces livelier television than consensus. Governments always want to be in control of domestic policy-making. They may make changes in return for advantages offered by others, in a process of bargaining. But they dislike adopting measures imposed from outside.

Cooperative economic diplomacy relies partly on bargaining but even more on persuasion. The secret is to convince your foreign counterparts to adopt policies that help you *on their own initiative*, not in response to suggestions from you. If it is their own idea, they will defend it much more robustly, though you cannot take the credit for it. This strategy depends on a thorough understanding of the domestic pressures at work on your partners, and the ability to mobilise internal forces that want the same as you do. Understanding and influencing what happens within your partner countries is the surest way to shape international negotiations in your favour. This strategy works best in conditions of mutual trust. Competitive diplomacy often involves keeping the other parties guessing. But cooperative diplomacy depends on openness, confidence and discretion. This encourages one party to float informal proposals in the hope of extracting a positive counter-proposal. The resulting agreement will always be made public, though the negotiation of this result may have to be done in secret.

Let me apply this analysis to economic diplomacy as I practised and observed it during four decades. My sustained involvement began in the

1970s, when the stable regime in force since World War II was collapsing in confusion. The IMF, World Bank and GATT were remarkable achievements of cooperative diplomacy, but the post-war instrument that impressed me most was the Marshall Plan. Its success came not so much from the generous provision of American finance, as from the obligation for the Europeans to work out their economic policies collectively. Because they were free to choose these policies, they were committed to them and did not regard them as imposed from outside. The OECD and the European Union are both heirs of the Marshall Plan.

But with time the cooperative impetus was undermined. As I saw early in my career, the newly independent countries turned the United Nations into a theatre of competitive diplomacy, seeking advantage at the expense of their ex-colonial masters. West European countries came together, as the Americans wanted; but then, under French influence, they defined Europe in opposition to the United States. The Americans, for their part, unilaterally removed the foundation of the monetary system. Finally, the Arab oil-producers provoked the first oil crisis in retaliation against the US for its support of Israel.

The oil crisis stimulated a revival of cooperative diplomacy. This influenced my outlook strongly, from my experience in the Treasury and Paris. I was present at the birth of the new economic summits, which mobilised collective action in the OECD, the IMF and the GATT. France and the United States gave up their rivalry and combined to launch a durable new monetary regime, based on floating exchange rates. US President Carter promoted coordinated measures whereby strong western economies would stimulate growth so as to revive weaker ones, like Britain. Germany was sceptical at first, but Chancellor Schmidt decided that fiscal stimulus was justified and used the international debate to overcome domestic resistance. The GATT concluded the Tokyo round of negotiations to reduce trade barriers, despite the pressures for protection. The IMF encouraged banks to lend on the surpluses deposited by OPEC to middle-income oil-importers, so that they could sustain their growth. In parallel western governments supported poor countries through aid loans and export credit. This breadth of cooperation has not been equalled since.

But everything changed in the 1980s, as this strategy revealed a fatal flaw. It focused on growth at the expense of checking inflation, which left the industrial states vulnerable to the second surge in oil prices. Reducing inflation through tight monetary policies now became the priority target, at the cost of a deep recession. Each country acted alone, leading to competition over whose interest rates would go highest. By this time I was Head of Economic Relations Department, while Margaret Thatcher became British Prime Minister. I supported her anti-inflation objectives and had earlier argued that putting sterling into the new European Exchange Rate Mechanism would oblige us to keep prices down. But after my experience in France I did not share her conviction that the private sector was always more efficient than government. She also strongly preferred competitive diplomacy, believing that cooperation only led to meaningless compromises. This provoked similar combative approaches around Whitehall. I had to face down Enid Jones over the International Tin Agreement, when I would have much preferred to strike a deal.

I was even more critical of the international impact of 'Reaganomics', which made it hard for other countries to escape from recession. But the US ignored the Europeans' complaints and even tried to dictate our economic policy towards Eastern Europe. The strong dollar made American exports uncompetitive and encouraged protectionism, while generous tax cuts produced a yawning budget deficit; the United States, from being the largest creditor, became the largest debtor in the world. Because of the long recession developing countries could no longer service their debts. But when Latin American countries threatened to default, the US mainly acted to protect its commercial banks and imposed tough corrective policies on the debtors. It was an unproductive period for economic diplomacy.

In Reagan's second term, James Baker, as US Treasury Secretary, rekindled the spirit of cooperation. The Plaza agreement of G5 finance ministers brought down the dollar and neutralised the pressures for protectionism. The new Uruguay Round of trade negotiations was launched in the GATT with a very ambitious agenda. But Baker's other initiatives were less successful, as he tried to impose his own ideas on others. His proposals for macroeconomic policy coordination, leading up to the Louvre agreement, did not convince Germany and Japan. The Baker Plan to end the debt crisis failed because the banks resisted his pressure to make new loans. His successor, Nicholas Brady, settled the matter by persuading the banks that they would never be repaid in full. I followed these events from the vantage-point of the OECD, which contributed some vital ideas to the trade negotiations. I admired the skill with which the OECD secretariat put good ideas into their members' heads, which they could later claim as their own. This was how the OECD advanced cooperative diplomacy, but could never take the credit.

Hitherto my time as an economic diplomat had been dominated by bad news: two crippling surges in the oil price and a sovereign debt crisis. But as FCO Economic Director I was lucky enough to witness the end of the Cold War, a historic period of good news. This generated tremendous excitement and optimism, but the transition from central planning to market economies was more difficult than expected. The change came so fast that the West was not prepared for it and sometimes could not agree on the right strategy. Our reactions were often improvised, with no clear idea of their long-term impact.

The programmes introduced to help the Central European countries worked well. Generous contributions of financial and technical assistance were coordinated through the G24. The EBRD was launched with amazing speed, to build up the neglected private sector in these countries. When the troubles of the Soviet Union threatened their initial recovery, the EU and the US offered new markets for their exports. The prospect of future EU membership gave them a long-term goal and the United States was happy to let the Europeans take the lead.

The Soviet Union was a much tougher problem and rivalry hampered agreement. The EU countries, led by Germany, wanted to reward Gorbachev with financial support and to integrate the Soviet Union into the international system. The United States and Japan, however, were disinclined to provide any funds without stronger evidence of reform. This led to two years of indecision. Nothing was agreed in 1990, except to conduct a study. In 1991 Gorbachev was invited to the London summit, but only got the form, not the substance of cooperation. By then the Soviet economy was close to collapse and we had to focus on short-term food aid and debt relief, rather than helping fundamental reform. A more decisive approach could have got the transition to a market economy in Russia off to a stronger start, with long-term benefits.

German reunification also created economic strains. I had always believed sterling should be in the EU Exchange Rate Mechanism (ERM). When the debate began on creating a European currency, I thought Britain should be part of that too. But Margaret Thatcher would not hear of it and I watched the tragedy unfold. Geoffrey Howe and Nigel Lawson favoured ERM membership, but their advocacy cost them their jobs. When John Major finally persuaded her to join, it was just at the wrong moment. The Bundesbank was tightening monetary policy, to offset loose fiscal policy caused by massive transfers to East Germany. The Germans gave priority to domestic factors and ignored the problems created for currencies linked to the DM, which now included sterling. If the pound had been an established member of the ERM, it might have survived. But as the newest arrival, it was the first target when the system came under pressure.

Britain's humiliating departure from the ERM aggravated the controversy that had raged ever since we had first tried to join the European Community. Supporters believed that the EU practised cooperative diplomacy, bringing benefits for all. Opponents argued that Commission and member states sought their own advantage at the expense of others and Britain was bound to lose out. Margaret Thatcher came to see the other European leaders as adversaries, while much of the British media claimed the EU was slanted against us. Many British officials became skilled at European diplomacy and were trusted by their colleagues. But instead of constructing mainstream EU programmes, they often had to negotiate 'opt-outs' and exceptions. The euro regime would have been more robust if we had helped to create it, while we could have avoided the mistakes in financial policy we made by staying outside. But the opportunity was lost.

The end of the Cold War had a profound effect on the entire international system. In the 1990s economic interdependence among OECD members mutated into 'globalisation' covering the whole world. There were new opportunities for cooperative diplomacy, in trade, the environment and finance, provided these embraced developing countries, especially the emerging powers of Asia.

Completing the European single market was a rare EU initiative that enjoyed the support of Margaret Thatcher. When I arrived as Economic Director, it was being attacked as giving advantages to EU members at the expense of others. I demonstrated that it was in fact cooperative, as non-EU countries would share its benefits. On my visits to the rising economic powers of East Asia, from Singapore to Korea, I argued that the liberalising impact of the single market should call forth commitments by others in the GATT Uruguay Round. I revived these arguments later, when I found EU-Canada relations beset by recurrent disputes. Canada's access to the EU single market and European access to NAFTA brought far greater benefits than any of the contentious issues. The fisheries crisis tested my approach to the limit. Canada was determined to prevent European fishermen from depleting endangered stocks, by force if necessary. We came within a whisker of a shooting war between the Spanish and Canadian navies. But an EU-Canada fisheries agreement that disciplined the Spanish trawlers restored cooperative diplomacy just in time. British advice behind the scenes helped to achieve this result; open support for Canada against Spain would have been ineffective.

While still in London, I helped Christopher Roberts to get a coherent British position on the GATT trade negotiations, backed by the whole of Whitehall. This strengthened his hand in arguing in the EU debates that the Commission should work for an ambitious package of agreements. Though agriculture held up the negotiations for three years, eventually external and domestic pressures combined to make the EU reform its Common Agricultural Policy. The Uruguay Round agreements emerged stronger from the delay, bringing benefits for industrial and developing countries alike. The new World Trade Organization involved stricter obligations than the old GATT, but developing countries were ready to embrace them. This seemed a good response to the advance of globalisation, which satisfied everybody. The WTO concluded further deals, including the financial services agreement, where I helped European and American firms to combine in support of a cooperative result. But as the new regime took effect, the developing countries became disillusioned. Instead of benefits for all, they considered that the rich countries were gaining advantages at their expense. When the WTO prepared to launch another negotiating round, the industrial states pursued new gains instead of responding to the needs of developing countries. I was in Seattle to see the trading system collapse in disarray.

Work on global environmental issues accelerated with the end of the Cold War. This made it possible to reach the agreements with universal participation that were required by these subjects. The initial impetus was positive. The UN environment conference at Rio reached a broad consensus on underlying principles and concluded legally binding conventions on climate change and biodiversity. But discord soon broke out. Developing countries argued they should not have to restrain their economic growth by limiting greenhouse gas emissions, because the industrial countries were responsible for emissions rising so fast. Under the 1997 Kyoto Protocol only industrial states were obliged to reduce their emissions. Then the United States, under pressure from the energy industry, also resiled from any obligations. Congress would not ratify the Kyoto Protocol and the US also stayed out of the Biodiversity Convention. Cooperative environmental diplomacy was losing momentum.

In finance, attention shifted to the debts owed by poor countries to governments and international institutions like the IMF and World Bank. Britain, France and Canada pioneered a scheme at the G7 summit to relieve these debts, which began modestly but was progressively improved throughout the 1990s. One by one, the advocates convinced the sceptical Americans, Germans and Japanese and finally won over the reluctant Fund and Bank staffs. By the end of the decade 100 per cent remission was offered on government debt and substantial relief was available on debt to institutions. Effective lobbying by NGOs helped to achieve this cooperative result.

The Halifax G7 summit of 1995, when I was in Canada, agreed a cooperative response to the default by the Mexican government. There were decisions to strengthen the IMF's policy surveillance, expand its resources and coordinate financial regulation. But the US and Britain resisted outside scrutiny of financial regulation, to preserve the competitive advantage enjoyed by New York and London. When Thailand, Indonesia and Korea provoked a contagious crisis in East Asia two years later, the IMF acted as if this too was caused by the governments and imposed tight monetary and fiscal policies. Asian countries resented this treatment and took steps to avoid having to call in the IMF again, by running large external surpluses and piling up currency reserves. But in fact the private sector had caused the crisis: it had taken advantage of weak regulation and become over-exposed internationally.

The reforms agreed at the IMF following the Asian crisis also looked like a good response to the demands of globalisation. The 'new architecture' created a finance ministers' group, the G20, which embraced emerging powers like Brazil, China and India. The Financial Stability Forum was set up to cooperate on regulation. But the United States prevented the new forum from doing any original work and, unlike other countries, refused a regulatory examination by the IMF.

The US and Britain trusted the markets to prevent irresponsible behaviour. When I was at LOTIS this trust was not misplaced. The banks and insurers that I represented were in favour of clear and predictable regulation, to prevent fraud and imprudent operations. But if the private sector should later be tempted by greed and arrogance, there were only weak defences to keep it in check.

In the first decade of the 2000s I was no longer an active player in economic diplomacy. But I remained a keen observer, especially of the G8 summits, which found a welcome new interest in the poor countries of Africa. These countries could easily have been marginalised by the advance of globalisation. But a group of African leaders took the initiative for the economic revival of their continent, realising that they had to assume responsibility for its problems. The G8 members were so impressed that they promised to back the Africans' efforts, so that the joint enterprise resembled the Marshall Plan. During the 1990s African economies had lost ground and aid had shrunk, with much of it diverted to Eastern Europe. Now aid for Africa rose strongly again, with a target of doubling the total, while 100 per cent relief was agreed for debts to the IMF and World Bank. The G8's commitment flagged by the end of the decade, but by then, mainly through their own efforts, many African countries were growing steadily and improving their standards of government.

Trade and the environment made less progress in the early 2000s. A new trade round was launched in the WTO, intended to benefit developing countries. But a package that satisfied all parties could not be agreed and the round could not be completed. Instead, countries resorted to bilateral or regional trade arrangements, which tended to raise barriers against non-members. In the environment, the US hardened its opposition to limits on greenhouse gas emissions, even as large developing countries like China became major emitters themselves. Hopes for a cooperative outcome rose when the US returned to the UN process, while China and other developing countries also entered the dialogue. The Copenhagen summit of 2009 was intended to agree a successor regime to the Kyoto Protocol, soon to expire. But agreement could not be reached and the debate continues.

'These are some of the darker features of globalisation,' I wrote in *The New Economic Diplomacy*. 'International financial markets develop on a scale that outstrips the ability of governments or central banks to control them.' Control was weakened further by the fragmentation of authority. Governments delegated monetary and financial policy to central banks, which often passed regulation to independent agencies. The markets were swollen by the flood of money from Asian countries investing their reserves in New York or London. Levels of debt, especially in the US and Britain, rose to extravagant heights. The banks invented strange new instruments that few understood; they appeared to dilute the risks but in fact concealed the potential losses. Some prophets warned that a crash would follow. But most people in rich countries were happy to borrow and spend, while governments congratulated themselves on buoyant growth.

When the credit crunch arrived in August 2007, governments could not believe what was happening and left their central banks to bear the brunt. A year later the collapse of Lehman Brothers unleashed the worst economic crisis since the Great Depression. Governments scrambled desperately to rescue failing institutions and poured money into their economies to offset the recession caused by the financial collapse. But the damage would take many years to repair, since these measures added to the excessive levels of debt that would need to be purged away. Governments became more than ever dependent on the backing of the markets, until they could bring their public finances back into equilibrium. I had seen the Canadian government come back from the brink in the 1990s and knew it could be done, given sufficient determination. But it would be a painful process.

International action focused on the G20, meeting at summit level. The emerging markets deserved their place at the table, as they followed more prudent policies and largely avoided recession. The IMF, which judged the crisis shrewdly after it broke, came back in demand again after a decade of neglect. There was a welcome spirit of cooperative diplomacy since the crisis became acute, with countries working together on macroeconomic policies, reforming regulation and strengthening the international financial system. But while measures were planned collectively, they were applied nationally. Some countries began taking action before international discussion was complete. Where consistency was lost in this way, competitive attitudes could easily develop later.

This review of four decades of economic diplomacy prompts a number of final thoughts. Cooperative diplomacy brings benefits for all, beyond what countries can achieve singly. But it is hard to achieve and even harder to sustain. It is often stimulated by a major disturbance, either negative, like the first oil shock, or positive, like the end of the Cold War. It is easily upset if cooperation is based on a faulty or incomplete strategy. But even without this, competitive diplomacy, where parties seek advantage at the expense of others, always tends to reassert itself. The end of the Cold War had a powerful cooperative effect on the regimes for multilateral trade, the global environment and international finance. But all three sectors were soon in trouble again, as industrial states misjudged the growing power of developing countries.

Throughout this period there was increasing reliance on open and competitive markets as a stimulus to growth and a source of discipline. This often led to neglect of the instruments of the state, because the market was seen as more efficient. But while the public sector makes mistakes, the private sector makes them too, and has its own failings and abuses. Lack of attention to the state has held back development in poor countries and left industrial economies exposed to the current financial crisis. The state is stronger in many of the emerging powers, especially China, but may intervene in ways that are unwelcome internationally. Western democracies need to re-define what the state can and should be doing in economic diplomacy.

What began as interdependence and is now globalisation means that economic diplomacy goes ever deeper into domestic policy. Governments have to persuade their electorates that they will share in the benefits that accrue to all from cooperation. But popular opinion usually likes to see the government gaining advantage competitively, at the expense of others, and the media encourages this. Governments therefore have to work harder to explain and justify the benefits of cooperation, bringing in other countries if necessary. Yet in fact they are reluctant to risk unpopularity by making these arguments. Some of the recent strategies for strengthening economic diplomacy, such as involving ministers and increasing transparency, can make this problem worse. Ministers give priority to domestic concerns, while transparency can inhibit sensitive negotiations.

There is a striking new opportunity to advance cooperative economic diplomacy, under the pressure of financial and economic turbulence. But my reflections make me cautious in my forecasts over what can be achieved through the G20. The early summits have been productive

beyond expectations and established positive interaction between the
G20, the IMF and the reformed Financial Stability Board. But the
programme of macroeconomic coordination to reduce international imbalances is very ambitious, going beyond anything attempted
for over thirty years. The G7 countries, after decades of dominating the
financial system, must learn to share power with the other G20 members,
deliberately holding back to encourage them to take the initiative. It will
require persistent vigilance to maintain a cooperative regime: there is a
high risk of slipping into competitive attitudes, with G7 and non-G7
looking for advantage at the expense of the others.

I shall continue to observe what happens, though my days of direct
involvement are receding into the past. I shall think of my successors
labouring away behind the scenes, in the way Lord Salisbury describes:

> There is nothing dramatic in the success of a diplomatist. His victories are
> made up of a series of microscopic advantages: of a judicious suggestion
> here, or an opportune civility there; of a wise concession at one moment,
> and a far-sighted persistence at another; of sleepless tact, immovable
> calmness, and patience that no folly, no provocation, no blunder can shake.

Yet life is more than diplomacy, as writing these memoirs constantly
reminds me. I have gained great pleasure from retrieving the records
going back over my life, a process which has revived my archaeological
instincts. Far more had been preserved than I expected: material about
my childhood carefully collected by my parents; letters that Dee and I
exchanged during our courtship and whenever we were parted later;
detailed accounts sent home by both of us from our posts overseas,
continued by Dee to her father right up to Canada; volumes of family
photographs, showing our children growing up and the places where we
lived. The letters on flimsy airmail paper and the fading pictures stir up
memories that come back more vividly than I can express on these pages.

I have enjoyed belonging to a nomadic profession. The Diplomatic
Service gave me a new job in a different place every three years or so.
Dee and I moved house eighteen times in thirty-five years. Profes-
sionally, I found that suited me. But in my personal life I have prized
constancy and stability. I have valued people and things I could trust and
rely on, and striven to be trustworthy and reliable myself. The greatest
sense of stability and contentment has come from being married to Dee,

and seeing our children grow up happily under her care. Together we were able to survive the shock of Charlie's accident and the pain of his death. In the intervening years he was able to live a full life, thanks to her dedication and to the loyalty he inspired in his volunteer helpers. During our courtship Dee foresaw that we would stay together because we loved each other tenderly, as well as passionately. Now we look forward hopefully to our golden wedding next year, as much devoted to one another as ever.

Before we got married I wrote Dee a poem about love and growing old. Now that we are old, it has all come true.

*To My True Love: Christmas 1960*
*(last verse added 2010)*

Let my halting pen rehearse
Through the mesh of this poor verse
Those delights that find a place
In my true love's form and face.

In the depths of your brown eyes
My lover's gaze untroubled lies,
Or marvels at the dancing light
Which the sparks of love ignite.

And as you walk, your upright grace,
Your slender waist in my embrace,
Transports me, feeling at my side
The balance of your buoyant stride.

But years can bow the figure trim;
Time can make the eyes grow dim;
Age can wear the smile away;
Where is love, if these decay?

Behind that firm and purposed gait,
That back irrevocably straight,
A chaste and constant heart appears,
To love and alter not with years.

Unreckoning love, whose power binds
Insolubly our hearts, our minds,
Moves our lips to smile in joy
Age is powerless to destroy.

And the soul behind your eyes,
Calm, compassionate and wise,
Looks undismayed on mirth or pain
And changes not; time stalks in vain.

*Half a century ago*
*I foretold what now I know:*
*While we live, our love endures,*
*As with age good wine matures.*

# Bibliography

This bibliography lists the main published sources for this book, divided into three parts. The first gives genealogical material used for Chapter 1, divided according to the different families. The second has memoirs and other works that I have consulted or quoted from, in alphabetical order by author. The third contains my own publications that I have drawn on, in order of writing.

## Genealogical material

Alfred Lawrence, *The Clan Bain with its Ancestral and Related Scottish Clans* (Inverness: Highland Printers Ltd 1963).

Norman Macrae, *Dingwall's Thousand Years* (Dingwall: North Star Proprietors 1923).

'Peter Bayne', in *Dictionary of National Biography*, Supplement Vol I (1901), 146–7, written by his elder son Ronald.

'George Christopher Hodgkinson', in *Dictionary of National Biography*, Vol XXVII (1891), 65.

M. J. Ross, *Polar Pioneers: John Ross and James Clark Ross* (Montreal: McGill Queens 1994).

'Noel Ashcroft', obituaries in:
    *Journal of the Geological Society*, Vol 105 (1950), lxix–lxxii;
    *Journal of the Mineralogical Society*, Vol XXXI (1956), 194–9.

P. Niggli, J. Koenigsberger and R. L. Parker, *Die Mineralien der Schweizeralpen* (Basel: B. Wepf & Co 1940).

Franz von Mandach, translated by Edward Kealy, *The History of the Oberen Gesellschaft zun Herren* (typescript, about 1933), on the early im Thurns.

'Johan Conrad im Thurn and his sons John Conrad and Everard im Thurn', biographies in Schaffhausen town archives, see www.stadtar-chiv-schaffhausen.ch.

## Memoirs and other works

Joel D. Aberbach, Robert D. Putnam and Bert A. Rockman, *Bureaucrats and Politicians in Western Democracies* (Cambridge, Mass: Harvard University Press 1981).

Diana Ashcroft, *Journey to Finland* (London: Frederick Muller 1952).

Christopher Audland, *Right Place, Right Time* (Stanhope, Durham: the Memoir Club 2004).

James Bartleman, *Rollercoaster: My Hectic Years as Jean Chrétien's Diplomatic Adviser* (Toronto: McClelland and Stewart 2004).

Richard Bayne (editor) *A Travelling Man: the Diaries and Other Writings of Charles Bayne* (privately printed 1992).

Jean Chrétien, *My Years as Prime Minister* (Toronto: Alfred A. Knopf 2007).

J. M. Cook, *The Troad: an Archaeological and Topographical Study* (Oxford: Oxford University Press 1973).

Duff Cooper, *Talleyrand* (London: Jonathan Cape 1932).

Leslie Fielding, *Kindly Call Me God* (London: Boerman Books 2009).

G8 Research Group, www.g8.utoronto.ca.

Denis Healey, *The Time of My Life* (London: Michael Joseph 1989).

Nicholas Henderson, *Mandarin* (London: Weidenfeld & Nicolson 1994).

Geoffrey Howe, *Conflict of Loyalty* (London: Macmillan 1995).

Douglas Hurd, *The Shape of Ice* (London: Little, Brown 1998).

Douglas Hurd, *Memoirs* (London: Little, Brown 2003).

Douglas Hurd and Edward Young, *Choose Your Weapons: the British Foreign Secretary* (London: Weidenfeld & Nicolson 2010).

Htin Aung, *The Stricken Peacock: Anglo-Burmese Relations, 1752–1948* (The Hague: Martinus Nijhoff 1965).

Simon Jenkins, *England's Thousand Best Churches* (London: Allen Lane 1999).

Keith Lightfoot, *The Philippines* (London: Ernest Benn 1973).

*North-South: a Programme for Survival*, Report of the Independent Commission on International Development Issues (London: Pan Books 1980).

Robert D. Putnam, 'Diplomacy and Domestic Politics: the Logic of Two-Level Games', *International Organization*, Vol 42. 4 (1988), 427–60.

Robert D. Putnam and C. Randall Henning, 'The Bonn Summit of 1978: A Case Study in Coordination', in Richard Cooper and others,

*Can Nations Agree? Issues in International Economic Cooperation*, (Washington: Brookings 1989).

Robert D. Putnam, *Making Democracy Work: Civic Traditions in Modern Italy* (Princeton, NJ: Princeton University Press 1993).

Robert D. Putnam, *Bowling Alone: the Collapse and Revival of American Community* (New York: Simon & Schuster 2000).

Andrew Roberts, *Salisbury: Victorian Titan* (London: Weidenfeld & Nicolson 1999).

Najib Saleeby, *The History of Sulu* (Manila: Filipiniana Book Club 1963, reprinted from the original edition of 1908).

Nigel Spencer, 'Early Lesbos between East and West: a 'Grey Area' of Aegean Archaeology', *Annual of the British School at Athens*, No 30 (1995), 269–306.

Margaret Thatcher, *The Downing Street Years* (London: HarperCollins 1993).


## My own publications

'Excavations at Lyneham Camp, Lyneham, Oxon', *Oxoniensia* Vol XXII (1957), 1–10.

'The Grey Wares of North-West Anatolia in the Middle and Late Bronze Age and the Early Iron Age and their Relation to the Early Greek Settlements', completed in 1963, published in *Asia Minor Studien* Vol 37 (Bonn: Rudolf Habelt 2000).

'Western Economic Summits: Can They Do Better?' *The World Today*, Vol 40.1 (1984), 4–11.

With Robert D. Putnam, *Hanging Together: the Seven-Power Summits* (London: Heinemann 1984); also editions in German (1985), Japanese (1986) and Italian (1987) and revised English edition (London: SAGE 1987).

'Making Sense of Western Economic Policy: the Role of the OECD', *The World Today*, Vol 43.2 (1987), 27–30.

'In the Balance: the Uruguay Round of International Trade Negotiations', *Government and Opposition*, Vol 26.3 (1991), 302–15.

'The Course of Summitry', *The World Today*, Vol 48.2 (1992), 27–30.

'International Economic Relations after the Cold War', *Government and Opposition*, Vol 29.1 (1994), 3–21.

'The G7 Summit and the Reform of Global Institutions', *Government and Opposition*, Vol 30.4 (1995), 492–509.

With Robert D. Putnam, 'The G-7 Summit Comes of Age', in Sylvia Ostry and Gilbert R. Winham (editors), *The Halifax G-7 Summit: Issues on the Table* (Halifax: Dalhousie University 1995), 1–14.

*Britain and Canada – 500 Years: Common Heritage, Shared Vision* (London: Foreign and Commonwealth Office 1997).

'What Governments Want From International Institutions and How They Get It', *Government and Opposition*, Vol 32. 2 (1997), 361–79.

'Globalization and the Commonwealth: International Economic Relations in the Post-Cold War World', *The Round Table*, No 344 (1997), 473–84.

*Opening Markets for Financial Services: the BI Guide to the Financial Services Agreement in the World Trade Organization* (London: British Invisibles 1998).

'Why Did Seattle Fail? Globalization and the Politics of Trade', *Government and Opposition*, Vol 35.2 (2000), 131–51

*Hanging in There: the G7 and G8 Summit in Maturity and Renewal* (Aldershot: Ashgate 2000).

With Stephen Woolcock, *The New Economic Diplomacy: Decision-Making and Negotiation in International Economic Relations* (Aldershot: Ashgate 2003, second revised edition 2007).

*Staying Together: the G8 Summit Confronts the 21st Century* (Aldershot: Ashgate 2005).

With Nigel Spencer, 'The Ceramics of the North-East Aegean Region from the Middle Bronze Age to the Early Iron Age', in Kyriacos Lambrianides and Nigel Spencer (eds), *The Madra River Delta: Regional Studies on the Aegean Coast of Turkey* (London: British Institute of Ankara Monograph 35, 2007).

*Burma and Tudor History: the Life and Work of Charles Bayne 1860–1947* (Bideford: Edward Gaskell 2008).

'Financial Diplomacy and the Credit Crunch: the Rise of Central Banks', *Columbia Journal of International Affairs*, Vol 62.1 (2008), 1–16.

# Index